The Nature of Early Memory

AN ADAPTIVE THEORY OF THE GENESIS AND DEVELOPMENT OF MEMORY

MARK L. HOWE
Department of Psychology, Lancaster University
Lancaster, United Kingdom

OXFORD
UNIVERSITY PRESS

OXFORD
UNIVERSITY PRESS

Oxford University Press, Inc., publishes works that furthers
Oxford University's objective of excellence
in research, scholarship, and education.

Oxford   New York
Auckland   Cape Town   Dar es Salaam   Hong Kong   Karachi
Kuala Lumpur   Madrid   Melbourne   Mexico City   Nairobi
New Delhi   Shanghai   Taipei   Toronto

With offices in
Argentina   Austria   Brazil   Chile   Czech Republic   France   Greece
Guatemala   Hungary   Italy   Japan   Poland   Portugal   Singapore
South Korea   Switzerland   Thailand   Turkey   Ukraine   Vietnam

Published by Oxford University Press, Inc.
198 Madison Avenue, New York, New York 10016

www.oup.com

Oxford is a registered trademark of Oxford University Press

Library of Congress Cataloging-in-Publication Data

Howe, Mark L.
Nature of early memory : an adaptive theory of the genesis and development of memory / by Mark L. Howe.
p. cm.
Includes bibliographical references and index.
ISBN 978-0-19-538141-2
1. Long-term memory in children. 2. Long-term memory in adolescence. 3. Memory. I. Title.
BF723.M4H693 2011
155.4'1312—dc22   2011005670

9 8 7 6 5 4 3 2 1
Printed in the United States of America
on acid-free paper

To Lynn, for making our memories the ones worth remembering.

Contents

PART I

THE SIGNIFICANCE AND EARLIEST SIGNS OF EARLY MEMORY

1

On the Importance of
Studying Early Memory

A childhood is what anyone wants to remember of it. It leaves behind
no fossils, except perhaps in fiction.
—Carol Shields, *The Stone Diaries* (Penguin Classics
Deluxe Edition, 2008)

Some people have tried to persuade me that my early memories are
not authentic . . . But I believe strongly in the power and persistence
of memory . . . In our brains, past and present coexist; they occupy,
as it were, adjoining rooms, but there are some rooms we never enter.
We seem to have lost the keys; but they can be retrieved.
—Hilary Mantel, "Father Figured" (*Daily Telegraph*; April 23, 2005)

When do we start remembering the experiences that make up our lives? Are we
able to remember the events that are our lives from the moment we are born (or
even earlier), or are there important developments (neurobiological, cognitive,
social) that predate such memory feats? More to the point, when we do begin to
remember life's events, are these vestiges of experience permanently etched in
different memory "rooms," or do they fade into a past, creating a fictional blend
with other, perhaps more recent experiences? If they do not become permanent
records of our past, what happens to them? Can these experiences still shape
the person we are and who we will become despite our inability to bring them
into conscious awareness?

These questions, ones that have perplexed scientists, philosophers, and
writers (among others) over the centuries, form the foundation of this book.
Such longstanding puzzles are important to address, not just because of their
theoretical preeminence, but also because their solution would have considerable pragmatic ramifications. Indeed, many lay people, members of the judicial

system, people working with children, and writers in the popular and scientific press frequently espouse the belief that,

> Hidden away in each of us is a permanent record of our past. The smell of a school canteen can conjure up long-forgotten images of childhood; vivid replays of past events can flash by at times of intense fear. Even if it is sometimes hard to recall experiences, they are permanently inscribed somewhere amid the billions of neurons in your brain
>
> (Furlow, 2001, p. 25).

This idea, that even the earliest of experiences survive intact in our neural structures, is not just a recent invention but one that dates back to some of the earliest known thinkers and philosophers (e.g., Aristotle, ca. 345 B.C./2001; Plato, 360 B.C./2004). At the beginning of the twentieth century, Thorndike (1905, pp. 330–331) recapitulated this notion when he stated, "Each mental acquisition really leaves its mark . . . Nothing of good or evil is ever lost. . . . Every event of a man's mental life is written indelibly in the brain's archives." Similar claims can be found in the writings of other luminaries, including Sigmund Freud (1916–1917/1963) and Otto Rank (1924/1994).

So entrenched is this notion that events experienced early in life are formative and remain permanently etched in our memories, exerting their influence throughout our lives, that many take it for granted in numerous areas of everyday functioning. For some, these beliefs go beyond simple ideation and can lead to (and indeed have led to) potentially serious consequences in their lives and the lives of others. Our courts are awash with claims of memories for traumatic experiences that are said to have occurred very early in life, memories so detailed that they appear to the layperson (e.g., juror) as highly believable. These early "memories" are said to be exerting a negative effect on the person's life, oftentimes having resulted in clinical depression, suicidal ideation and behavior, post-traumatic stress disorder (PTSD), and other maladies in adulthood. Indeed, claims abound that even if one cannot consciously recollect these memories, the residue of these early experiences can still affect behavior in adolescence and adulthood. For example, the vestiges of early experience (remembered or not) have been said to shape subsequent violent behavior (Karr-Morse & Wiley, 1997).

Beliefs about the permanence of early memory have also served as the basis for some modern therapeutic interventions. In fact, it has been claimed that memories of very early experiences (ostensibly imprinted on the nervous system) shape a child's future psychological health (e.g., Janov, 2000). According to some, these memories are not limited to postnatal experiences, but can arise during the birthing process itself. For example, some therapists have linked the desire for sexual bondage to memories of entanglement with the umbilical cord during birth, or proposed that the fear of being crushed is linked to memories of a prolonged birthing process caused by the narrowness of the mother's pelvis (see, e.g., Janus, 1993).

The idea that we can remember being born is not as uncommon as it once was, having appeared in a number of popular books where it has been claimed that remembering our birth is the rule, not the exception (e.g., Chamberlain, 1990, 1998). According to these writers, birth memories are "deeply hidden in the unconscious mind (and) usually announce themselves indirectly. They appear in association with some triggering event, such as watching people fall through space in a movie, seeing someone pinned down in a fight, or perhaps just watching a fish wriggling and struggling on a fishing line" (Chamberlain, 1998, p. 92). Like the previously hypothesized existence of repressed memories of sexual abuse, birth memories and memories of intrauterine life are said to lie hidden deep in the unconscious recesses of our neural hardware, but also that they can, under appropriate conditions, become part of our consciousness (see Chamberlain, 1998; Janov, 2000).

So strong is this belief that our early experiences survive intact in memory that a number of therapeutic procedures have been developed that encourage the patient to contact these memories in order to "cure" some current, maladaptive behavior. One infamous case reported in the popular press occurred during a "rebirthing" therapy session. Based on the belief that psychological disturbances can have their roots in unconscious memories of the trauma experienced during the birthing process, therapists Connell Watkins and Julie Ponder and their assistants wrapped Candace Newmaker in a blue flannel sheet, laid her on the floor in a fetal position, and covered her with large pillows. As the therapists and their assistants applied their weight to the pillows that were on top of Candace, Candace was urged to be "reborn" to her adoptive mother, Jeane Newmaker, sitting nearby, by wriggling and struggling to get out from under the pillows. Unfortunately, the 70-pound Candace was unable to get free from the weighted pillows, began shrieking that she could not breathe and that she was going to die, and eventually she did die (for an account of this tragedy, see Lowe, 2001).

Apparently, not only do we need to be cognizant of unconscious memories during and after the birth process, but according to some, of intrauterine experiences as well.

> We must push the envelope back to womblife if we are to understand and treat all manner of later disorders. Just when some of us caught on that birth trauma affected us for a lifetime, now we must consider prebirth events as even more important in shaping our lives. We "do not get over it, nor do we grow out of it" (Janov, 2000, p. 211).

Similarly, there are those who would have us believe that children and adults can remember past lives (e.g., Shroder, 2001) and that these past-life memories affect current behavior, including one's physical and psychological health (e.g., Bowman, 1998). Of course, these "theories" are not backed by any rigorous scientific investigations (see Spanos, 1996). Indeed, at best, there may be some clinical observations that appear to be consistent with such claims, and at worst, much of this "theorizing" is the product of armchair speculation. Moreover, the majority of this observational "evidentiary" base involves tautological and circular reasoning about simple observations. For example, unexplained behaviors, such as a person's fear of loud noises, are attributed to that person's musings when in an altered state of awareness. Such musings might include a hypnotized five-year-old's "memory" of being in a war during a past life (Bowman, 1998) or an adult's comments about their past life experiences when questioned under the influence of LSD or during age-regression hypnosis (see Hepper, 1997). Alternatively, others have examined both mothers' and children's narrative accounts of the birth process, where the data consist of an analysis of agreements and disagreements in their accounts of this event (e.g., Chamberlain, 1990, 1998). Of course, it is not clear what such narrative comparisons tell us about memory of those experiences because there is little evidence that preverbal experiences (of which being born must surely be one) can be talked about once language has developed (e.g., Richardson & Hayne, 2007; Simcock & Hayne, 2002). Moreover, it is by no means clear that if a narrative is produced, it is a narrative about a memory for the target event and not simply a recounting of something that has been discussed with the parent well after the event occurred.

Given the lack of scientific credibility for ideas concerning memories of past lives, intrauterine memories, or memories of birth experiences, what types of events are we capable of remembering and at what age are we capable of remembering them? Although early experience undoubtedly plays a role in subsequent development, are these experiences encoded in such a way as to make them accessible to consciousness later in life? If not, do these experiences still influence our behavior later in life despite their absence from our awareness? Perhaps their effects are already embedded in who we have become, their influence already established at the time they have been experienced. If so, there may be no need to explicitly remember these events as they are now a part of what it is we have become. As an example, is it necessary to remember the event or events that led up to knowing how to add numbers together? Probably not, but it may be necessary to remember how to add numbers together. Similarly, is it necessary to remember every time we have eaten at a restaurant to know how to behave in a restaurant? Obviously not, as long as we remember what behaviors are expected of us when we are in a restaurant.

Although these examples illustrate an important distinction between semantic knowledge/memory (e.g., appropriate restaurant behavior) and episodic or autobiographical knowledge/memory (e.g., remembering a specific experience of ourselves in a restaurant), a distinction that will be important throughout this book, it also illustrates another key point about experience: In order for an experience to have an effect on us, it is not necessary for us to have a conscious memory of that event. The event itself has an impact at the time it is experienced, changing us (for better or worse) as the experience itself is occurring. Moreover, these experiences need not be indelibly etched as separate and individual episodes in the brain, neither as a memory nor as a change that cannot be altered by subsequent experience. Human plasticity (both neural and behavioral), whether it has to do with the effects of prenatal stress or postnatal experience, is critical to our understanding of how events, remembered or not, can shape us, sometimes for the worse (e.g., the impact of child maltreatment) but at other times for the better (e.g., resilience once the maltreating experience is removed) (Nelson et al., 2007; Pollak et al., in press; Rutter et al., 2007a, 2007b; for reviews, see Marshall & Kenney, 2009, and Belsky & Pluess, 2009). Thus, to a large extent, conscious, explicit memory for single episodic events may not always be a prerequisite to learning, knowledge acquisition, or human development.

So, what do we remember and when? These are the questions that form the core of this volume. The short answer is that the earliest we begin remembering events is around 18 to 24 months of age. Although we have evidence that memory is operating before that, when we talk about being able to remember specific experiences in a more than fragmentary fashion (e.g., hazy images), the earliest reported memories have be dated to when the individual was 1½ years old, and even here, such memories are extremely rare (Usher & Neisser, 1993) and may occur only in individuals with unusual memory abilities (Price, 2008).

In the first part of this book, I examine the beginnings of memory very early in life. As it turns out, the emergence of memory early in life is essential to the flexibility with which infants adapt and learn about their environment. Although the functioning of memory relatively early in life provides humans (and some nonhumans) with an evolutionary "edge" early in life (see Chapter 10), it has not always been easy to investigate the nature of earliest memory. As we will see in Chapter 2, the study of memory prior to language acquisition is difficult at the best of times, although it is clear that such memories exist. Like the study of memory in nonhuman animals (see Chapter 4), the study of memory in human infants has been facilitated by a number of extremely clever paradigms that have been devised to provide us with considerable insight into the nature of early, nonverbal memory. As we will see, we are born well prepared to form memories very early in life, despite not being able to bring these experiences to conscious awareness in later childhood and adulthood. Although the neural underpinnings responsible for encoding, storage, consolidation, retention, and retrieval of memories for our experiences develop very early in life (see Chapter 3), our experiences are not available to later conscious recollection unless formed sometime after 18 to 24 months of age (see Chapters 4 and 5). Even then, such memories can be highly fragmented and are susceptible to influences of a whole host of factors that promote forgetting, not retention.

In the remainder of this volume, I examine what happens to memories that are formed after the period of infantile amnesia. Again, like with earlier memories, the development and retention of these later semantic and episodic autobiographical memories are critical to human adaptation. That is, they not only provide us with an understanding about how the world we live in operates (semantic autobiographical memory or one's knowledge base) as well as memories for key past experiences (episodic autobiographical memory), but also allow us to plan for future events—a sort of "anticipatory map" for future behaviors (see Chapter 10). This latter part of this volume sets forth ideas about the relevance of consciousness to early memory (Chapter 6); the role of distinctiveness, emotion, and stress in children's memory (Chapters 7 and 8); and the importance of a flexible, reconstructive memory system that, although frequently accurate, sometimes leads us down a path where memory illusions become memory truths (Chapter 9).

In the final chapter (Chapter 10), I make explicit a point that is woven throughout this volume and something that is perhaps all too obvious—that is, that memory, both the semantic and the episodic aspects of autobiographical memory, is adaptive. Indeed, although perhaps a trivial idea in its inception, memory as described in this book has been essential to evolutionary adaptation in humans and nonhumans alike. Although this truism may be self-evident in any number of observations, perhaps the most important advantage accrued from having the memory system that we do is that adaptive change can (and frequently does) occur in ontogenetic time (within an individual's lifespan) and does not have to await the more tedious process of phylogenetic change (across evolutionary time). The emergence of this autobiographical memory system is contingent on the co-emergence of the "self," a self that is thought to arise out of the very memories it now serves to organize. Self-consciousness and autobiographical memory stand in a dynamic relationship, with the self forming the interpretation of these experiences and shaping the memories that are formed from these experiences. In turn, these memories (or reconstructions of experiences based on these memories) help define the self and our interpretation of who we are and what we might become through planning future behaviors.

We may never know the evolutionary pressures that transformed earlier and more basic (sensory and perceptual) memory systems into the relatively sophisticated one we possess today. However, it is clear that the key adaptive functions of this new system lie in the role it plays in the emergence of self-consciousness and in its role as a support system for guiding future decisions and behaviors that enable survival (and, perhaps, reproductive success). The following chapters, then, provide an account of the emergence and development of this early autobiographical memory, a memory system that is inherently dynamic and self-organizing. These memories are important, not simply because they are dynamically intertwined with our self-consciousness, but because they are meant to insure our survival by preserving some aspects of the self while altering others, even when such changes modify the contents of our memories.

2

Studying Memory in Nonverbal Human Organisms

> I shall suggest, on the contrary, that all communication relies, to a
> noticeable extent on evoking knowledge that we cannot tell, and that
> all our knowledge of mental processes, like feelings or conscious
> intellectual activities, is based on a knowledge which we cannot tell.
> —Michael Polanyi, chemist, philosopher, 1891–1976

The study of memory in humans has been dominated by verbal remembering protocols. Frequently when we ask children to remember an event, what we intend is that they provide us with a narrative account of some prior experience. Indeed, the study of autobiographical memory has been dominated by narrative accounts of past events elicited by verbal stimuli such as individual words (e.g., Morrison & Conway, 2010; Usher & Neisser, 1993) or requests to "tell us about your earliest childhood memory" (for a review, see Howe, 2000). Although a detailed discussion of these findings is deferred until Chapter 5, the question that is the main concern of this chapter is how we elicit memories from nonverbal humans (a discussion of nonverbal recollection in nonhuman animals can be found in Chapter 4). If much of what is in memory is stored nonverbally (see Paivio, 2007), then there must be ways we can access and express memories in a nonverbal fashion as well.

There are three main paradigms used to study memory in nonverbal (primarily human) organisms: visual habituation, mobile conjugate reinforcement paradigm, and deferred and elicited imitation. In what follows, I review the research in each of these three areas and what they tell us about the development of very early memory. Along the way, evidence about whether these tasks can be used to distinguish between *implicit* (not consciously accessible) and *explicit* (consciously accessible) memory is discussed. As we will see, whether this is a useful distinction is yet to be determined. Useful or not, recent work concerning the storage of early traumatic experiences in an implicit memory system will be considered, and the effects of these "memories" on subsequent nonverbal behavior and the health of the organism will be reviewed.

Visual Habituation Paradigm

Visual habituation is one way researchers have allowed nonverbal organisms to show us what is stored in their memory, as they are unable to tell us verbally. Due to limited motor skills, infants have only a finite repertoire of behaviors they can use to express their memories (e.g., leg kicks, sucking, visual fixation). The visual paired-comparison task (VPC) is particularly advantageous as it is one memory task that can be used across the entire first two years of life, or what is called "the period of infancy."

The VPC was originally designed to examine perceptual development in nonhuman animals (e.g., chicks, infant chimpanzees—see Fantz, 1957, 1958b) but was quickly adapted for use in the study of infant humans (Fantz, 1958a). Following the demonstration of visual habituation in human infants, the VPC has been used to study early memory development (Fantz, 1964). The procedure involves two stages: a period of familiarization followed by a test. During familiarization, infants are presented with a pair of identical visual stimuli for either a fixed period of time or a predetermined time period in which the infant is looking at the relevant stimuli. After a delay, the infant is tested using another pair of stimuli where one stimulus is the same as the ones seen before and the other stimulus is new. The primary dependent measure is the amount of time the infant looks at each stimulus during the test. Memory for the original stimulus is inferred when infants look longer at the novel stimulus than the original stimulus—that is, they exhibit a novelty preference. Forgetting is inferred when the infant looks at both stimuli for similar amounts of time—that is, they exhibit no preference.

These inferences are based primarily on Sokolov's (1963) comparator theory of the orienting response. In this theory, the infant is said to form an internal representation of the original stimulus, at which point the stimulus ceases to elicit an orienting response, and the infant stops looking at the stimulus display. During the test, the familiarized stimulus, being stored in memory, does not elicit attention; whereas the novel stimulus, not being previously stored in memory, elicits attention. More precisely, the degree to which each stimulus elicits attention at test is a direct function of the discrepancy between the internal representation and the external reality (Sokolov, 1963). Given sufficient familiarization, the old stimulus should elicit little attention, with the majority of the infant's looking time (or longer periods of looking time) going to the novel, previously unseen stimulus. This latter *novelty preference* is frequently interpreted as an index of memory strength for the original stimulus.

Developmentally, the amount of fixation time necessary to form an internal representation decreases with age, the rate at which visual habituation occurs increases with age, and the length of the delay between familiarization and test increases with age (for reviews, see Colombo & Mitchell, 1990, 2009). What this means is that stimulus encoding is faster, and the length of the time over which the internal representation is viable in memory increases with age. These changes in memory (speed of encoding and the length of time information remains in storage) that occur with age during infancy using the VPC paradigm are similar to those seen in other methodologies (see later in this chapter).

The question remains, what is it about infant memory that the VPC is actually measuring? The problem here is that there are additional ways to interpret the outcome of these tasks, ones that are not always consistent with Sokolov's (1963) model (see Colombo & Mitchell, 2009). For example, some researchers have proposed that the null preference does not represent complete forgetting. Instead, the null preference can represent a transition phase where the memory for the original stimulus, although weaker, is nonetheless, still present. Thus, depending on the length of the delay between familiarization and test, infants' memory for the original stimulus (or their ability to access the memory representation) can change from relatively strong (novelty preference) to intermediate (null preference) to weak (familiarity preference) (see Bahrick et al., 1997; Bahrick & Pickens, 1995; Courage & Howe, 1998, 2001). These and more recent studies (e.g., Richmond et al., 2007) have confirmed that a null preference is not indicative of complete forgetting and that early infant memory can be expressed in terms of novelty preference, null preference, and familiarity preference, depending on the accessibility of the representation in memory.

Since its inception, the VPC has been used, not only to study memory in infant nonhuman and human animals, but also in children (e.g., Overman et al., 1993) and adults (e.g., Richmond et al., 2004). Although not without its critics, the VPC has frequently been interpreted as a measure of explicit or declarative memory. For example, McKee and Squire (1993) studied human patients with medial temporal lobe (MTL) damage using the VPC task, where the delay between familiarization and testing ranged from two minutes to 24 hours. Whereas adults without MTL damage exhibited novelty preferences across delays of an hour, those with MTL (hippocampal) damage exhibited null preferences after delays as short as two minutes. Because declarative or explicit memories are dependent on an intact hippocampus (among other things, see Chapter 3), these and other, similar results (e.g., Pascalis et al., 2004; Zola et al., 2000) have led a number of researchers to conclude that the VPC task measures explicit or declarative memory (Manns et al., 2000; Nelson et al., 2006).

Despite this more recent evidence, there still remain questions about whether the VPC represents a measure of nonverbal explicit or declarative memory.

For example, as we will see in Chapter 3, the neurobiological development of brain systems that subserve explicit memory is thought to be somewhat protracted, extending to the latter part of the first postnatal year. It is not clear how this neural time frame squares with research using the VPC that has demonstrated that three-month-olds can remember visual stimuli after considerable delay (Courage & Howe, 1998, 2001). Although the VPC is an example of a hippocampal-dependent memory (Pascalis et al., 2004), that does not necessarily make it an explicit (consciously available) form of memory (Kunst-Wilson & Zajonc, 1980).

Alternatively, perhaps the evidence concerning the neurobiological readiness of the explicit memory system has overestimated the postnatal age at which these systems are available in the infant's memorial repertoire. That is, it may not be that basic memory processes are controlled by two independent neuroanatomical systems that mature at different rates—one that regulates implicit or procedural memory and the other controlling explicit or declarative memory. Rather, it may be that the types of information infants versus older children and adults select to encode changes across development. This more recent *ecological model* holds that it is not the memory systems themselves that change, but rather that what the organism attends to (and hence encodes and stores) changes with development, and that it is this change that is responsible for what has been interpreted as an ontogenetic shift in basic memory processes (Rovee-Collier & Giles, 2010). Before considering these alternatives in more detail, I turn to a review of some of the research that has led to this new ecological conceptualization, the conjugate reinforcement paradigm.

Conjugate Reinforcement Paradigm

The *mobile conjugate reinforcement* paradigm consists of three main stages: a *baseline* stage, in which a ribbon is tied to the infant's ankle but not to an overhead mobile, so kicks do not move the mobile; an *acquisition* stage in which the ribbon is now attached to a hook that moves the mobile when the infant kicks; and a *retention test* stage where, following a delay interval whose length can be varied systematically, the ribbon is again connected to the infant's ankle but kicking does not move the mobile. During this latter test phase, infants are shown the same mobile as that during acquisition or one that differs in some way from the original. Infants whose kick rate during test is higher than that during baseline are said to recognize the mobile, and those responding at the baseline rate are said to not remember the mobile.

This is a very powerful paradigm for a number of reasons. First, the retention interval can be varied systematically, allowing researchers to determine the length of time information is accessible in infant memory and how this develops. Second, what goes on during the retention interval can be varied (from presenting no additional stimuli to presenting competing information), enabling researchers to examine the influence of the type and timing of additional experiences on infants' memory. Third, the properties of the stimulus (mobile) can be systematically changed at test, allowing the researcher to understand the properties of the stimulus display that are important and that get encoded and stored in infants' memory at various stages of development.

What the research using this paradigm has shown is that the duration of retention increases monotonically over the first six postnatal months. For example, two-month-olds typically forget the relevant contingency after one or two days, whereas six-month-olds can remember for as long as 14 days (e.g., Hill et al., 1988). More important, even very young infants can remember after long delays if they receive periodic reminders of the contingency during the retention interval. These reinstatement (reintroducing the original training conditions) or reactivation (exposure to only a fragment of the original event) procedures serve to prime memory for the earlier-learned contingency, increasing its accessibility in memory. For example, when three-month-olds are briefly exposed to a memory prime (sitting under the mobile for three minutes while the experimenter moves it) after a period when they normally would have forgotten the contingency (e.g., 13 or 27 days post-training) and are then tested for retention 24 hours later, forgetting is alleviated and the infants' responses are elevated to levels akin to those observed at the end of acquisition. These results have been obtained throughout the infancy period, and in some instances, infants have been able to retain memories for 4½ months and sometimes much longer (for reviews, see Rovee-Collier & Cuevas, 2009a, 2009b).

Using a variety of other memory paradigms, the effects of reinstatement and reactivation have been observed not only with infants but also in toddlers, older children, and adults, as well as in nonhuman animals (e.g., Campbell & Jaynes, 1966; Howe et al., 1993; Spear & Parsons, 1976). Other factors have also been found to affect the length of time infants can remember, factors such as the amount and distribution (massed versus spaced) of training. Again, these variables have similar effects on memory in toddlers, older children, adults, and some nonhuman animals. However, despite the similarity of these effects across age and species, or perhaps in part because of it, the type of memory being tapped by this paradigm has been a topic of considerable debate. Specifically, some view this type of memory as being similar to that observed in operant conditioning (i.e., procedural or implicit memory), and not what we would consider explicit or declarative memory for a specific event or episode (e.g., see Bauer, 2007; Mandler, 2004).

One basis for this argument is that the patterns of generalization, extinction, and reinstatement seen using this paradigm are more typical of effects seen in implicit than explicit memory. A key point here concerns the issue of generalization of learning. In young infants (two- and three-month-olds), memory is highly specific, and they fail to recognize the training mobile at test when even a single element has been changed. Indeed, even minor modifications to the context in which the contingency was learned (e.g., changes in the fabric of the crib liner) can produce profound changes in measures of infant retention (see Rovee-Collier et al., 1992). Rovee-Collier and her colleagues have provided considerable evidence that memory in infants is highly context-dependent, a dependency that includes many aspects of the experimental setting, including the room, ambient odors, the experimenter, and even the infant's affective state. Young infants encode a variety of these components of the incidental context, which then become part of the memory trace associated with the learning experience. If the external context at the time of testing is altered from that of acquisition, infants' exhibit impaired retention (for a review, see Rovee-Collier & Cuevas, 2009a).

However, the importance of context specificity in memory may be more apparent than real when trying to decide whether the mobile conjugate reinforcement paradigm measures implicit or explicit memory. For example, although explicit memory is said to exhibit considerable flexibility and is not so contextually bound, it does contain information about both the external and internal context in which the learning episode occurred. Although such information does not have profoundly detrimental effects on retention, depending on how memory is cued, such features can interfere with remembering, depending on the nature of the retrieval cues (for recent research on context-dependent memories, see Howe & Malone, in press). Moreover, infants do not always exhibit such high levels of context specificity. For example, when infants are trained in multiple contexts, context-specificity effects tend to vanish (Amabile & Rovee-Collier, 1991; Rovee-Collier & DuFault, 1991). Finally, although apparent in very young infants, the degree of context dependence declines with age across the infancy period (see Rovee-Collier & Cuevas, 2009a, 2009b).

More problematic for the claim that the mobile conjugate reinforcement paradigm is a measure of explicit memory are the requirements that such memory, unlike implicit memory, is available to conscious awareness, and that explicit associations can be formed among discrete learning episodes. Concerning conscious awareness, it is difficult to establish, in the absence of verbal recollection, whether an individual is consciously aware that they have remembered something. Although it is clear that infants may be consciously aware, it is not easy to establish that they are aware that they have remembered something they have experienced in the past.

However, it is clear that infants' memory, like toddlers', older children's, and adults', is associative, and includes not only associations among components of the mobile stimulus itself, but also between components of the mobile and the stimuli that constitute the incidental context (see Rovee-Collier & Giles, 2010). Critically, as development proceeds, the importance of incidental context wanes as infants begin to focus attention on salient components of the stimuli themselves. As Rovee-Collier and Cuevas (2009b, p. 168) point out,

> Very young infants of all species can learn and remember numerous associations between events that co-occur or share a common member or affordance (function). These associations can enter into relationships with previously acquired associations in a complex mnemonic network. As the network expands and becomes increasingly interconnected, their memory performance becomes increasingly flexible.

As we will see throughout this book, it is the establishment of this knowledge base, the individual concepts, their interconnections, and their restructuring with age, learning, and experience, that provide some of the keys to understanding memory and its development.

The issues concerning whether the conjugate reinforcement paradigm measures implicit or explicit memory rests on the critical assumption that these are two different memory systems whose developmental trajectories differ. As seen in Chapter 3, there is neurobiological evidence indicating that there are different substrates that subserve these different types of memory, and that they appear to come on-stream at different times developmentally. However, multiple memory systems need not be invoked in order to explain memory development, even memory development in early infancy. Indeed, in Rovee-Collier and Cuevas' (2009b, p. 170) ecological perspective, the underlying memory process

> . . . does not change ontogenetically, but the content of what is learned and remembered does. Instead of asking *whether* infants remember over the long term, research in this tradition focuses on *what* they remember and under what conditions they remember it.

Rather than relying on the emergence of different memory systems across development, this ecological perspective states that

> . . . at each point in development, infants of all species epitomize a successful evolutionary adaptation . . . [where] they rapidly learn the relationships that define their niche and confer survival and reproductive advantage . . . . To meet each new set of ecological demands,

infants select particular aspects of episodes to learn and remember until their niche changes again (Rovee-Collier & Cuevas, 2009b, p. 168).

Again, it is the importance of what infants need to know in order to adapt effectively to their environment that is critical in this perspective. With additional variation in environmental demands as well as in what the organism has experienced and learned, what gets encoded and stored changes, and what is in memory gets restructured and reorganized in ways that optimize performance to enhance survival. Although developmental changes in the neural mechanisms that serve learning and memory are important, they are not the whole story. Indeed, according to this ecological model, fundamental memory processes themselves do not change ontogenetically. What does change with development is what immature organisms select to encode about events and episodes and what more mature, adult organisms learn from experiences (see Rovee-Collier & Giles, 2010).

Deferred and Elicited Imitation

The two main paradigms that have been used to study early explicit memory are *deferred imitation* and *elicited imitation*. In deferred imitation, infants (as young as three to six months of age and upward) witness a behavior, one that they have not previously experienced: for example, leaning over at the waist and tapping one's head on a pad that subsequently lights up. The delay between witnessing the modeled behavior and the opportunity to imitate that behavior can range from hours, to days, to weeks and even months. Showing the infant or toddler the object involved in the original demonstration cues the opportunity for imitation following the delay. Although it would be easier in this example to light up the pad by simply touching it with one's hand, infants and toddlers routinely use their heads as per the demonstration (e.g., Meltzoff, 1988a, 1988b).

Deferred imitation is said to measure explicit memory because it requires the conscious recall of a specific prior event (see Bauer, 2007; Mandler, 2007). Moreover, these explicit memories are formed following a single observation, in the absence of prior practice, and are retrieved without perceptual support from the to-be-remembered information (i.e., although the objects are available to cue behavior, the imitative act itself is not perceptually cued) (see also de Haan et al., 2006). Finally, explicit memory is said to exhibit *representational flexibility*. This term has been defined in a variety of ways, including "a quality that permits inferential use of memories in novel situations" (Eichenbaum, 1997, p. 554) and "animals can learn relations among stored items and then express this relational knowledge in novel situations" (Squire & Kandel, 1999, p. 99). Both of these definitions of flexibility stress the inferential or relational component of explicit memory. Developmental researchers, on the other hand, have defined representational flexibility somewhat differently, as being "the ability to retrieve memories with cues and in contexts that are not identical to those originally encoded" (Jones & Herbert, 2006, p. 200).

Representational flexibility, at least in terms of this latter definition, has been shown repeatedly in deferred-imitation studies. For example, memory for an imitated sequence has been demonstrated with objects that varied in size, shape, material composition, and color from the original ones (e.g., Klein & Meltzoff, 1999). Moreover, infants and toddlers can generalize imitation across alterations in the appearance of the room at testing and that used to demonstrate the original actions (e.g., Klein & Meltzoff, 1999), in the context at test and that used at original learning (e.g., the child's home rather than the experimental lab; Klein & Meltzoff, 1999), and changes in the individual who demonstrated the original actions and the person who is present during testing (e.g., Hanna & Meltzoff, 1993).

As we saw in the previous section, two- to three-month-old infants' memory as measured in the mobile conjugate reinforcement paradigm is highly context-specific. That is, if either the mobile or the context is altered, then retention is disrupted. Similarly, using the conjugate reinforcement paradigm or other operant paradigms (e.g., the operant train paradigm; see Rovee-Collier & Cuevas, 2009a, 2009b), six-month-olds fail to demonstrate retention when there is variation in the original and test stimuli. This also holds for infants up to six months of age in deferred-imitation tasks as well. Indeed, representational flexibility is not observed in early memory (including imitation tasks) until infants are at the end of their first postnatal year of life. For example, in the operant train paradigm, nine-month-olds exhibited no retention when tested with a train that differed from the one used during original encoding, but 12-month-olds showed similar levels of retention regardless of whether the train was the same or different (e.g., Hartshorn et al., 1998). Similar findings have been obtained in deferred-imitation tasks (e.g., Klein & Meltzoff, 1999).

These findings are consistent with the research that will be reviewed in the next chapter that shows that the neurobiological substrates necessary to sustain explicit memory do not reach a sufficient level of maturation until the latter part of the first year of life. However, there are other aspects of the research on the properties of early memory that pose a serious challenge to this neurobiological timeframe. Indeed, perhaps most problematic when using deferred imitation as a marker for the onset of explicit memory is the finding that even very young infants (three- and six-month-olds) exhibit deferred imitation after a single 60-second demonstration and do so even after delays of up to three months (e.g., Barr et al., 1996; Barr et al., 2003; Barr et al., 2001;

Campanella & Rovee-Collier, 2005). If the neural hardware involved in the creation of explicit memories does not mature sufficiently to support such memories until near the end of the first postnatal year, three-month-olds should not be capable of deferred imitation. Either this timeline is wrong and explicit memory is available very early in life, or deferred imitation, at least in its earliest form, does not require explicit memory.

Interestingly, although the retention function associated with deferred imitation appears to increase linearly with age, there is no evidence of discontinuity at the end of the first year of life, the time when explicit memory presumably emerges (see Barr et al., 1996). Alternatively, explicit memory may be available earlier than anticipated, but additional neurobiological changes are necessary for true representational flexibility to emerge. Of course, it may be that the distinction between implicit and explicit memory is useful only as a conceptual tool, and that such systems are not really distinct neurobiologically or behaviorally— that is, multiple memory systems may be more a matter of fiction than fact (also see Rovee-Collier & Cuevas, 2009a, 2009b; Rovee-Collier & Giles, 2010).

Regardless of what sort of memory deferred imitation measures, preverbal infants exhibit this behavior very early in life, and, like the memory data generated by the conjugate reinforcement paradigm, the delay interval over which such memories are retained increases with age; also, duration of retention is affected by the number of times the memory has been retrieved and the length of the interval between successive retrievals. These findings have also been obtained in a related paradigm; namely, the elicited-imitation task. Here, infants or toddlers are shown multi-step sequences (e.g., making a shaker) where the individual parts are put together in a specified sequence. Some of these sequences are termed "enabling," meaning that the children must follow a specific order in order for the sequence to work, while others can be created using any order. This allows for two measures of performance: getting the individual moves correct and getting them in the correct sequence. In order to insure that the behaviors are unique, infants and toddlers are given the objects involved in the task to see whether they spontaneously form the desired object. Given that they do not, they are then shown how the object (e.g., shaker) is constructed from the parts. Following a delay, they are then given the parts and asked to "make the shaker" (see Bauer, 2007).

Unlike deferred imitation, the elicited-imitation paradigm uses verbal descriptions of the target actions and the event outcome during the demonstration, the infant is allowed to practice the target actions after the demonstration and prior to the test, and the test itself usually begins with verbal cuing. Despite these procedural differences, the elicited-imitation paradigm, like the other paradigms discussed so far, has also shown that as infants and toddlers get older, the length of time they can retain information in memory increases (for a review, see Bauer, 2007). However, although the differences between the elicited- and deferred-imitation paradigms have been considered trivial in the past, subsequent research has shown that they are quite important and affect memory performance. For example, the opportunity to practice the target actions following the demonstration increased the long-term accessibility of information in memory as well as infants' and toddlers' ability to generalize the target actions to novel test stimuli (Hayne et al., 2003). Moreover, the use of verbalizations during the demonstration phase and verbal prompts during testing has also been shown to increase long-term retention and generalization (Hayne & Herbert, 2004). Thus, both the use of immediate imitation and verbal cuing introduce a confounding factor; namely, increased flexibility in responding. That is, immediate repetition of the demonstrated behavior and verbal cuing of those behaviors at encoding and at test are two variables that are known to increase representational flexibility. What this means is that this paradigm may artificially inflate memory flexibility and enhance the probability that the memories formed in imitation paradigms are not tied to specific materials and contexts.

What Measures of Memory in Preverbal Humans Tell Us About the Development of Early Memory

All three measures of memory in preverbal human infants converge on the same set of findings; namely, what gets encoded changes with age and experience, how durable those memories are increases monotonically with age, and the flexibility with which memories can be used also increases with age over the first two postnatal years. It is clear that the neurobiological systems that support encoding, storage, consolidation, retention, and retrieval are available and operating very early in life, perhaps even before we are born (e.g., DeCasper & Spence, 1986; also see Chapter 4 in this volume), at least in rudimentary form. Although there are clear advances in these neurobiological substrates that continue throughout development (see Chapter 3), these developments by themselves are not responsible for changes in early memory development. Indeed, as seen in this chapter, many advances in memory are the result of experience, experience that gives rise to changes in the content and structure of children's knowledge base, which, in turn, leads to changes in what children encode, store, and remember. This cycle begins early in life and continues throughout childhood (Ceci et al., 2010) and into adulthood.

The research reviewed in this chapter also calls into question the utility of the distinction between implicit and explicit memory systems. That is, if explicit memory is what is being measured by imitation tasks, tasks that even young three-month-olds can perform, then explicit memory must be available before the neurobiological systems said to serve this form of memory have matured (see Chapter 3). As already suggested, perhaps imitation tasks measure a very rudimentary form of explicit memory, one whose limitation is representational flexibility. As maturation proceeds, neurobiological developments, along with experience and a growing knowledge base, lead to reductions in content and context-specificity and these memory-limiting tendencies are replaced by increased representational flexibility.

Although the division between implicit and explicit memory is a useful heuristic, it is not clear how this dichotomy stands up to the empirical evidence concerning early memory development (see Rovee-Collier & Cuevas, 2009a, 2009b; Rovee-Collier & Giles, 2010). Indeed, such a dichotomy may be more descriptive than explanatory. What this means is that additional research is needed to uncover the mechanism or mechanisms that drive memory development in preverbal infants, toddlers, and children. As described throughout this volume, an adaptive model of memory and its development does just that. That is, early memory, whether it is implicit or explicit, helps the organism encode, store, and retain key data about the environment in which it lives, information that is essential to its survival. However, before articulating this theory in greater detail, additional background concerning extant research and theory concerning early memory and its development is in order so the stage can be set for this adaptive model of memory development.

In the final section of this chapter, I review another aspect of the implicit-explicit memory debate, one that concerns the retention of early traumatic experiences by preverbal infants and toddlers. Although the role of stress, trauma, and maltreatment in memory development will be discussed more thoroughly later in this volume (see Chapters 7 and 8), I review what is known about implicit memory of early stressful experiences in predominantly preverbal infants and toddlers. Such experiences have been viewed by some as critical in a child's development, and they believe that even though explicit recollection of the traumatic episode may not be possible, such memories continue to play a critical role in many if not all aspects of a child's development.

Exposure to Trauma During the Preverbal Period, and Ensuing Memory

There are well-documented studies demonstrating that infants can "remember" stimuli presented in utero (see detailed analysis of these studies in Chapter 4). By "remember," I mean that they show early preferences for stimuli that are the same as (or similar to) those experienced in utero, not that infants can explicitly or consciously remember the in utero experiences per se. That is, although infants clearly are not remembering the in utero episodes themselves, prenatal experience can influence initial preferences for certain stimuli following birth.

Of course, additional postnatal experiences can change these preferences just as easily. Indeed, there is good evidence that such preferential responses based on prenatal experiences are quickly extinguished by postnatal experience. That is, preferential responding is replaced by newer, more recent experiences that are more relevant to the infants' current set of needs and level of functioning (again, see Chapter 4 for a more detailed discussion).

Like prenatal experiences, early-learned postnatal responses are replaced by more mature reactions as the organism develops. For example, research with rat pups has shown that, as they mature, pups exhibit at least three different types of reaction to fearful stimuli, with each newer one replacing an earlier, more immature response. If the pup has only a single experience with a specific fearful situation, this immature reaction might continue into adulthood if that stimulus is not encountered again during development. However, if this experience is repeated, then more mature responses can be elicited and used in future encounters with these stimuli (see Yap et al., 2005). Thus, although it may be possible to retain immature responses into adulthood (e.g., as when one experiences a single, one-time traumatic event), something that may be a source of certain phobias (see Richardson & Hayne, 2007), more often than not these responses are replaced by more mature reactions as the organism develops.

What about early, preverbal experiences in humans? It is possible that some preverbal memories might serve as the basis for later phobic reactions to certain stimuli. However, because these memories are usually thought to be implicit, the rememberer will not be able to consciously recollect the experience that serves as the basis for this reaction. Of course, as we have already seen in this chapter, early-acquired memories can be updated if they are reactivated and recoded at later points in development. Thus, it is not clear to what extent early, preverbal experiences are retained across development.

A case in point comes from studies of pain early in life. In particular, consider the circumcision of newborn males, something that can lead to changes in later reactions to other painful experiences. For example, baby boys who were circumcised without local anesthetic cried significantly more and exhibited greater behavioral and physiological distress to an immunization injection four to six months later than boys who had been circumcised with anesthesia and those who were not circumcised (Taddio et al., 1997). This and other research (e.g., Taddio et al., 2002) suggests that painful experiences might be remembered implicitly and cause changes in reactions to later painful experiences.

What is not clear is just how long such implicit memories are retained in the absence of repetition of such painful experiences. Of course, infants will not have explicit memory for such events, and thus these memories will not be rehearsed or reinstated via the normal conscious, cognitive mechanisms that can increase the longevity of explicit memories.

However, there are other, non-experimental studies of early trauma that suggest such memories may not be solely implicit. For example, a number of clinicians have examined memories for early childhood trauma, particularly in children who were preverbal at the time of the traumatic event (Gaensbauer, 1995, 2002, 2010; Terr, 1988, 1994). Because children cannot talk about the traumatic experience(s), oftentimes they are seen to reenact part, or all, of the event. Many clinicians consider these reenactments to be "behavioral memories" (Terr, 1988) that are based on implicit memories for these traumatic events (e.g., Siegel, 1995). Others suggest that explicit memory may be involved in these experiences, even those that occur very early in life, and that these experiences may be open to conscious inspection (Gaensbauer, 2002, 2010; Paley & Alpert, 2003). From a therapeutic standpoint, the latter idea could lead to a very different set of interventions than the former—indeed, the ability to consciously introspect on such traumatic experiences might permit a variety of different therapies involving reconceptualizing and reorganizing such experiences with respect to the self (e.g., Gaensbauer & Siegel, 1995).

According to Gaensbauer (2010), explicit memories of early trauma may be the result of the activation of mirror neurons. Mirror neurons were originally indentified in studies of the ventral premotor cortex in macaque monkeys (Gallese et al., 1996). Rather than firing for elementary movements, neurons in this region are activated when macaques are carrying out goal-directed actions such as grasping and manipulating objects. Critically, these neurons fired not only when macaques were actually grasping and manipulating objects, but also when they observed other macaques executing the same actions. That is, executing behaviors oneself or watching another execute the same behaviors resulted in the activation of the same neural network. Thus, because of this visuomotor identity, these neurons were given the name *mirror neurons*.

Subsequent research discovered that mirror neurons were not just mediating visuomotor representations of another's act but also comprehension of the meaning of that action (Rizzolatti et al., 2004). The ramifications of mirror neurons as an underlying neural mechanism for imitation and social cognition were recognized immediately, not just for nonhumans but also for humans (e.g., see Meltzoff & Prinz, 2002). In the human brain, mirror neurons appear to be widespread, being found not only in the premotor areas associated with hand movements, but also in areas associated with mouth movements and language (e.g., Studdert-Kennedy, 2002), extending beyond the prefrontal cortex into areas in the temporal, parietal, and frontal lobes and including connections to limbic areas that are associated with emotion (Carr et al., 2003; Iacoboni, 2007). Indeed, the mirror neuron system is now thought to play a critical role in the processing of emotion in faces, social cognition, and the development of empathy (e.g., Decety & Meyer, 2008; Enticott et al., 2008; Kaplan & Iacoboni, 2006).

Research on mirror neurons strongly suggests that their purpose is not simply to facilitate veridical imitation of an action by others, but rather, to enhance the comprehension of the goals of that action and the motivation behind the action (e.g., Ferrari & Gallese, 2007). The mapping of observed actions by others onto the equivalent neural structures in oneself facilitates this understanding, and it has been given a variety of labels, perhaps the most relevant of which for current purposes is *participatory memory* (Fogel, 2004). It is because of this shared mental mapping between self and other that infants become aware of specific mental and emotional states associated with particular actions and at the same time come to appreciate the resonance between their own actions and those of others (e.g., see Meltzoff & Brooks, 2007).

Importantly, returning to the question of whether such "participatory memory" can exist early in life, and particularly in the preverbal infant, the answer appears to be yes. Indeed, there are many studies that now show that even newborns have the capacity to imitate a range of mouth movements (lip and tongue) as well as emotional facial expressions (e.g., Meltzoff & Moore, 1977). Together, this body of work strongly suggests that mirror neurons are present very early in life and are active, at the very least, in the first few postnatal days (also see Berenthal & Longo, 2007; Lepage & Theoret, 2007). This is not to say that the infant is immediately aware of the meanings of, or motivations behind, observed behaviors. This will depend on the infants' current cognitive abilities, including self-conscious awareness of their own actions, ability to discriminate between self and other, and their understanding of thoughts and emotions.

Interestingly, although mirror neurons may be activated automatically and implicitly, such pathways are arguably available to subsequent conscious inspection. This is only possible if the activation of mirror neurons gives rise to some kind of lasting memory trace (e.g., see Stefan et al., 2008). The residue of imitation, as we saw earlier in this chapter, can create memories lasting many months. Thus, it may be possible that memories based on mirror neuron activation while simply observing another's behavior can be long-lasting, even in preverbal infancy.

If this is true, then there is no reason not to suppose that traumatic experiences might give rise to memories that, although initially activated automatically and implicitly, can be consciously accessed at a later time. That is, infants and toddlers may reenact (imitate) events witnessed, traumatic or not, automatically and without intentional awareness. Such reenactments might constitute the "behavioral memories" discussed by Terr (1988) or the "participatory memories" referred to by Fogel (2004). As Gaensbauer (2010) has argued, these memories are not simply veridical copies of the original actions, but contain the goals and motivation behind the witnessed behaviors. Indeed, concerning traumatic experiences, Braten (2007, p. 305) argued,

> ... the victim may come to experience engagement in the bodily motions and feelings of the abuser, not just the suffering. That leaves the victim with a compelling bodily and emotional remembrance that increases the likelihood of circular reenactment of abuse in peer relations or towards younger children later in ontogeny ... no conceptual or verbal "memory" is required for experiences of abuse in felt immediacy to give rise to reenactment.

Thus, according to Braten (2007) and Gaensbauser (2010), among others, memories of early traumatic experiences in preverbal infants can be stored and, like imitation found for other witnessed behaviors early in life, can be repeated (reenacted) later in childhood. Although this reenactment might occur automatically, such reenactments can be explored consciously, just like other, explicit memories. Indeed, Gaensbauer (2010, p. 20 and 22) states,

> ... there is good reason to believe that even if these reenactment pathways are triggered automatically, they are at the same time accessible to conscious awareness and to neural pathways associated with declarative memory systems .... [At the very least,] even though a traumatic reenactment may be initially driven by a subconscious, automatic recapitulation of "memories" mediated by the mirror neuron system, the behavioral actions and affects associated with the reenactment are available for conscious processing.

Thus, although reenactment can occur without conscious recognition by the actor, leading the observer to believe these are implicit memories, the externalization of these mirror neuron "memories" can lead to the creation of explicit "memories" for these earlier experienced events, ones that can then be interpreted and explored consciously.

As intriguing as these ideas are, to date there are no scientific investigations that directly examine these claims when it comes to memories of traumatic experiences. Although there is clear evidence for the existence of mirror neurons and the important role they play in early social cognition and imitation, it is not clear that they play the same role in children's "recollection" of early traumatic experiences. What evidence exists is anecdotal and consists primarily of case studies of children's play therapy sessions. Interpretation of the child's reenactment behaviors is provided by the therapist, usually in light of prior knowledge about the trauma that was witnessed or experienced by the child. Although case studies provide extremely valuable information, there can be multiple interpretations of the observed behavior. If one did not already know the circumstances of a child's trauma, reenactment behaviors (e.g., stabbing actions, hitting people on the leg, physical fights with dolls) (see Gaensbauer, 2010), although clearly involving aggression and fighting, do not unambiguously indicate what the therapist already knows; namely, that this child had witnessed their father being fatally stabbed in a fight. The problem here is a familiar one: there are multiple interpretations of just about any behavior. Traumatic, like non-traumatic, experiences affect different children in different ways—there is no one-to-one correspondence (i.e., the familiar one [behavior]-to-many [interpretations] problem). Although the mirror neuron hypothesis does contain room for creative variations in how children reenact similar traumatic experiences, the problem still remains as to how we can unambiguously decipher what the child's current behavior indicates about the contents of their memory of a traumatic experience.

Not to put too fine a point on this, but consider a drawing by a 10-year-old child depicting an attacker with enormous knives, slashing two individuals who are prostrate, with blood gushing out of their bodies. At first glance, this would appear to be a child's attempt at illustrating a terrible nightmare. But instead, it gives an insight into the deeply disturbed mind of a boy who was brought up in a dysfunctional home and, despite his tender years, routinely watched sick horror movies. Worse, who would have known that the "artist" drew this image (inspired by the 18-rated horror movie *Halloween*) only weeks before he (Jon Venables) and Robert Thompson (both then only 10 years of age) abducted and murdered two-year-old James Bulger in 1993.

Based on such drawings, it was impossible to know that the artist was going to murder anyone in the future. Although this example is not one of a traumatic memory being reenacted, the same point holds for "postdiction" (or back-engineering) as it does for prediction. Until future research focuses squarely on such issues, neither an individual behavior nor a set of loosely related behaviors, in the absence of additional evidence, can provide unambiguous evidence about the nature of a traumatic act that may be perpetrated in the future or one that has been perpetrated in the past.

Although we have yet to develop a sophisticated methodology for unambiguously deciphering the contents of memories that are enacted only behaviorally, as mentioned earlier, this does not mean that such case-based evidence does not provide useful information for the study of early memory development. In addition to developing technologies for "parsing" these nonverbal expressions of memory, the idea that mirror neurons may play a significant role in early memory development, particularly in the development of consciously accessible memories, is intriguing. Importantly, to the extent that such neurons play a key role in the development of empathy, something that turns out to be associated with the development of self-recognition, which itself is related to the emergence of autobiographical memory, studying that role may provide for additional insights into how this adaptive memory system emerges and develops in human and nonhuman animals alike. I return to these issues and a number of related matters throughout the remainder of this volume.

Concluding Comments

The study of memory in nonverbal humans involves the use of some very creative paradigms. Together, these research efforts have shown that memory exists very early in life, even prenatally. Implicit memory is certainly operative at birth (and even earlier) and continues to play an important role in infants' and toddlers' learning about the environment in which they live. Although there is controversy concerning the timing of explicit memory, at the very worst, the hardware associated with the formation of consciously accessible episodic (and semantic) memories is available by the end of the first year of life. Although we can remember much earlier in life than was previously thought, later chapters will show that these memories are not well remembered later in life, are poorly organized, and tend to be highly fragmented.

In this chapter I have also discussed the usefulness of the distinction between implicit and explicit memory. Indeed, the utility of this distinction has been questioned in both the experimental and clinical memory literatures. Although the jury may still be out, this theme will recur throughout other chapters in this book.

Finally, early memory, like memory throughout the lifespan, provides an extremely important and evolutionarily adaptive function. Whether we are talking about memories of traumatic or more everyday experiences, infants and toddlers take from those episodes knowledge that is critical for survival. They learn about how their world operates and extract information relevant to developing and revising a knowledge base that will permit their adaptation to that world. At first, these memories rely heavily on their context. As development unfolds and experiences accrue, this reliance on context diminishes, and what gets encoded and stored in memory changes. The information stored in memory can be retained for longer and longer periods of time, and previously stored information is modified and reorganized in the infant's developing knowledge base about the world in which it lives.

This dynamic interplay between what is in memory, how that directs what then gets extracted from the environment, and in turn how what has been extracted alters what is in memory, makes for an extremely powerful and adaptive system. Not only does this system serve the preverbal infant and toddler inasmuch as it permits the reconstruction of episodes that have been experienced in the past, it also allows the organism to construct scenarios that will guide future behaviors. As I document in the next chapter, the neural hardware that permits the operation of this quite sophisticated memory system is itself exceedingly elegant.

3

Neurobiological Development and the Beginnings of Early Memory

> The brain is a marvellous mechanism. Our feelings of love and hate, of good and evil, our appreciation of ugliness and beauty in the world around us, the values toward which we aspire, the injustices which we strive to correct—all these mental riches which form the most treasured part of life for us are somehow generated by the interaction of present experiences with the residue of our past stored in the brain.
> —E. Roy John (from *Mechanisms of Memory*, 1967)

> Whenever you read a book or have a conversation, the experience causes physical changes in your brain. It's a little frightening to think that every time you walk away from an encounter, your brain has been altered, sometimes permanently.
> —George Johnson (from *In the Palaces of Memory. How We Build the Worlds Inside Our Heads*, 1991)

As we have just seen in the previous chapter, early memory development, particularly in the first two years, is quite remarkable indeed. Infants go from being able to remember single actions over a 24-hour period to remembering more complex action sequences for up to three months, and later, to being able to remember sequences for up to a year (see Chapter 2). Of course, it is not simply the quantitative aspects of memory that change as infants develop, but the qualitative components of early memory also develop. That is, older infants not only acquire information more rapidly than younger infants, and retain that information over longer intervals, but they also encode more and different features from the stimulus array than their younger counterparts and can use these richer memories more flexibly across different contexts (see Chapter 2).

The main business of this chapter is to examine the neurobiological developments that are *correlated* with these changes in memory. I stress "correlated" because, although the changes in neurological functioning occur in parallel with the changes we observe in memory at the behavioral level, there are still serious conceptual and methodological problems with assumptions about direct causal relations. Indeed, like other brain-behavior–linked changes that depend on neural plasticity early in life (e.g., phoneme discrimination; see Kuhl, 1993; Kuhl et al., 1992), it is the dynamics of the organism–environment interaction that eventuate in change (also see Marshall & Kenney, 2009; Nelson, 2000). As Greenough, Black, and Wallace (1987) pointed out some time ago, these early interactions may be of two types: *experience-expectant,* in which specific environmental features must be present for neural programming to occur, and *experience-dependent,* in which an individual's particular experiences affect neural programming. Experience-expectant features are thought to be invariant for a given species, occurring in all environments common to that species early in development (e.g., the expectation that an infant experiences normal speech patterns with a properly functioning auditory system). These expected experiences produce specific patterns of neural activity that target the synapses necessary for the development of the system in question. These experiences "sculpt" the neural activity, creating "permanent" synaptic patterns necessary for typical development. If these experiences do not occur, or the pattern of activity is abnormal, then development may go awry (discussion of the effects of a maltreating environment and its potential effects on memory development can be found in Chapter 8). Experience-dependent features are the aspects of the environment that are unique to individuals in the species (e.g., the particular language heard) and form the basis of individual differences. Thus, exploring these dynamics of early adaptation to the environment can enhance our understanding of both invariant characteristics across a species and individual differences.

Of course, memory development (like development in other domains) cannot be simply reduced to changes that occur during neurological development (also see discussion in Ceci et al., 2010). That is, although the changes that occur in the brain during development may be necessary for memory to function, such developments are not sufficient to account for all of the changes we see in early memory development. In fact, as we will see, much of the basic neurological hardware necessary for memory to function properly is in place and operating quite well very early (by the end of the first year) in development.

The final chapter concerning the neuroscience that underpins the emergence of early memory has yet to be written. Despite the unfinished nature of our knowledge in this area, this rapidly progressing research domain does provide us with a number of important insights into the neural underpinnings of memory development. Before we can begin our exploration of this research, however, it is important to be more precise in the distinction that has been drawn between nondeclarative (or implicit/procedural) memory and declarative (or explicit) memory. Nondeclarative memory (or memory without conscious awareness) is said to include the acquisition of motor skills (e.g., riding a bike), priming (e.g., when a concept comes to mind easily and rapidly because it, or some other concept highly associated with it, was encountered previously), and classical conditioning (for a more complete typology, see Squire & Zola, 1996). In declarative memory, participants are consciously aware of the contents of their memory and use deliberate processes to recollect, manipulate, and re-store information.

The origin of this distinction can be found in the study of patients who had become amnesic as a result of surgery that removed portions of their medial temporal lobe (MTL) (Scoville & Milner, 1957). The MTL has been associated with declarative, episodic memory for some time, and comprises the hippocampal formation (dentate gyrus, hippocampus proper [which includes the cornu ammonis or CA fields], subicular complex, and entorhinal cortex); the perirhinal cortex; and the parahippocampal cortex (the amygdala is also part of the MTL and will be described in detail later when we examine the role of stress, emotion, and arousal on memory; see Chapters 7 and 8). For these particular patients, the severity of the amnesia was correlated with the extent of hippocampal removal. Patients with severe amnesia could not learn new information (beyond their immediate memory span) but could remember events two to three years prior to surgery. Additional testing of one severely amnesic patient (H.M.) showed that he could learn new perceptual-motor behaviors (nondeclarative memory) despite having no conscious awareness of the training he received (declarative memory) (Corkin, 1968; Milner et al., 1968). The finding that the hippocampus is involved in declarative memory but perhaps not in nondeclarative memory was initially interpreted within a unitary memory framework (e.g., Milner et al., 1968) but was later taken as evidence that there must be two, dissociated memory systems—the explicit or declarative memory system that depends on the integrity of highly interconnected structures in the MTL (hippocampus, dentate gyrus, and subiculum) and adjacent cortical areas surrounding the hippocampus and the amygdala (perirhinal, entorhinal, and parahippocampal cortices); and the implicit or nondeclarative memory system that depends on many different areas in the MTL that are not integrated (Cohen & Eichenbaum, 1993; Squire, 1992).

Not all theorists view nondeclarative and declarative memory as separate systems. Indeed, many prefer to see them simply as different memory tasks, ones that require different types of processing in order to be successful, but that these different processes are applied to a single memory system (e.g., Roediger et al., 1989, 1990; Toth & Hunt, 1999). A more detailed discussion of these matters is not critical to understanding the neural basis of early memory. For the purposes of reviewing the literature on the neural underpinnings of memory development, it is simply important to acknowledge that the distinction between nondeclarative and declarative memory has been a useful heuristic when studying the neural basis of memory development. For the moment, then, we can remain agnostic as to whether nondeclarative and declarative memory represent different memory systems or are simply different processes used to access a unitary memory system, and simply consider the findings relevant to the neurological basis of memory development.

Neural Underpinnings of Nondeclarative Memory Development

As discussed in Chapter 2, it is difficult to evaluate whether memory performance in nonverbal organisms is declarative or nondeclarative, as it is not clear how consciousness can be assessed. That is, it is not obvious how we can evaluate whether the behavioral measure of memory (e.g., a change in response rate in the conjugate reinforcement paradigm) is mediated by conscious awareness of a retrieved memory (declarative) or is simply a change in response rate due to conditioning, one that does not enter conscious awareness (nondeclarative memory). Recall that one solution to this problem has been to design tasks that share other characteristic features of declarative memory and that produce behaviors quite different from those observed on nondeclarative tasks. Unfortunately, this gives us only an indirect measure at best, and a seriously distorted measure at worst, of whether the organism has conscious awareness of the contents of its memory.

A more promising approach is one that takes advantage of our knowledge concerning the neural substrates of nondeclarative and declarative memory. Rapid progress in this area of research has been facilitated by the growth in neuroimagining techniques (e.g., functional magnetic resonance imaging, fMRI, e.g., Thomas & Tseng, 2008; magnetoencephalography, MEG, Otsubo & Snead, 2001), eye tracking studies (e.g., Richardson & Kirkham, 2004), and electroencephalographic (EEG) research examining event-related potentials (ERPs) (e.g., Reynolds & Richards, 2005). Because nondeclarative memory covers a number of different tasks (skill learning, priming, and conditioning), each is generally associated with its own neural substrate (neocortex, striatum, and amygdala/cerebellum, respectively; see Squire & Zola, 1996). Although each of these tasks needs to be studied on its own if we are to get a more complete picture of how nondeclarative memory develops (also see Lloyd & Newcombe, 2009), there is evidence that all of the structures that permit these different forms of nondeclarative memory are functional very early in life (some even at birth or earlier) (Nelson, 1995, 1997; Richmond & Nelson, 2007; for a recent overview, see Bachevalier, 2008). For example, the cerebellum (critical to conditioning) develops rapidly near the end of the prenatal period and has adultlike myelination (the wrapping of oligodendrocytes around axons) patterns by the third postnatal month (Nelson, 1995, 1997). Indeed, such structures (the cerebellum as well as specific deep nuclei in the brainstem) may subserve some of the simple conditioned responses newborns exhibit (e.g., DeCasper & Fifer, 1980; see Chapter 4). By contrast, as we see next, there is a more protracted period of development for neural structures that support declarative memory.

Neural Underpinnings of Declarative Memory Development

The hippocampus and other MTL structures are critical to declarative memory. Studies of early brain development have shown that although much of the hippocampus is formed early in gestation, the dentate gyrus is one of the hippocampal subfields that is slower to develop (for a review, see Seress & Abraham, 2008). Indeed, the cytoarchitecture does not appear adultlike until the end of the first postnatal year. In addition, there is protracted development of inhibitory interneurons within the hippocampus, with these cells continuing to mature throughout infancy, reaching adult morphology somewhere between two and eight years of age (Seress & Abraham, 2008). This relatively late development of GABA-ergic interneurons may be critical to the development of declarative memory, as there is evidence they play a key role in attention and recognition memory (Kahana, 2006). Thus, although the hippocampus is formed before birth, the slower maturation of the dentate gyrus and the inhibitory interneurons delays the growth of the MTL-related memory system until about two years of age (Seress & Abraham, 2008). As we have seen in Chapter 2, this timeframe is only roughly consistent with behavioral data that shows that there are signs of a very rudimentary declarative memory system early in postnatal life. However, there continue to be advances in encoding, storage and consolidation, and retrieval that are seen throughout infancy and early childhood. In the remainder of this chapter, I outline the growth in various neural mechanisms that underlie these subsequent developments in encoding, storage and consolidation, and retrieval.

ENCODING

As already mentioned, older infants encode more information more quickly than younger infants (Hayne, 2004, 2007; Rovee-Collier & Cuevas, 2009a, 2009b). For example, using the visual paired-comparison (VPC) task, older infants need a much shorter familiarization time (i.e., the time it takes to habituate to a presented stimulus, a measure that is used as an index of how long it takes to store new information in memory) than younger infants (e.g., Rose et al., 2001). Similarly, 12-month-olds require half the demonstration time six-month-olds need in order to exhibit deferred imitation (e.g., Barr et al., 1996). These age-related differences become much less apparent by the end of the first postnatal year, with one- to four-year-olds exhibiting similar novelty preferences given equivalent familiarization times (Hayne, 2004, 2007). What this suggests is that declarative memory emerges early in the first year of life and that at least some of the age-related changes in declarative memory must be related to developments in encoding.

These developmental changes in encoding are likely to be mediated by changes in speed of processing (see Rose et al., 2004). Indeed, recent longitudinal ERP studies support this hypothesis (Webb et al., 2005). Importantly, the hippocampus is not a likely contributor to the development of encoding, because lesions to the hippocampus do not impair memory performance as long as testing occurs immediately rather than after a delay (see Richmond & Nelson, 2007). The most probable neurobiological sources for changes in encoding are the developments that occur in the association cortices. These cortices are involved in the initial registration and temporary maintenance of information (e.g., Markowitsch, 2000), and there is much evidence that the prefrontal cortex, in particular, undergoes considerable postnatal development (for reviews, see Benes, 2001; and Bourgeois, 2001).

Richmond and Nelson (2007) suggest that a major contributor to these changes is the rapid myelination that occurs during the first postnatal year. Although myelination begins in the fifth fetal month, it continues throughout the first two decades of life, with the most rapid changes occurring during the first postnatal year (also see Paus et al., 2001). During this time, the cerebral cortex undergoes rapid myelination, starting with the occipital cortex, followed by the frontal and parietal lobes at around eight months of age, and then the temporal lobe by 12 months of age (Ballesteros et al., 1993). Because myelination allows for more efficient transmission of electrical impulses, it would seem to be a likely candidate for the underlying neural substrate related to the behavioral changes witnessed in the speed of encoding that occur over the first postnatal year.

STORAGE AND CONSOLIDATION

Of course, changes in encoding are but one source of memory development. Indeed, when levels of encoding are carefully equated across age, developmental differences in declarative memory still exist. For example, when Howe and Courage (1997b) equated learning across infants, they found that, as expected, younger (12-month-old) infants took longer to learn the same amount of information as older (15- and 18-month-old) infants. By the end of the learning session, all children had correctly encoded the to-be-learned information and were able to correctly remember it at test. However, following a three-month retention interval, 18-month-olds remembered more than the 15-month-olds, who in turn remembered more than the 12-month-olds.

Similar findings have been obtained in tasks with younger infants. For example, using the VPC task, Rose (1981) demonstrated that whereas six- and nine-month-olds displayed the usual novelty-preference response immediately following familiarization, only the nine-month-olds exhibited a novelty preference following a delay. Using an imitation paradigm, Barr and Hayne (2000) showed that, even when levels of immediate imitation were equated, six-month-olds only retained the imitative response for 24 hours, whereas 12-month-olds remembered it for a week. These and other, similar findings (e.g., Bauer et al., 2000) suggest that the development of declarative memory involves much more than changes in encoding. Instead, there must be other, related changes in infants' ability to remember information, and some of these may involve changes in the retention of information once it has been encoded. Indeed, the ability to retain information in memory for longer and longer periods of time is a major contributor to declarative memory development across infancy as well as into childhood and adolescence (Howe, 2000).

Bauer (2004, 2005, 2007, 2009) has cogently argued that these age differences in retention are most likely due to correlated achievements in storage and consolidation. This suggestion is supported by the observation that not only do older infants retain more information over a longer retention interval than younger infants, but also that older infants exhibit greater savings than younger infants following relearning opportunities (Bauer, 2005).[1] Additional support for this perspective comes from ERP studies of infant imitation (Bauer et al., 2003; Bauer et al., 2006). Based on studies such as these, changes in infants'

---

[1] Reactivation of memory usually involves the re-presentation of a part (or sometimes all) of the original learning stimuli, the context, or both. Interestingly, there is evidence that when a stored memory trace is reactivated, it becomes labile and possibly subject to change or erasure (see Lee, 2009). This raises concerns about the pliability of memory, something that may have positive effects (e.g., lead to the reorganization of memories; see Kaang et al., 2009) or negative effects (e.g., information loss or overwriting; see Hupbach et al., 2009). Fortunately, nonhuman animal research has shown that reconsolidation occurs more rapidly than the initial consolidation of memory, so traces remain labile for considerably shorter periods upon reactivation (e.g., Debiec et al., 2002). As discussed in the various chapters in this volume, reconsolidation has a number of important consequences for memory development, including how children's knowledge base becomes reorganized.

ability to keep information intact in storage for longer and longer periods has been attributed to developments in the dentate gyrus. That is, consolidation of information in declarative memory, a process that can take hours, days, months, and even years, is dependant on the maturation of the dentate gyrus, something that, as we saw earlier, continues to develop into the latter part of the first postnatal year.

To see how consolidation operates, recall that it is well documented that newly acquired information has to go through additional processing in order to be remembered later. This additional processing, or consolidation, takes a very labile trace of immediate perceptual experience and transforms it into a more durable and integrated memory trace of that experience. This process involves the integration and stabilization of inputs from various cortical regions, a task that is believed to be accomplished by MTL structures (including the hippocampus and the dentate gyrus). More specifically, the hippocampus, parahippocampus, and entorhinal and perirhinal cortices bind into a single memory trace the distributed neocortical representation of what has been experienced (e.g., Eichenbaum & Cohen, 2001; Kandel & Squire, 2000). Association areas also contribute by linking the current experience to information already stored in the cortex. The perirhinal and parahippocampal cortices serve as an interim storage mechanism. Here, the vestiges of current experience (the pattern of neural activation) are rehearsed and maintained while the hippocampus is busy linking and elaborating relations between the current experience and representations of experiences from the past already in long-term storage. As a result of these processes, the current experience becomes consolidated and fused into a single episode, one that is associated with previously stored experiences (Eichenbaum & Cohen, 2001).

Developmentally, it is known that aspects of the temporal-cortical network responsible for consolidation undergo more protracted changes in the first few postnatal years. What this means is that the processes responsible for the consolidation of memory traces may not be operating very efficiently early in life, something that might affect the longevity of early experiences in memory. As already noted, although many of the MTL structures of the temporal-cortical network develop early (e.g., the hippocampus), others do not (e.g., the dentate gyrus) (see Seress & Abraham, 2008). For example, at birth the dentate gyrus possesses only 70% of the number of cells found in adults, meaning that roughly 30% develop postnatally. Moreover, the morphology of the structure of the dentate gyrus does not appear adultlike until 12 to 15 months of age. Finally, synaptic density is also delayed relative to other regions of the hippocampus, with dramatic increases not appearing until 12 to 15 months, peaking at around 16 to 20 months. This rapid period of growth, or synaptogenesis (where the number of synaptic connections grows to exceed those found in adults), is followed by a period of stability, and then excess (or unused) synapses are pruned back to adult levels by around four or five years of age (Eckenhoff & Rakic, 1991).

The functional significance of this relative delay in the maturation of the dentate gyrus presents us with somewhat of a puzzle when it comes to understanding its role in memory and its developmental course. In particular, memory does not always depend on the dentate gyrus—one course (the "long route") involves projections from the entorhinal cortex into the hippocampus via the dentate gyrus, whereas another course (the "short route") bypasses the dentate gyrus. Although both versions support memory formation (e.g., Nelson, 1995, 1997), there is speculation that the storage of more stable declarative memories must take the long route (whereas the short route may actually be associated with retrieval, not storage; see Gluck & Myers, 2001). This speculation is consistent with some recent adult neuroimaging studies that have shown higher levels of activation in the hippocampus and MTL structures during the encoding of information that is subsequently remembered than of information that is subsequently forgotten (for a review, see Henson, 2005). Moreover, research using high-resolution fMRI has shown that the dentate gyrus tends to be disproportionately active during the consolidation of new associative memories, but other areas (e.g., the subiculum) are more active during retrieval (e.g., Zeinah et al., 2005).

Interestingly, the prefrontal cortex (PFC) is also thought to be involved in the flexible use of stored information. As documented in the previous chapter, infants frequently fail to use stored information in a flexible manner, often requiring the same context to be present at retrieval as at encoding. This extreme encoding specificity limits the usefulness of stored information, as it precludes the ability to form relational representations. Importantly, then, to maximize the use of relational information when forming memories, the maturation of the dentate gyrus (and the associated inhibitory interneurons) should be accomplished as quickly as possible. Indeed, while such development is protracted, most researchers agree that the maturation of the dentate gyrus and inhibitory interneurons is sufficient that, by at least the age of two years (and perhaps earlier), they are functioning at levels that are adequate for the formation of declarative memories (Seress & Abraham, 2008). This finding also squares reasonably well with some of the behavioral memory data reviewed in this book. However, it may not be until three to five years of age, when synapses are pruned back to those levels seen in adults, something that permits neuronal interconnectivity to match that of adults, that we should see fully functioning MTL processing and a reasonably adultlike declarative memory system (e.g., Goldman-Rakic, 1987; Seress & Abraham, 2008).

It is not just the more protracted development of the dentate gyrus that may affect memory development, but so, too, do changes in the association areas of the cortex (Bachevalier, 2008). Although cortical synaptogenesis begins around the 17th to 24th week prenatally, it is not until the seventh prenatal month that all six layers of the cortex have developed. Despite the fact that synaptogenesis begins around the same time in all cortical areas, different cortical areas mature at different rates due to differences in when pruning of unused connections begins (e.g., Bourgeois et al., 2000; for a review, see Casey et al., 2005). For example, it is well established that pruning begins around the second or third year of life in the human primary visual cortex, but not until much later in childhood (in fact, until adolescence) for the prefrontal cortex (see Huttenlocher, 1979, 1994; Huttenlocher & Dabholkar, 1997). Other changes in the prefrontal cortex, including myelination, also continue well into adolescence (e.g., Johnson, 1997; Schneider et al., 2004). Indeed, some neurotransmitters (e.g., acetylcholine, dopamine) do not achieve adult levels until the end of the first and second decades of life (see discussion in Benes, 2001).

RETRIEVAL

The preceding discussion of the PFC leads inexorably to the topic of retrieval. This is because retrieval of memories from long-term storage is said to depend on activation of the PFC (e.g., Markowitsch, 2000). Imaging studies have shown high levels of activation in the PFC when people are trying to retrieve long-term memories (for reviews, see Maguire, 2001; Nyberg, 1998). Indeed, as will become important later in the discussion concerning the beginnings of autobiographical memory, functional neuroimaging research has shown the importance of prefrontal activation not only in remembering autobiographical events but also in the processing of self-related information (Levine, 2004). Critically, it has been suggested that as pruning progresses in the PFC, there is an increase in the efficiency of intracerebral information transfer, something that in turn results in a more rapid integration of sensory and self-related information, a phenomenon that is key to the emergence of autobiographical memory (see Thatcher, 1997).

Interconnectivity and the Temporal-Cortical Network

Of course, the story of the neural basis of memory development is more than one about the maturation of brain structures. Critically, the story becomes more complete once we understand that it is the set of connections among structures (the paths of communication) that is also key to memory development. Indeed, disruptions in memory can occur due to disruption of connections between structures, even when those structures themselves are intact. For example,

Yasuno and colleagues (1999) documented impoverished memory for temporal order when connections between the hippocampus and frontal cortex were disrupted in the absence of lesions in either structure.

The development of connectivity has often been synonymous with the study of myelination (see earlier in this chapter). Although it is clear that connectivity increases with development, there is little research on how this proceeds in different neural networks, and very little knowledge concerning connections between specific structures involved in declarative memory. There is some research with nonhuman primates to suggest that the period between the end of the first year of life and the beginning of the second year of life is important for the development of connections between the cortex and MTL structures (e.g., Bachevalier & Mishkin, 1984). Additionally, we have already seen that connections between the entorhinal cortex and the hippocampus (the so-called short route) develop earlier than those that link the entorhinal cortex to the hippocampus via the dentate gyrus (the so-called long route).

Recent research (Mabbott et al., 2009) has examined one of the major pathways between the MTL and the PFC: the uncinate fasciculus (Schmahmann et al., 2007). Using diffusion tensor imaging (DTI), Mabbott et al. (2009) found that proficiency in recall in nine- to 15-year-olds was related to the integrity of this connective pathway. However, because research of this sort has only recently become available, our knowledge of the development of interconnectivity is not as advanced as our knowledge of the maturation of neural structures themselves.

In the past, theorists have relied on a somewhat different approach to studying connectivity; namely, the "functional maturity" of the temporal-cortical network that subserves declarative memory. This network functions as a whole only after each of its components and their interconnections have reached an optimal level of functioning, something that in turn is linked to achieving adultlike synaptic levels (Goldman-Rakic, 1987). What this means is that long-term declarative memory should have emerged by the end of the first year of life, with significant changes during the second postnatal year, and continued development for a number of years after that (at least until adultlike synaptic levels are achieved—by the third to fifth postnatal year: Goldman-Rakic, 1987; Seress & Abraham, 2008). Specifically, putting together what has been reviewed in this chapter, with the exception of the dentate gyrus, MTL components of the network reach maturity between the second and sixth postnatal months (Paldino & Purpura, 1979), and the cortical components along with the connections within the MTL (those involving the dentate gyrus of the hippocampus) as well as between the MTL and the cortex should reach functional maturity by the end of the first year and over the course of the second year. The network would continue to mature over the coming years, based on the fact that synaptogenesis increases in the dentate gyrus between eight and 20 months (Eckenhoff & Rakic, 1991), and in the prefrontal cortex from eight to 24 months (Huttenlocher, 1979; Huttenlocher & Dabholkar, 1997). This network may not be complete for some time and is contingent on pruning differences between the dentate gyrus, up until four or five years of age (see Eckenhoff & Rakic, 1991), and the prefrontal cortex, whose pruning extends throughout adolescence (Huttenlocher & Dabholkar, 1997).

Later Developments in the Neural Substrates of Declarative Memory

Included among the developments that take place during the final maturation phases of the cortical-temporal network are changes in metamemory and strategy use, and these developments have been related to changes in the prefrontal cortex (e.g., Nelson et al., 2006) as well as improvements in relational processing or binding related to changes in the MTL (e.g., Newcombe et al., in press). For example, Chiu and colleagues (2006) found that story recall was initially mediated by activity in the MTL in seven- and eight-year-olds, but by activity in both the MTL and prefrontal cortex in 10- to 18-year-olds. This additional involvement of the prefrontal cortex with older children was correlated with increases in rehearsal and other encoding strategies. In a similar vein, Menon, Boyett-Anderson, and Reiss (2005) found that there was decreased involvement of MTL structures and increased interaction between the MTL and prefrontal structures with age in a picture-encoding task involving 11- to 19-year-olds. They suggested that these differences may be correlated with improvements in strategy use, source memory, and awareness that occur across childhood.

Relational memory skills, or binding, also improves across childhood. For example, Sluzenski, Newcombe, and Kovacs (2006) demonstrated that six-year-olds are better able to bind information in animal-environment pictures than four-year-olds, and six-year-olds did not differ from adults. Improvements in binding elements together in a memory trace often leads to better episodic recall, something Sluzenski and colleagues (2006) observed in their work. Such improvements may be correlated with later developing components of MLT systems (Newcombe et al., in press).

Finally, there is an interesting line of research that has emerged recently examining the role of sleep in the consolidation of nondeclarative and declarative memories. Research with adults has shown that sleep, not wakefulness, facilitates the consolidation of newly encoded information—declarative memory benefits from slow-wave sleep (SWS), whereas nondeclarative memory benefits from both rapid eye movement (REM) and Stage 2 sleep (for reviews, see

Born et al., 2006; Fogel et al., 2007; Smith, 2001; Walker & Stickgold, 2004). Interestingly, REM sleep is also associated with the consolidation of emotional memories (see Hu et al., 2006; Wagner et al., 2001).

Similar effects for the consolidation of declarative memories have been observed in children (Backhaus et al., 2008; Wilhelm et al., 2008). This is a particularly interesting finding because the relative amounts of SWS, REM, and Stage 2 sleep are known to change with development (Brehmer et al., 2007; Garcia-Rill et al., 2008; Ohayon et al., 2004). In fact, these differences in the relative amounts of different types of sleep may be responsible for developmental differences in the type of memory consolidation that is supported during children's sleep. That is, although children's (six- to 11-year-olds) consolidation of declarative memories improved with sleep, there were no benefits for nondeclarative memory (e.g., Fischer et al., 2007; Wilhelm et al., 2008). It may be that, for children, sleep preferentially supports the consolidation of declarative or hippocampus-dependent memories. More recently, it has also been shown that sleep facilitates children's consolidation of declarative emotional memories, as it does with adults, but unlike in adults, there was no difference between a wakeful interval and sleep when it came to consolidating children's nondeclarative memories (Prehn-Kristensen et al., 2009). Additional research along these lines might advance our understanding of the neural bases underlying developmental changes in the consolidation of nondeclarative and declarative memories during the course of early childhood and adolescence.

Summary and Concluding Comments

As infants, we come into this world with the neural plasticity necessary to take advantage of the multitude of new experiences that await us. Experience-expectant and experience-dependent processes that can affect much of our neural development also help sculpt our memory systems in such a way that we can adapt to the environment we find ourselves in—by adapt, I mean create dynamic memory representations that allow us to predict, within a reasonable tolerance, where in our environment we can find food and shelter, and satisfy the other basic needs relevant to our survival. We come prepared, as it were, to encode and store experiences, detect regularities in these experiences, and extract the meaning or gist from the memories we construct of our experiences, so that the world we live in becomes knowable and somewhat predictable. We come prepared to create (construct) records of experiences and retrieve (reconstruct) these records when needed in order to make sense of the world we live in, something that allows us to plan future actions and behavior. Repetition of experience not only reactivates previous memories (leading to their reconsolidation: see footnote 1), but signals that such an experience may be important, so that perhaps the synapses involved in the memory trace for that experience are not lost through subsequent pruning. Even in the earliest days of infancy, regularities are discovered (e.g., through habituation), and once they become familiarized and stored in memory, we turn our attention to something novel, perhaps discovering the exception to the habituated "rule."

It is clear from the research reviewed in this chapter that the neural mechanisms necessary (although perhaps not sufficient) for these "feats" of memory are in place early in life. The structures necessary for nondeclarative memory are functional by birth at the latest and in the last trimester prenatally at the earliest. By contrast, the neural structures and connectivity between these structures necessary for declarative memory are functional at the latest by the end of the second postnatal year and at the earliest by the end of the first postnatal year. However, when it comes to declarative memory, it is also clear that, consistent with the behavioral evidence concerning memory development, there are important neurological changes (e.g., connectivity, myelination) that continue throughout infancy and childhood, and into adolescence. These changes may be linked to increased speed-of-processing, leading to better encoding; more efficient or faster consolidation, leading to better retention of information over longer and longer retention intervals; and more flexible retrieval plans, leading to better access to information that is available in storage regardless of the context in which it was acquired.

These and other changes in declarative memory will be discussed in greater detail in the remaining chapters of this book. I have purposely not discussed the effects of early trauma on the neural substrates of memory, nor have I discussed the role of the amygdala and other related structures on early memory development. Instead, with this chapter as backdrop, these effects will be discussed in detail in later chapters concerning the role of emotion, stress, and trauma in memory development (particularly Chapters 7 and 8).

Of course, it should be remembered that memory is more than the neural underpinnings that subserve it (e.g., structures, connections, networks). Indeed, often there can be a fundamental disconnect between what memory behaviors infants exhibit and our understanding of the neural substrates necessary to achieve these memory feats. However, to the extent that changes in the brain can help us understand which components are responsible for declarative memory and when they mature, we may be able to construct a much more complete science of the nature of early memory and its development.

PART II

INFANTILE AMNESIA, AUTOBIOGRAPHICAL MEMORY, AND THE REMEMBERING SELF

4

Infantile Amnesia in Human and Nonhuman Animals

> I remember, I remember,
> The house where I was born,
> The little window where the sun
> Came peeping in at morn.
> —Thomas Hood ("I Remember," 1826)

> My earliest memory is from when I was eighteen months old
> and I was in my crib. My uncle's poodle, Frenchie, woke me up,
> and when I opened my eyes, there he was, his big brown eyes
> staring at me in curiosity, and I started crying.
> —Jill Price (from *The Woman Who Can't Forget: A Memoir*, 2008, p. 26)

How far back can we remember into our childhoods? Is it really possible that we can recollect an experience from eighteen months of age or even earlier? Are our memories from childhood, the ones thought to be formative of the person who we have become, stored somewhere just waiting for the right cue to unleash them into our conscious awareness? Or have these experiences somehow never been properly encoded, or perhaps subsequently altered in memory, making them wholly inaccessible to conscious awareness as we mature? The purpose of this chapter as well as the subsequent one is to answer these longstanding questions.

Infantile amnesia was a term first used by Freud (1905/1953) over 100 years ago to refer to that period very early in an organism's life when memories that are formed tend to be short-lived or become inaccessible after a relatively short time frame. Although defined slightly differently by species, this unique memory phenomenon occurs in humans and nonhumans alike. For nonhumans, "infantile amnesia" typically refers solely to the more rapid forgetting of information that is associated with immature organisms as opposed to the slower rates of forgetting associated with more mature members of the species. Critically, this more rapid forgetting in younger than older animals occurs even when levels of initial learning have been equated (see Arnold & Spear, 1997; Campbell & Spear, 1972). Much of the nonhuman animal research concerning accelerated forgetting during infancy has been conducted with rats. A general consensus has emerged that one cause of this more rapid forgetting has to do with young rat pups' greater susceptibility to interference effects in memory (Smith & Spear, 1981), a condition, as we will see, that is also thought to pertain to young humans (Kail, 2002).

For humans, "infantile amnesia" refers not only to more rapid forgetting early in life, but also to our inability to remember early experiences as maturation unfolds (i.e., in later childhood and adulthood). Although increased susceptibility to interference effects is thought to be one possible contributor to the frailty of early memory in humans, it is by no means the sole factor. In fact, depending upon encoding and retrieval conditions, young infants may not be any more susceptible to interference effects than older children and adults (see Howe, 2000; Rovee-Collier et al., 2001).

Both historical and current explanations of this phenomenon have fallen into two different camps. The first camp focuses on *retrieval* mechanisms. The basic premise here is that information that is stored early in life remains intact in storage, but fluctuations in its retrievability as development proceeds make it more difficult to remember, and hence, infantile amnesia results (Freud, 1914/1938; Hoffding, 1891). This hypothesis and its modern variants assume that storage is permanent and that the inability to recall early experiences is simply a matter of retrieval failure. These failures of remembering could hypothetically be circumvented when the appropriate retrieval cues reoccur in the environment (external or internal; e.g., see Nash's, 1987 discussion of the hypnotic age-regression literature). In essence, this argument amounts to an extreme version of the encoding specificity principle, in which contextually dependent memories survive intact and can be "recovered"[1] only when the original encoding context is reinstated. Of course it is extremely difficult, if not impossible, to reinstate the original encoding context at the best of times, and particularly the state of mind experienced during infancy. In addition, there are considerable data

---

[1] This assumption is similar to that used when it is argued that early memories, especially so-called "repressed memories," are alleged to have been recovered given the sudden appearance of a particular environmental cue (e.g., watching a television program). This argument falters for the same reason as that for recovering memories from the period of infantile amnesia. As well, because storage is not a permanent repository for encoded information, traces stored in memory interact with newly formed traces as well as with the processing of incoming information, altering and changing what is in storage. That is, memory storage is a dynamic, not static, system, one in which the contents can be altered by the encoding, storage, consolidation, and retrieval of new information.

(reviewed later in this chapter) that rule out any pure retrieval account of infantile amnesia.

The second camp focuses on *storage* mechanisms. The basic premise here is that in young organisms, memory storage is extremely fragile, and that infantile amnesia is directly caused by the labile nature of storage so early in the maturation process (Kohler, 1929, 1941). The storage-based explanation has fared somewhat better than the retrieval-based explanation. For example, there is considerable evidence that, although memory is much better in infancy than originally thought, storage is nonetheless relatively fragile in the immature organism (Rovee-Collier et al., 2001). Given that storage is not a permanent repository of encoded information, particularly in the immature organism, then no matter what retrieval remedies are brought to bear, recall of early experiences may be impossible. Indeed, the volatility of memory storage due to the ravages of interference, decay, and forgetting has been well documented over the years (e.g., Loftus & Loftus, 1980), and that it is fundamentally more labile in infancy is well known (Hayne, 2004).

As attested to throughout this book, it is well established that infants form memories early in life. The infantile amnesia puzzle is one that asks the question, what happens to these early memories? This issue concerning the fate of these early memories is key to many theories of development because they almost all place special emphasis on the formative nature of early experiences. For example, for Freud, early experience was pivotal in development, including the formation of neuroses. Many later theories of social, emotional, and personality development also gave early experience an anointed place in our development (e.g., see Ainsworth & Bowlby, 1991). In fact, early research demonstrated the profound effects of adverse experiences in infancy (in this case, social isolation) on subsequent development (Harlow et al., 1971; Skeels, 1966), something that has been more recently investigated in institutionalized children (see Chapter 8). The question that needs answering is whether *memories* of these very early and formative experiences, ones that can, it is alleged, result in aberrant adult outcomes, are still available to conscious inspection as adults, or whether they are forever lost to infantile amnesia, potentially exerting their effects without our awareness (also see Kagan, 1996).

As this chapter unfolds, I will examine the nature of infantile amnesia in both human and nonhuman animal populations. Because a review of the underlying neurobiological developments relevant to memory structures and systems has already been presented (Chapter 3), the emphasis in this chapter will be on the behavioral and cognitive factors related to infantile amnesia in humans and nonhumans (also see Howe, 2008a). Another reason for excluding an additional consideration of these neurobiological changes here is that their timing, at least in humans, is at odds with the empirical findings that autobiographical memories, a sign that infantile amnesia has ended, can begin around the end of the second year of life (see Chapter 5; Howe et al., 2009a). What this means is that neurobiological constraints themselves may not be at the source of infantile amnesia at all. Although there are clear advances in neocortical structures and their interconnections that continue during early maturation, some of which might contribute, albeit indirectly, to the demise of infantile amnesia (see the later discussion in this chapter; also Levine, 2004), it is reasonably well accepted that neither age nor neurological developments by themselves control memory longevity after the basic neural "hardware" essential for declarative memory has been laid down near the end of the first year of life (e.g., Bauer, 2004; Howe, 2000, 2004a). Instead, the termination of infantile amnesia, like changes in other areas of memory, is most likely controlled by alterations in the basic processes of encoding, storage, consolidation, retention, and retrieval that drive memory across development as well as, perhaps, across species. Although such changes may have obvious neurobiological correlates, their origins may have more to do with the development of an organism's knowledge (cognitive) structures than with additional neurobiological change by itself. In what follows, I review this literature on behavioral and cognitive factors associated with infantile amnesia, first for nonhuman animals and then for humans.

Behavioral and Cognitive Factors in Infantile Amnesia

NONHUMAN ANIMAL POPULATIONS

Research on behavioral and cognitive manifestations of infantile amnesia in nonhuman animal populations has focused almost exclusively on the faster forgetting in immature organisms. In addition, more recent questions have arisen concerning whether nonhuman animals might also possess autobiographical (or even episodic) memory. This latter question asks whether nonhuman animals are "stuck in time" (for reviews, see Roberts, 2002; Zentall, 2005, 2006). If they are stuck in time, then nonhuman animals cannot travel (cognitively) into the past and thus do not have what Tulving (1985, 1989, 1993) refers to as *episodic memory*. Tulving has suggested that there are two types of memory systems, one "episodic" and the other "semantic." He has argued that a key difference between these systems is that whereas episodic memory involves autonoetic consciousness (personal awareness of remembering), semantic memory involves only noetic consciousness. In this latter type of consciousness, organisms access general information but do not experience a specific awareness of having experienced it in time.

This distinction has also been linked to "remember-know" judgments. Here, episodic memory is fundamental to *remember* judgments because the organism is aware that this particular experience occurred in the past. However, *know* judgments, although they involve a sense of familiarity, do not carry with them a sense of personal, past experience. Importantly, this sense of time is also involved in being able to plan for the future. Tulving suggests that nonhuman animals possess the ability neither to mentally travel back in time nor to travel forward in time (but see Zentall, 2005, 2006). More specifically, Tulving has argued that despite nonhuman animals' possessing knowledge of the world (e.g., general relationships between stimuli and events) derived from specific episodes, they do not encode temporal information that allows them to travel back and re-experience the past episodes—that is, they have semantic memory but not episodic memory. Indeed, episodic memory may be a uniquely human form of memory, dependent on the development of frontal lobes and conscious awareness (Tulving & Markowitsch, 1998). That is, although nonhuman animals can certainly learn from previous experiences and can anticipate future events, Tulving and Markowitsch (1998) would argue that they do not explicitly (declaratively) retrieve past episodes or make plans for the future.

Interestingly, if semantic memory is a more primitive form of remembering, one that does not require conscious recollection of the episode in which the knowledge was acquired, then what we retain from the infantile amnesia period may have been stored in this semantic memory system (also see Newcombe et al., 2007). That is, all animals (human and nonhuman) can learn from experience; the question is whether when we remember, we also remember the circumstances of how we came to have that knowledge. For example, I know that Ottawa is the capital of Canada, but I do not remember how I came to know that fact. It may be, as Tulving has suggested, that episodic/autobiographical memory is a later-evolving system, one that is uniquely human and requires the advent of a self. More detailed discussion of this possibility is deferred until later chapters (Chapters 5 and 10).

The question for nonhuman animals, then, is whether they possess the what, where, when, and even the "who" of previous experiences, as well as whether they can plan for future events. It is unlikely that we will ever establish directly whether nonhuman animals (or preverbal humans) have autonoetic consciousness. This is because such measures usually entail verbal reports and elaboration of one's phenomenological experiences. In their absence, there are no agreed-upon nonverbal, behavioral markers of conscious experience (Griffiths et al., 1999). Indeed, any model of episodic memory that requires conscious awareness may only apply to language-using organisms of language-using age. With the exception of putatively language-savvy apes and parrots, there would appear to be no litmus test that would establish that an organism was re-experiencing the past when remembering an episode or planning for the future (also see Clayton et al., 2003).

If we accept the futility of using phenomenological criteria in language-challenged organisms to establish the existence of episodic memory, we may then have to settle for providing only indirect evidence. Indeed, researchers have focused on behavioral criteria in an attempt to establish that nonhuman animals (and preverbal humans) do have episodic (or episodic-like) memory. The three main behavioral criteria, ones that are consistent with Tulving's definition of episodic memory, that are required in order to establish that nonhuman animals have a similar episodic-like memory system are: (1) the *content of memory* (recollecting what happened where and when); (2) the *structure of memory* (having an integrated "what-where-when" representation); and (3) the *flexibility of memory* (deploying information in a flexible fashion). Concerning memory content, it is clear that for memory to be episodic, the "when" of what-where-when must be evident (Clayton et al., 2003). The critical point here is that although a number of different episodes can share "what" and "where," they cannot share "when."

However, memory content, although necessary, is not sufficient to guarantee that memory is truly episodic. For example, I know that through the process of confederation, the federal Dominion of Canada was formed on July 1, 1867. Yet no one alive today could claim to have an episodic memory for when Canada became a country. The point here is that organisms can acquire the "what," "where," and "when" of an episode without having experienced the event itself. This is why Clayton and colleagues (2003) added memory structure and memory flexibility to their criteria. Concerning memory structure, the "what," "where," and "when" of an episode must be well integrated in the memory trace for that experience, such that the retrieval of any one component acts to retrieve the others. Finally, concerning the flexibility of memory, because organisms have conscious access to episodic memories (i.e., they are, by definition, declarative), they are *flexible* (whereas nondeclarative memories are viewed as inflexible and inaccessible to consciousness). What this means is that animals should be able to flexibly deploy memories in new situations.

Using all three of these criteria, episodic-like memories have been demonstrated in western scrub jays (*Aphelocoma californica*; Clayton & Dickinson, 1998, 1999; Clayton et al., 2005; Clayton et al., 2001, 2003; Dally et al., 2006), pigeons (*Columba livia*; Zentall et al., 2001), black-capped chickadees (*Poecile atricapillus*; Feeney et al., 2009), magpies (*Pica pica*; Zinkivskay et al., 2009), rats (*Rattus norvegicus*; Eacott et al., 2006; Norman & Eacott, 2005; for a recent review, see Eichenbaum, 2007), meadow voles (*Microtus pennsylvanicus*; Ferkin et al., 2008), honeybees (*Apis mellifera*; Pahl et al., 2007; Zhang et al., 2006), dolphins (*Tursiops truncates*; Mercado et al., 1998), rhesus monkeys (*Macaca mulatta;* Hoffman et al., 2009), white-faced saki monkeys (*Pithecia pithecia;* Cunningham & Janson, 2007), and gorillas (*Gorilla gorilla;* Schwartz et al., 2005). Indeed, there is considerable evidence that many nonhuman animals possess episodic-like memory that contains all three of the key properties: memory content, memory structure, and memory flexibility. Concerning *memory content,* King, an adult male western lowland gorilla, remembered not only the order of previous events, but also correctly remembered where the events occurred (see Schwartz et al., 2005). As well, western scrub jays have been shown to remember not only the what-where-when of specific food-caching episodes, but also which other scrub jay (the "who") was watching them while they were hiding food, and altered their re-caching behavior accordingly (Dally et al., 2006). Concerning *memory structure,* rhesus monkeys have been shown to not only remember the what, where, and when components individually, but that these elements were well integrated in a single memory trace (Hoffman et al., 2009). Even more compelling evidence for the integration of what-where-when components in nonhuman animal memory has been demonstrated with great apes (specifically, chimpanzees, bonobos, and orangutans) who encoded information about what had been hidden (e.g., grape or frozen juice), where it was hidden (in which two out of three baiting locations), and when (how long ago: five minutes to an hour) it had been hidden in a single, integrated memory trace (Martin-Ordas et al., 2010). Finally, concerning *memory flexibility,* pigeons not only exhibit what-where-when memory (e.g., Skov-Rackette et al., 2006) but also have been shown to exhibit flexibility in its use by accurately reporting whether they had recently been pecking, even when such reports were unanticipated (Singer & Zentall, 2007; Zentall et al., 2001; Zentall et al., 2008). This same memory flexibility has been shown in dolphins when they correctly reproduce recently performed behaviors when such performance was not anticipated (for a review, see Hampton & Schwartz, 2004).

The remaining question, when attempting to determine whether nonhuman animals possess episodic or episodic-like memory, focuses on future planning (for recent overviews, see Raby & Clayton, 2009; Zentall, 2005, 2006). Although this research agenda is more recent, there are some promising findings. Indeed, there are some suggestive studies of prospective memory (remembering to do something in the future; e.g., take medication every four hours) in nonhuman animals. For example, hummingbirds remember to revisit blossoms at a rate commensurate with their regeneration of nectar. Males will even interrupt their courtship in order to revisit blooms after their nectar has been replenished (e.g., Gill, 1988). Of course these behaviors do not unequivocally demonstrate prospective memory because it is not clear whether such time–place associations are cognitive in nature or that these behaviors are not being driven by internal timing mechanisms found in many animals (e.g., Gibbon et al., 1984).

Somewhat more convincing evidence exists concerning anticipation in the western scrub jay. These birds, given relevant previous experience, can successfully anticipate which food caches will become inedible or be pilfered by other birds, and adjust their caching behaviors accordingly (e.g., re-cache food when other jays are not present; see Emery & Clayton, 2001). Indeed, western scrub jays, when given food to cache when they are not hungry in the evening, tended to cache that food in locations in which they anticipated hunger the following morning (Raby et al., 2007). Finally, great apes also show evidence of future planning (Dufour & Sterck, 2008; Mulcahy & Call, 2006; Osvath & Osvath, 2008). For example, orangutans and chimpanzees consistently selected the proper tool that would allow them access to a food reward in the future in a room different than where the tool was selected (Osvath & Osvath, 2008). These and other experiments are beginning to demonstrate that a variety of nonhuman animal species may also possess the future planning skills that are associated with a fully functioning episodic memory system (but see Suddendorf et al., 2009, for a critique).

Some theorists have suggested that this research agenda is somewhat misguided and that we will never know what another species' mental experiences are like (Shettleworth, 2007). Others are not so pessimistic but do remain skeptical about whether these studies actually demonstrate that nonhuman animals' memories are episodic or even episodic-like (e.g., Roberts, 2002; Suddendorf & Busby, 2003a, 2003b; but see Clayton et al., 2003). Indeed, the question as to whether nonhuman animals have a potential for autobiographical memory, at least as measured by these three behavioral criteria, remains an area of intense scientific debate and research. Concerning the debate, there are those who suggest that because there is considerable anatomical similarity in (human and nonhuman) mammals in the hippocampal and parahippocampal regions of the brain (Manns & Eichenbaum, 2006), the functional role of these neural regions in declarative memory must also be highly similar and conserved across these species. Furthermore, because the hippocampal and parahippocampal regions are critical for declarative, episodic memory (e.g., de Hoz & Wood, 2006; Tulving & Markowitsch, 1998), these cross-species similarities can serve as the foundation for the claim that episodic (and perhaps autobiographical) memory may exist in a variety of mammalian species and is not special to humans.

However, these arguments may beg the question concerning the autonoetic component (the remembering self) of Tulving's episodic memory. It is possible that this autonoetic component of human conscious recollection is epiphenomenal and is not a requirement of the memory itself across different species—that is, perhaps the autonoetic experience is a feature of *human consciousness* and not an aspect of episodic memory per se (also see Ferbinteanu et al., 2006). If this were the case, then episodic memory could exist in many species and could be accurately measured behaviorally in human and nonhuman species alike, but it is only humans who have the phenomenological experience that they are remembering something from the past. As Manns and Eichenbaum (2006) have pointed out, there can be many differences among species in the psychological properties of episodic memories, including autonoetic experiences. However, these differences are more likely to be due to variations in (a) the neocortical inputs to the hippocampal and parahippocampal regions as well as (b) the neocortical circuitry that mediates their outputs, determining their behavioral expression, and not the consequence of between-species differences in the hippocampal and parahippocampal regions themselves.

Because there is considerable additional research needed before we can close the book on episodic (and autobiographical) memory in nonhuman animals, it is premature to suggest that nonhuman animals experience infantile amnesia in all the senses that humans do. That is, if episodic memory is not present in these species, then it is difficult to argue that early experiences that were encoded in infancy are later forgotten following maturation, the hallmark of infantile amnesia in humans. However, that these same organisms experience more rapid forgetting during infancy, a second key component of infantile amnesia, is not disputed; although, as with episodic memory itself, the cause of this form of infantile amnesia may not be the same across human and nonhuman animal species.

To examine these (and other) questions, Richardson and his colleagues (Kim et al., 2006; Richardson et al., 1986; Richardson et al., 1983; Weber et al., 2006; Westbrook et al., 2002; Yap et al., 2005) have examined the properties of early memory in rat pups. What this research has shown is that younger rat pups forget information more rapidly than older rat pups. More important, this research has demonstrated that many of the behavioral markers that index infantile amnesia in human infants turn out to be not too dissimilar to those observed in nonhuman animals. That is, both human and nonhuman infants forget more quickly than older members of their species, and there is an increase in what can be recollected following the administration of reinstatement treatments. That reinstatement is operative early in life turns out to be quite important, because it has been used to temper arguments about storage failure as the sole cause of infantile amnesia. That is, memories cannot be reactivated (e.g., by a reminder) unless they were present in storage in the first place. Instead, what this finding shows is that at least some aspects of infantile amnesia (faster forgetting) may be the result of retrieval failure rather than failures of the storage variety.

To illustrate, recent research with rat pups has shown that the effects of infantile amnesia can be mitigated by the injection of naloxone prior to training a fear response (Weber et al., 2006). Critically, this shows that central opioid receptors are involved in the regulation of the retrieval of fear memories in rat pups.

Interestingly, although younger rat pups retain fear conditioning for relatively short periods of time, the administration of the gamma-aminobutyric acid (GABA$_A$) receptor partial inverse agonist FG7142 alleviated infantile amnesia (Kim et al., 2006). Gamma-aminobutyric acid is the major inhibitory neurotransmitter in the mammalian central nervous system (Wong et al., 2003), and GABA$_A$ receptors are especially abundant in the amygdala, a structure critical to fear responses (Davis et al., 1995). Although GABA receptors are known to play an important role in forgetting regardless of the age of the organism, these results demonstrate that FG7142 facilitates the retrieval of a "forgotten memory" and show, for the first time, that GABA receptors play a prominent role in the forgetting of fear memories from infancy. Thus, it may be that forgetting early in life (infantile amnesia) and forgetting in adulthood simply represent quantitative, not qualitative, variation in forgetting mechanisms. That the same treatment facilitates retrieval in adults also facilitates the same process in infancy is consistent with such a memory-continuity hypothesis.

Of course, there is also extensive evidence that storage factors play a role as well in infantile amnesia. We should not forget about the exceedingly robust finding that immature organisms exhibit more rapid forgetting of information than more mature organisms. Of course, the longer any memory has been in storage without rehearsal or reminders that reinstate that trace, the more likely it is to be forgotten. Obviously, early memories, which have had more opportunity to be forgotten than memories stored more recently, should be more difficult to access (e.g., Joh et al., 2002). Like the research on retrieval, there is good pharmacological evidence that post-training injections of glucose, epinephrine, or norepinephrine facilitate storage and consolidation in adult rats (Flint & Riccio, 1999; Gold et al., 1982), and these same agents mitigate the effects of infantile amnesia in rat pups. Thus, both storage and retrieval play a role in infantile amnesia, at least in nonhuman animals, and appear to behave in a manner consistent with a memory-continuity theory. That is, they are affected by the same manipulations (both pharmacologically induced and experimentally induced; e.g., reinstatement) in infancy and adulthood.

Finally, despite the presence of infantile amnesia during the induction of fear responses in rat pups, Richardson and his colleagues have shown that this fear response is time-locked in memory. That is, because the rats' fear response is expressed in age-appropriate ways, ones that unfold with development (Yap et al., 2005), learned fear is expressed in terms of the age at which the animal was first trained (time of encoding) and not the age at which it was tested (Richardson & Fan, 2002; Richardson et al., 2000). Interestingly, these memories can be updated by subsequent experience and the expression of fear recalibrated to a more mature response if a similar fear experience occurs at an older age (Yap et al., 2005).

Results such as these have implications for whether and how single versus multiple fear events (including acute versus chronic adverse experiences) occurring early in life may be remembered and expressed later in adulthood (also see Sevelinges et al., 2007). That is, although the experiences themselves may not be explicitly remembered, the response bias established early in life may serve as the basis for behaviors in adulthood (and may even serve as the basis for certain phobic responses; also see Richardson & Hayne, 2007). For language-using organisms, results such as these raise the additional question of whether experiences that have occurred before the vocabulary (receptive or productive) necessary to encode and communicate those experiences is acquired can ever be expressed linguistically. If responses are truly time-locked at encoding and language is not available at that time, then the answer to this question may be no. Of course, should an experience that elicits a specific response (e.g., fear) be repeated at a later time, earlier nonverbal memory for that original experience can be updated by re-encoding processes operating during the elicitation of this more mature response. This suggests that earlier established nonverbal memories can be updated if they are reactivated, re-encoded, and reconsolidated later in development. To the extent that this update includes relevant language that has been acquired since the time of the original experience, the answer to the question of whether language-using organisms can have a verbal memory for that event may be yes. I will return to these questions in the next section when I consider behavioral and cognitive factors relevant to infantile amnesia human populations.

HUMAN POPULATIONS

As in their nonhuman counterparts, studies of memory with preverbal human infants are, as we saw earlier (Chapter 2), difficult at best. This is because tasks must be nonverbal, both in terms of the task instructions as well as the types of responses indexing remembering. Moreover, like nonhumans, preverbal humans cannot provide us with an unambiguous indication of their conscious state during recollection. In spite of these problems, experiments using a wide range of tasks have established beyond a reasonable doubt that human infants do possess declarative, episodic memory; if not before the end of the first year of life, shortly thereafter.

In Chapter 2, I provided a relatively complete review of memory from birth to two years and will not repeat it here. Instead, I will focus on several key paradigms and outcomes that illustrate the precocity of infant memory relevant to the discussion of infantile amnesia. I begin by reviewing reports concerning memory for operantly conditioned events very early in life, including memory for in utero conditioning experiences. Although there is some recent work on in utero habituation (e.g., Dirix et al., 2009), perhaps the most well-known research on the recollection of in utero experiences is that by DeCasper and his associates (DeCasper & Fifer, 1980; DeCasper & Prescott, 1984; DeCasper & Spence, 1986, 1991; Spence, 1996; Spence & Freeman, 1996). These researchers have shown that newborn infants can recognize the prosodic characteristics of a story heard in the last trimester of their prenatal life and have determined the factors that affect this recognition memory. More specifically, newborns prefer their mother's voice to a non-maternal voice (DeCasper & Fifer, 1980), and they prefer the sounds of a passage that had been recited frequently by the mother during the third trimester to the sounds of a passage she never recited (DeCasper & Spence, 1986).

Studies with nonhuman animals have shown that when prenatal experience with the maternal call is either altered or absent, ducklings will exhibit either an atypical response or an inability to detect the maternal call (Gottlieb, 1985; also see Lickliter & Virkar, 1989, for similar research with newborn quails). This research with nonhumans parallels that with humans and suggests that early pre-natal experience with the maternal voice may be critical to normal development, including, in humans, the later acquisition of language (see Lecanuet & Schaal, 1996; Moon & Fifer, 2000; Reynolds & Lickliter, 2002). Indeed, these results are consistent with theories concerning the importance of experience-expectant mechanisms in early development (Greenough et al., 1987; also see Chapter 3). These findings are also consistent with theories in which the foundation of speech perception and language acquisition may be laid down before birth (Kuhl, 1988; Lindblom, 1992). Of course, fetal learning is affected by both the amount of previous experience (e.g., see Kisilevsky et al., 2003) with the relevant information (i.e., the number of times stories or rhymes have been recited by the mother) as well as the timing of these experiences in relation to fetal maturation (particularly with regard to the autonomic nervous system) (also see Krueger et al., 2004).

It is important to point out that "memory" for in utero experiences is expressed as a conditioned response. For example, in the work by DeCasper and his colleagues, newborns respond to auditory stimulation shortly after birth by changing their pattern of nonnutritive sucking. Thus, in order to hear the mother's voice (or to hear her read the familiar passage) infants would have suck faster (or slower, depending on the response condition) on a nonnutritive nipple. Thus, the claim is not that infants emerge from their intrauterine environment with a set of declarative, episodic memories for their experiences (as some have claimed is possible—see Chapter 1). Rather, they emerge with a set of response preferences, ones that include the rather adaptive preference for the maternal voice (or call).

It is not just prenatal experience that may have important implications for subsequent development: so, too, do very early postnatal experiences. Like prenatal experiences, early postnatal experiences can have effects on later behavior in humans in much the same way they do in nonhuman animals (e.g., fear conditioning in rat pups). For example, Taddio and colleagues (1997) examined the effects of circumcision in neonates who either were or were not anesthetized on their response to a subsequent immunization injection at four to six months of age. Compared to control infants receiving the injection who were uncircumcised as well as those who had been circumcised with anesthetic, males who had been circumcised without an anesthetic showed greater behavioral and physiological distress during the injection. In a related study, infants born to mothers with diabetes and who received repeated heel lances during the first 24 to 36 hours displayed more intense pain reactions to a subsequent venipuncture than control infants (Taddio et al., 2002). These reactions occurred not just during the procedure itself but also during skin preparation and cleansing.

Studies such as these demonstrate that prior experience, even in very young infants, leads to learning about which cues are relevant to anticipating pain even when those stimuli are not themselves painful (e.g., cleaning the skin). The question remains, what exactly is it that is being "remembered," and for how long do such memories persist? Much of the research used to address this question has been conducted with older children (e.g., those over two years of age). However, there is some research showing that younger children remember and report more pain than older children for the same procedures (e.g., venipuncture; see Fradet et al., 1990; Goodenough et al., 1997, 1998). It is also clear that there are individual differences in pain severity even when the same procedure has been administered to different children (e.g., temperament; Schechter et al., 1991). Unfortunately, much of this research has conflated memory for the painful experience itself and memory for pain expression, so what is being remembered is not the pain per se, but rather pain-related behaviors or even the child's expectation of pain based on their previous experience (for a review, see von Baeyer et al., 2004). Although, as detailed later in this book (Chapters 7 and 8), children do remember events associated with trauma and stress, this does not necessarily mean that they have an accurate recollection of pain itself. At best, we can say that the cues that are associated with painful experiences, even ones that are not painful in and of themselves, serve to set off anticipatory conditioned responses that signal impending pain, even in very young infants. It is unlikely, however, particularly prior to the offset of infantile amnesia, that children will form lasting declarative memories for pain itself or the episode that produced a painful response. That is, like fear memories in rats, although early traumatic and painful experiences leave their mark, one that can be updated by similar, later experiences, it is extremely unlikely that individuals will ever gain complete access to declarative memories for these early experiences. Indeed, as we will see in a number of subsequent chapters in this book, early memories, even those for painful and traumatic experiences, cannot be accessed intact and therefore a coherent narrative account of such experiences cannot be created (also see Richardson & Hayne, 2007).

As infants mature, their memory skills show remarkable development. For example, as we saw in Chapter 2, infants are able imitators, and as they grow older, they model more and more complex behaviors and can hold such information in memory for longer and longer delays (for a review, see Meltzoff, 1995). It is important to remember that even this seemingly rudimentary test of infant recollection was seen as an index of their declarative memory skills. This was because the behaviors that were being modeled were novel for the infant, no verbal instructions were given, and the actions to be imitated were not performed by infants prior to the test of retention. Thus, it was argued, this type of imitation was based on stored representations of previous experience and as such indexes declarative memory.

Indeed, across all of the different types of paradigms used to study early memory that were reviewed in previous chapters, declarative memory appears relatively early in infants. Overall, data from a number of different experimental procedures used to examine memory in human infants, including conjugate reinforcement (e.g., Rovee-Collier et al., 2001), novelty preference (e.g., Courage & Howe, 1998; Courage et al., 2004), deferred imitation (e.g., Hayne, 2004; Meltzoff, 1995), elicited imitation (e.g., Bauer, 2004), and behavioral reenactment (e.g., McDonough & Mandler, 1994; Sheffield & Hudson, 1994), all demonstrated that, as in many of our nonhuman counterparts: (1) infant age and longevity of memory are positively correlated; (2) length of retention is affected by factors such as distribution of practice (spaced was better than massed) and the match between cues at encoding and test; and (3) retention can be prolonged given appropriate reminders (i.e., reinstatement). Together, these findings show that although it is fragile and short-lived, even very young infants can show signs of declarative memory. With development, declarative memory becomes more durable, with traces becoming better integrated, more stable over time, and less susceptible to decay and interference.

Although it is clearly impressive, young infants' memory is still not as robust as that of children who have matured beyond the infantile amnesia threshold. In fact, it would seem that experiences before the age of two years may be mysteriously "time-locked" and inaccessible to later conscious recall. Recollection, if any, is disjointed and fragmentary at best (Bruce et al., 2005, 2007), with individuals not being able to construct a coherent narrative about those early experiences (Simcock & Hayne, 2002). As will be shown in the next chapter, it is not until around the age of two years that memories become more stable and can be retrieved later in childhood and adulthood (Crawley & Eacott, 2006; Dudycha & Dudycha, 1933; Eacott & Crawley, 1998; Kihlstrom & Harackiewicz, 1982; Newcombe et al., 2000; Usher & Neisser, 1993). Here again, these memories are not well integrated and tend to be more fragmented than those formed in later childhood.

What do we mean by *fragmented memory*? In contrast to the better articulated, more detailed narratives for events that we have from later childhood and adulthood, consider the following examples of "memory fragments" from participants who were asked to describe their earliest personal memories (both participants estimated these memories to be from the age of two to three years of age). Here, one participant recalls, "I remember playing in the kitchen sink with a toy army man, not really sure how I reached the sink, but I remember that there was music!" Another participant recollects, "I remember sitting in my parents' bedroom, observing my mother as she did some house cleaning. There is nothing else to the memory, but I remember having a very different perspective of the room at the time." (Bruce et al., 2005, p. 572).

Research on earliest memories can also involve the use of memory probes instead of free recall of one's earliest memory. Here, investigators ask about very specific, ostensibly significant events (e.g., birth of a sibling, death of a relative, traumatic experiences). Interestingly, regardless of which procedure is used, there does not appear to be any specific trend in the content of earliest memories. That is, although such recollections are not of commonplace everyday events (e.g., what one had for lunch on the fifth day of April when one was two years old), neither are they particularly emotional or traumatic (e.g., Bruce et al., 2005). More frequently the recollections we do have from around the age of two are decontextualized segments from the past, ones that are simple recollections of sensory experiences, behaviors and actions, or a feeling (see earlier examples of fragments; also see Bruce et al., 2005, 2007).

As seen earlier in Chapter 3, neurobiological changes can certainly drive many of the developments in memory that occur during the first postnatal year, but they do not, by themselves, account for many of the changes in the longevity of human episodic memory. Instead, there are a number of changes that occur during cognitive development that may help explain the transition from infantile amnesia to true autobiographical remembering. Although many such changes exist around this transitional period (for a review, see Courage & Howe, 2002), the key development driving autobiographical memory is the onset of the cognitive self (Howe & Courage, 1993, 1997a; Howe et al., 2009a). A more detailed discussion of these changes will be deferred until the next chapter.

But what makes these episodic memories more durable? Briefly, memory traces consist of collections of primitive elements (e.g., features, nodes) that are integrated into a single cohesive structure in memory. The better the information in the trace is integrated, the more likely it is to be retained over time, and the less susceptible it is to interference. Less well-integrated traces lose their distinctiveness and are more likely to recede into the background noise of other faded memories. More specifically, as development unfolds, our proficiency with organizing information increases with changes in our knowledge base. As our knowledge structures change and become reorganized in more efficient ways, we are better able to group information in memory into cohesive structures that are more stable and relatively permanent. Of course, these assumptions are consistent with most models of memory, and they are helpful in organizing the extensive literature on children's memory development and in accounting for the offset of infantile amnesia and the onset of autobiographical memory, at least in humans. The key event that heralds the transition from storing events that have happened (early episodic memories) to events that have happened "to me" (autobiographical memory) is the acquisition of one of the most powerful memory organizers, the self. Although the specific details of this transition will be laid out in the next chapter, the critical point here is that because a recognizable self contributes features that increase the cohesion of a memory trace, such traces are no longer event memories but memories of events that "happened to me." That is, they are autobiographical.

Before turning to a more detailed discussion concerning the parameters responsible for the onset of autobiographical memory, an important question remains to be answered here; namely, what happens to memories from the infantile amnesia period? Although it has already been pointed out that such memories are fragmentary at best, do they remain time-locked or can they be later retrieved and recoded using newly acquired language skills? For humans, the period of infantile amnesia is also one in which language skills are relatively impoverished; and the acquisition of language was thought by some to herald the end of infantile amnesia (see Allport, 1937; Schachtel, 1947). Some current theories of infantile amnesia also emphasize the importance of language (for a recent review, see Reese, 2009). However, to the extent that infantile amnesia is similar in human and nonhuman animals, the role of language in the offset of infantile amnesia can be questioned and may turn out to be epiphenomenal rather than causal. What evidence exists indicates that language is not causative in the offset of infantile amnesia, although it is one way in which humans can increase the durability of memories, through verbal rehearsal and verbal elaboration. Thus, it may be that whereas language is not germane to our nonhuman counterparts, it may be one of those neocortical inputs and outputs to the hippocampal and parahippocampal areas discussed earlier that varies across species and is important to later developments in autobiographical memory (see the discussion in Chapter 5).

It is clear from Chapter 2 that infants can recall past events behaviorally in the absence of language. More important, there is little evidence that these early memories are accessible to verbal report, given that they were encoded and stored prior to the offset of infantile amnesia. Some exceptions exist, but these are limited to conditions in which early memories were tested under conditions of high contextual support (e.g., Bauer & Wewerka, 1995, 1997). Many other studies in which the degree of contextual support was limited have failed to produce narrative accounts of early memories (Simcock & Hayne, 2002, 2003). In these latter studies, although children did not possess the relevant vocabulary when the events were being stored in memory but had acquired the vocabulary by the time they were asked to report the prior events, verbal ability was not related to memory performance. As well, these children's sparse verbal reports of previous events could not be accounted for as simply poor memory per se, because these same children were able to accurately recognize photographs of the previous event, as well as reenact them behaviorally.

Summary and Conclusions

Several important conclusions can be drawn from this review of infantile amnesia. First, the recent literature on neural structures related to episodic/declarative memory shows that humans share a number of important anatomical, functional, and developmental similarities with nonhuman animal species. Despite these similarities, there are clear cross-species variations in memory performance as well as in the manner in which these memories can be expressed. Such differences may be small relative to that which we share across species in terms of early memory development, and these differences are likely due to well-documented and substantial differences in neocortical inputs and outputs. Second, perhaps because of this similarity in hippocampal and parahippocampal neuroanatomy, functionality, and developmental trajectory, humans also share with nonhuman animals an episodic or episodic-like memory, one that develops with maturation. Regardless of species, human and nonhuman animals alike can code the *what, where, when,* and even *who* of past events and use that information to guide future behavior.

Third, human and nonhuman animals share a main limitation of early episodic memory; namely, infantile amnesia. In particular, (1) for younger organisms, there is faster forgetting of information than in more mature organisms, (2) memories laid down by younger members of the species tend to be more susceptible to interference than those encoded and stored by older members of the species, and (3) for those species that recall past events, memories for early events encoded during the infantile amnesia period are less accessible later in life than memories for events that occurred after the infantile amnesia period. For humans, infantile amnesia wanes at around two years of age, and this shift is aided by corresponding developments in the cognitive domain.

Because of these cross-species commonalities in both episodic memory and associated infantile amnesia, it may be intellectual folly to explain the end of infantile amnesia in uniquely human terms. In a similar vein, Hayne (2004) has argued that, due to these stark similarities, we are forced to conclude that infantile amnesia and its end must be explained using basic processing explanations of memory and its development. Thus, the end of infantile amnesia must be due to changes that occur at the level of encoding, storage, consolidation, or retrieval that drive the development of episodic memory. When species-unique capacities play a role in the ebbing of infantile amnesia, they do so only to the extent that they directly influence these basic processes.

For humans, these basic process changes lead to an increase in the facility with which information can be organized and integrated in memory. Advances in children's knowledge base and its organization, whether they have to do with the self or other constructs (e.g., "four-footed animals," "vegetables"), allow children to better organize the storage of incoming information. This, in turn, allows for the construction of memory traces that are much better integrated and hence more resistant to forgetting. Because the neurological components necessary for episodic/declarative memory are in place and operating in the first year of life (see Chapter 3), what drives memory development are changes in knowledge (cognitive) structures that serve encoding, storage, retention, and retrieval processes—changes that make these basic processes more robust. As discussed in the next chapter, the key knowledge structure that forces the offset of infantile amnesia and the onset of autobiographical memory is the development of the *cognitive self*. As observed in that chapter, it is of more than passing interest to note that this cognitive self may be present in species other than humans. The quintessential test for the cognitive self, mirror self-recognition, has also been reported for a variety of nonhuman species (for a review, see Gallup, 1979). Although many animals simply respond to the image as if they were viewing a conspecific, nonhuman primates (given a period of exposure to mirrors) will respond to the contingent movement cues and use the reflective properties to locate objects. Although it is speculative to say so, it may be that the end of infantile amnesia in some other nonhuman species can also be heralded by changes in cognitive structures, ones that are similar to what human infants acquire as their cognitive self.

Regardless of the veracity of such a claim, it is clear that the common cross-species ingredient that brings about the end of infantile amnesia is some change in the organisms' ability to encode, store, consolidate, or retrieve event memories. Whether that is through the advent of new knowledge (cognitive) structures or some other (cognitive) mechanism deserves further research. That various species possess different neocortical structures that moderate hippocampal and parahippocampal functions is most likely the phenomenon whose study will give us further insight into the mechanisms that modulate basic episodic memory processes and that contribute to the waning of infantile amnesia and the onset of autobiographical memory.

So, what is the fate of early memories? As we saw earlier, events that can be remembered behaviorally during the infantile amnesia period (also see Chapter 2) are not subsequently recollected (at least not verbally) (e.g., Bauer et al., 2004; Simcock & Hayne, 2002, 2003). Of course, these events were neither traumatic nor life-changing, but simply innocuous laboratory-contrived events. It is interesting to note that the degree of emotion may not be important, as there is converging evidence that adult participants' recall of events, traumatic and otherwise, is limited by this infantile amnesia barrier, one that stretches across the first two years of life (e.g., Eacott & Crawley, 1998; Usher & Neisser, 1993). So, do memories for early events remain in storage despite our inability to bring them to conscious awareness during later childhood or adulthood, remaining forever inaccessible and irretrievable?

Recall that many theorists believe that, despite our inability to consciously recollect early life events, they remain with us and continue to influence our future behaviors (see Kagan, 1996). Of course, there is clear evidence that early experience by itself does not determine future outcomes and that subsequent experiences can alter that path (e.g., Richardson & Hayne, 2007). Indeed, even the bizarre behavior of six-month-old isolated macaques can be changed if they are subsequently placed with younger female monkeys over a four- to five-month period (Suomi & Harlow, 1972). In fact, there is considerable research that shows that a strong form of early experiential determinism is not tenable (see Chapter 8; also see Howe, 2000). In light of these considerations, there is little reason to suppose that our early experiences continue to exist in memory in isolation and that they have not been updated by more recent memories for experiences.

Of course, it is possible that implicit or procedural memories that have not been altered by subsequent experience (given that such a memory is possible) are still accessible implicitly and they continue to influence our behaviors as adults. Indeed, there is some evidence that early implicit memories may survive intact in humans (Newcombe et al., 2000), and even stronger evidence of this was presented earlier in this chapter for early fear responses in rats (e.g., Yap et al., 2005). If early postnatal responses are not altered by subsequent experience, then it may be that earlier, immature responses could still control the behavior of the more mature organism. To the extent that these response patterns are controlled by implicit memories, the organism would not be consciously aware of these earlier experiences that form the basis of their current behavior.

However, as we will see in subsequent chapters, direct evidence for these claims is absent in the literature. Indeed, to the contrary, the literature is replete with examples that contradict rather than confirm such intuitions (for reviews, see Hardt & Rutter, 2004; Howe et al., 2006b). What remains unclear, and deserves additional research, is how implicit memories can be altered by subsequent experience. Only future research will help us understand the fate of these early implicit memories, especially those acquired during the period of infantile amnesia. Until this evidence is forthcoming, it may be reasonable to assume that their fate is similar to that of early explicit memories—that is, they are malleable, subject to interference, and can be as easily updated as explicit episodic memories throughout the maturation process.

5

The Onset and Early Development of Autobiographical Remembering

Just remember that the things you put in your head are there
forever, he said. You might want to think about that.
You forget some things don't you?
Yes. You forget what you want to remember and
you remember what you want to forget.
—Cormac McCarthy (*The Road*, 2006, p. 11)

As this volume attests, memories can be formed very early in life. What happens to our earliest autobiographical memories has been a matter of intense debate for well over a century (e.g., Freud, 1905/1953; Henri & Henri, 1895). As it turns out, most do not survive, at least not in a form that allows them to be reliably retrieved. Although early experiences may be formative, the remnants of these experiences cannot be brought back into consciousness. Early memories tend to be poorly organized and very fragmented—pieces of the past that, at best, may be simple images but contain few hints as to their meaning or importance. Most often, though, such memories seem to disappear without a trace.

Interestingly, it may be that these very early experiences are "remembered" implicitly as semantic memories (i.e., memories about the world that are not tied to a specific time, place, or person). *Semantic memory*, or one's knowledge base, contains important information about the world we live in; information necessary for our survival. For example, to remember that certain snakes are poisonous may be key to our survival (depending where we live), but it may not be as important to remember the time or place where we learned this fact. As Newcombe, Lloyd, and Ratliff (2007) pointed out, even for potentially more mundane information (although not so mundane if you are hungry and searching for food), it may be more important to remember the word "banana" as well as the properties of bananas (e.g., they are edible, they taste sweet) than to remember the circumstances surrounding the acquisition of this knowledge.

Thus, the vestiges of early experiences may be retained in semantic, not episodic, memory (Newcombe et al., 2007).

This is consistent with the adaptive nature of autobiographical memory espoused in the current volume. Indeed, as concluded in a prior monograph, memory generally, and autobiographical memory specifically,

> ... is conceptualized as being fundamentally adaptive in the sense that it seeks to store meanings or the gist of experiences so that the world people live in becomes as knowable and predictable as possible. In essence, memory serves as a record of the meaning of experiences, so that people can not only understand the world but also anticipate and plan for the future ... people extract gist or meaning from experiences and distill it to the point where they can derive a generic representation of how their world operates. This can be seen even in the earliest days of infancy, where regularities are discovered and amalgamated into some form of coherent memory trace that may represent some initial attempt at categorization. Once habituated, infants then turn their attention to novelty to discover the exception to the rules contained in the previously idealized prototype ... (which) in turn may result in the modification of the earlier stored trace or in the storage of a new trace, one whose distinctiveness from the previous experience confers memorability. Thus, memory involves a balance between the old, similar, and predictable (e.g., generic or categorical representation) and the new, distinctive, and unpredictable (e.g., episodic representation of distinctive experiences)
>
> (Howe, 2000, pp. 139–140).

Thus, the idea that autobiographical memory contains both semantic knowledge (how the world operates without respect to how, where, when, or with whom we learned it) as well as episodic knowledge (remembrances of personally experienced events themselves) is not new (see Howe, 2000; Newcombe et al., 2007). Although "autobiographical memory" is more typically defined as memories for personally experienced events, autobiographical recall itself often contains fragments of personally experienced events laced with semantic knowledge that serves to "fill in" some of the missing gaps in what is our somewhat fallible, reconstructive memory. A more in-depth discussion of the details of these and related ideas is deferred until later in this volume.

As discussed in Chapters 2 and 4, although these early experiences may serve as the basis for later predispositions and behaviors (e.g., avoiding certain snakes or the development of phobic reactions to specific aversive stimuli; the development of anxieties, or even aspects of our adult personality), the memories of these experiences cannot be brought to mind. There does come a time, however, when we can remember these experiences from our early childhood. This is not because these experiences are particularly important, emotional, or even distinctive (e.g., Fivush & Hamond, 1990; Reese, 1999), but because we begin to organize them in a manner that permits longevity, a manner in which they become part of ourselves.

Indeed, the experiences remembered from early in our life can be somewhat surprising in terms of their content. That is, what is remembered does not necessarily represent the most salient aspect of those events, at least not from an adult's perspective. For example, one two-year-old talked about going to get diapers, and not about the birth of her baby brother (Nelson, 1989). Of course, by adult standards, the birth of a sibling is considerably more important than the more mundane event of purchasing diapers. Similarly, Fivush and Hamond (1990) found that whereas 2½-year-olds may report more mundane aspects of novel events, the emphasis on the mundane is attenuated in older preschool children, and by the age of four years, the emphasis is on the novel and distinctive components of events (also see Cleveland & Reese, 2008).

Because organization is an important key to the durability of memories, once we begin to imbue memories with our sense of self, they become better organized and can be remembered for longer periods of time. The onset of this sense of self, although benefitting the longevity of memories, does not make them impervious to subsequent interference, distortion, or forgetting. Like all of memory, these remembrances are reconstructive and hence prone to error. However, the importance of this apparent waning of infantile amnesia is that it gives way to the retention of experiences that are linked to the emerging sense of self.

The enduring interest in the beginnings of autobiographical memory has increased recently mainly because of its important mental health and forensic consequences. Questions concerning the accuracy and durability of adults' memories of childhood experiences need answers, particularly when memory is the only evidence in, for example, trials concerning historical childhood abuse. I, along with my colleagues (Howe & Courage, 1993, 1997a; Howe et al., 2003 2009a), have maintained that the necessary, although not sufficient, foundation for the onset of autobiographical memory is the coincident emergence of the cognitive self. The *cognitive self* is defined as the objective sense of self that embodies unique and recognizable features and characteristics that constitute one's self-concept, or the "me" aspect of the self. This sense of the self differs from a related facet of the self, one that comprises the more subjective aspects of the self as a thinker, knower, and causal agent, or "I" (for a more in-depth review, see Courage & Howe, 2002). The cognitive self becomes stable at about two years of age and serves as a new organizational scheme in memory, one around which events can be encoded, stored, and retrieved as personal. That is, memories for events are no longer traces of things that have happened, but rather, they are memories of events that happened to "me." These memories are now imbued with recognizable features of one's self, a self that continues, albeit modified by experience and development, across time. Subsequent developments in basic memory processes (e.g., encoding, storage, and retrieval), knowledge of the world, formal learning, as well as language and other aspects of social cognition, serve to elaborate and refine characteristics of the self and help shape the nature and durability of autobiographical recall.

Much of the research on autobiographical memory has focused on the factors that underlie age-related changes, although age alone is not necessarily the best predictor of what is recalled. Indeed, there is now considerable research to indicate that there are a number of individual and group differences in cognitive (e.g., self-concept, knowledge), biological (e.g., stress reactivity, gender), emotional (e.g., traumatic vs. non-traumatic; attachment status), linguistic (e.g., narrative skill), social (e.g., parent–child interaction styles), and cultural (e.g., self vs. community focus) factors that contribute to the recollection and reporting of personally experienced events.

In this chapter, I trace the beginnings and early development of autobiographical memory, including the role of individual differences in earliest memories. I begin by providing some background on autobiographical memory research, followed by a brief overview of the literature on the emergence of autobiographical memory in infants and young children. After that, I review some of the individual difference factors that affect the onset, durability, content, and fluency of autobiographical memory for routine and emotional events. I will also discuss how the transition from infantile amnesia to autobiographical memory may be more seamless than originally thought—that is, this transition may be more a matter of continuous development than one of abrupt change. Along the way, I discuss whether autobiographical memory is an adaptation unique to humans or whether nonhuman animals also possess a memory system that is similarly autobiographical. Finally, I conclude with an integration of the two theoretical perspectives that have dominated the recent debate on the origin and development of autobiographical memory—the emergence of self versus the nature of sociolinguistic interactions between the child and others.

Autobiographical Memory and the Self

Autobiographical memory has often been defined as memory for the events that have occurred in one's life (e.g., Conway & Rubin, 1993). Such memories involve the who, what, where, when, and how of the events we experience, our emotional reactions to those events, the personal significance of those events, and our reflections on them. Autobiographical memory forms our personal life history, something that in turn helps define who we are. Autobiographical memory is frequently considered to be a special case of event memory. However, it differs from traditional definitions of event memory in the sense that there is personal involvement or ownership of the constituent events that it entails. That is, autobiographical memories are usually thought of as being specific personal events that happened at a specific point in time and in a particular place (e.g., one's first day at school) rather than generalized pieces of semantic knowledge about events related to the self (e.g., that one attended school). However, as already pointed out, more recent accounts of autobiographical memory also include decontextualized, semantic knowledge that has been gleaned from such personalized experiences.

The importance of the relationship between autobiographical memory and the sense of self has long been recognized in the adult literature (e.g., Conway, 2005; Conway & Pleydell-Pearce, 2000; McAdams, 2001; Skronowski, 2004). Here, autobiographical memories are said to contribute directly to the development and maintenance of a viable and stable self-concept. In addition, the self is thought to direct the ways in which autobiographical memories are encoded, stored, and retrieved, such that relevant autobiographical knowledge structures remain consistent with one's current self-concept or "working self" goals (e.g., Conway & Pleydell-Pearce, 2000; Ross & Wilson, 2000). Thus, the relationship between the self and autobiographical memory is a dynamic and interactive one wherein the self constructs (and reconstructs) the past, and the past constructs (and reconstructs) the self. Indeed, numerous studies have shown that autobiographical recollection is best for events pertaining to the self (i.e., are personally consequential), especially the self in times of transition (e.g., Conway, 1996; Csikszentmihalkyi & Beattie, 1979; Rubin et al., 1998). The loss of this critical self–event memory relationship that can occur in some amnesic conditions can be devastating for the individuals and their families who are affected (e.g., Conway & Fthenaki, 2000), something that is perhaps best documented in studies of Alzheimer's disease.

Although there is a large literature on autobiographical memory in older children and adults, there is considerably less research on its emergence and early development. This may be a consequence of problems with the way in which autobiographical memory has been operationalized, particularly as it applies to research with very young children (and other nonverbal organisms). That is, what is said to constitute evidence that an event memory is autobiographical is a verbal report of that memory that contains confirmation by the individual that the event is an autobiographical one (i.e., the ability to recollect the who, what, where, when, and how of the event). Obviously, because infants and very young children are considerably less proficient than older children and adults in their language and narrative skills, such confirmation is rarely, if ever, possible. Because of this, researchers are left to infer the autobiographical status of a memory from the younger child's nonverbal behavior (e.g., behavioral reenactment of previously experienced events), and several researchers have shown that young children's nonverbal behaviors may provide a reliable and valid index of their autobiographical memories (see Howe et al., 2003). Of course, as children become proficient language-users with more sophisticated narrative skills, their autobiographical memories become consistent with the verbal requirements in the definition of autobiographical memory above, and they can be evaluated in more traditional ways. In what follows, I provide an overview of theories pertaining to the onset and early development of autobiographical memory, ones that set the stage for understanding the important individual differences in the early development of autobiographical memory.

How Does Autobiographical Memory Emerge and Develop Early in Life?

THE IMPORTANCE OF SELF-RECOGNITION

Courage and I (Howe & Courage, 1993, 1997a; Howe et al., 2003) have argued that the necessary (though not sufficient) condition for the emergence of autobiographical memory is the development of the cognitive self late in the second year of life. This achievement sets the lower limit on the age at which memories of specific episodes and events can be encoded, stored, and retrieved as personal. In essence, this burgeoning cognitive self provides a new knowledge structure whereby experiences are organized as autobiographical. As seen in earlier chapters, prior to the articulation of the self, infants do learn and remember, but these experiences are not coded as events that happened to a "self." It is only after the onset of the cognitive self that the recollection of autobiographical events from childhood becomes more abundant. Moreover, like advances in other aspects of memory development, these changes in autobiographical recollection are due in large part to corresponding increases in storage maintenance (including consolidation and reconsolidation processes) as well as to strategic retrieval processes. Importantly, it is more than mere coincidence that the timing of the onset of the cognitive self coincides approximately with the timing at which studies have dated the earliest autobiographical memories that have been recalled by adults (e.g., Eacott & Crawley, 1998; Usher & Neisser, 1993).

Research concerning the nature and early development of the cognitive self has a long history. Of most relevance to the onset of autobiographical memory is the emergence of the objective, categorical (i.e., cognitive) aspect of the self described by William James (1890/1961) as the "me" component of the self. The initial unambiguous sign of the emergence of the cognitive self occurs when children recognize that their mirror image is an image of themselves. This is typically evaluated using the mirror self-recognition (MSR) test. Here, the child is familiarized with their mirror image and then, once the mirror is removed, a dot of face paint is surreptitiously placed on the child's nose. When the mirror is reintroduced, the child who recognizes the marked image as "me" will touch his or her own nose, as opposed to touching the mirror image or engaging in other mirror-directed reactions. Coincident with the onset of MSR, infants start to exhibit other signs of self-awareness, including embarrassment when shown their images; and later, around 22 months, they provide a correct verbal label of the image (see Courage et al., 2004). Despite evidence from research with photo and video materials showing that infants can and do discriminate their facial and other body features from those of other infants beginning around four or five months (Bahrick et al., 1996; Legerstee et al., 1998; Rochat & Striano, 2002; Schmuckler, 1995), it is not clear what level of self-knowledge can be attributed to these discriminations (but see Nielsen et al., 2006).

However, visual self-recognition is only one facet of the self concept. Indeed, the self concept (and self-awareness) implies more than recognition of one's physical features and is a fundamental aspect of social cognitive development that has its origins in the early weeks of life and continues to develop throughout childhood and adolescence (for reviews, see Butterworth, 1990; Cicchetti & Beeghley, 1990; Damon & Hart, 1988; Lewis, 1995; Neisser, 1993, 1995; Rochat, 1995, 2001). Povinelli and his co-investigators (Povinelli & Simon, 1998; Povinelli, et al., 1996, 1999) have demonstrated that mirror self-recognition may be just the first step toward the recognition of the objective self as "temporally extended." For example, they found that two-year-old children who were able to recognize themselves on-line failed to do so after even a brief delay. It was not until about five years of age that children fully understood the relationship between the present self and the recent and more distant past selves. Although the self continues to develop, most authors agree that the achievement of MSR is a developmental milestone (Asendorpf & Baudonniere, 1993; Butterworth, 1990; Kagan, 1981; Lewis, 1994; Meltzoff, 1990; Neisser, 1993) and that a critical step is reached when children are able to represent themselves as an object of knowledge and imagination.

The important point is simply that, at about the age of two years, the cognitive self, a new organizer of information and experience, becomes available and facilitates the structuring and personalization of memories for events that become what is termed "autobiographical memory." That childhood memories become more numerous after the onset of the self is anticipated in this theory because (1) features associated with the self increase, providing a larger knowledge base which encoding processes can reference with; (2) improvements in the basic processes that drive memory (encoding, storage, and retrieval) that occur across development (attention, strategy use, knowledge, and metamemory) facilitate memory functioning in general and autobiographical recollection in particular (see Bjorklund et al., 2009); and (3) certain neurocognitive developments (e.g., prefrontal cortex) relevant to this expanding knowledge base (see Bauer, 2009) about the self occur in this time frame.

NEUROBIOLOGY AND THE SELF

Although I have reviewed the underlying neurobiological developments that are thought to contribute to memory development in Chapter 3, it is of more than passing interest that there are additional neurological developments relevant to the development of the self. Indeed, prefrontal areas related to autobiographical recall and the self undergo considerable developmental change—for example, cortical gray matter volume increases until age four and then declines (synaptogenesis followed by pruning; see Pfefferbaum et al., 1994). Functional neuroimaging studies have shown that portions of the anteromedial prefrontal cortex are involved in processing self-related information and autobiographical recall (see Levine, 2004). Although I would not argue that there is any direct link between these neurobiological changes and the offset of infantile amnesia, the cognitive advances that drive the onset of autobiographical memory may have their neural correlates in early changes in the prefrontal cortex (also see Lewis & Carmody, 2008).

Interestingly, other research has found that it may not just be frontal regions that are associated with the self and the onset of autobiographical memory, but also the interaction between hemispheres as mediated by the corpus callosum. For example, Christman, Propper, and Brown (2006) found evidence that enhanced interhemispheric interaction was associated with earlier offset of infantile amnesia. More specifically, callosal-mediated interhemispheric interaction appeared to affect the ability to retrieve autobiographical memories but did not affect the encoding of autobiographical memories.

IS SELF-RECOGNITION UNIQUELY HUMAN?

The simple answer to this question is no. Like the similarities observed in Chapter 4 between human and nonhuman animals in their experiences of infantile amnesia and the development of an episodic, or episodic-like, memory system that allows them to re-experience the past and anticipate the future, self-recognition is not unique to humans. To date, MSR has been demonstrated in the Hominoidea (i.e., humans and great apes), dolphins (*Tursiops truncates*), and Asian elephants (*Elephas maximus*) (although some have argued that corvid birds are also capable of MSR). Gallup (1970) demonstrated that MSR was present in our closest relatives, the chimpanzee (*Pan troglodytes*). He exposed mirror-naïve chimpanzees to mirrors and observed three stages of behavior: (1) *Exploratory behavior* directed to the mirror itself and *social behavior* as if interacting with a conspecific; followed by (2) *mirror* or *contingency testing* behavior in which the animal was testing the contingencies of its own behavior with that of the reflected image; which in turn was followed by (3) *self-directed behavior* in which the chimpanzee would use the mirror to examine parts of its body that could not be viewed without the mirror. Gallup then conducted the "mark" test in which the chimpanzee was marked with an odorless substance that the animal could only see when viewing itself in the mirror. As with humans, chimpanzees passed this MSR test if they touched the mark on their bodies and not the one reflected in the mirror. Similar success has been obtained with the other great apes, including bonobos (*P. panicus*), orangutans (*Pongo pygmaeus*), and gorillas (*Gorilla gorilla*) (for a review, see de Waal, 1996). However, attempts to elicit MSR using Old and New World monkeys has not been successful although they can succeed at discriminating between "self" and "other" (e.g., capuchins [*Cebus apella*]; see de Waal et al., 2005).

Importantly, these same stages have been observed in non-handed animals. Moreover, when marked, non-handed animals exhibit similar self-directed, not mirror-directed, behaviors. For example, bottlenose dolphins orient immediately to the marked area on their own body and not to the reflected mark in the mirror (Reiss & Marino, 2001). In a recent study with Asian elephants, three adult females (Maxine, Patty, and Happy) were exposed to an eight-foot by eight-foot elephant-safe mirror in a secluded location (outside of the public exhibit area) of the Bronx Zoo (Plotnik et al., 2006). All three elephants exhibited similar behavioral stages to that previously witnessed with dolphins and great apes in MSR studies. That is, initially the elephants explored the mirror (e.g., looking under and over the mirror), although they did not exhibit any social behaviors toward the mirror during this first stage. Following this, all three females exhibited mirror testing and contingency behaviors (e.g., non-stereotypic trunk and body movements, rhythmic head movements in and out of the view of the mirror). In the third, self-directed behavior stage, the elephants engaged in behaviors that indicated they were exploring parts of their body that were normally unseen by using the mirror (e.g., they explored the inside of their mouths using their trunks in close proximity to the mirror). Finally, when the mark test was administered, one of the elephants (Happy) passed the test by touching her head where the mark was located with her trunk significantly more often than other areas that were unmarked. That the other two elephants did not pass the mark test is consistent with research with other species (e.g., chimpanzees) that shows that not all individuals pass the MSR test (see Povinelli et al., 1993). However, like these other species, all three elephants continued to exhibit self-directed mirror behavior, suggesting that their own reflection was of interest even if the mark itself was not.

From this research it is clear that humans and some nonhuman animals pass the MSR test. What, if anything, is the common denominator that links these animals in their ability to pass the MSR test? Could a common denominator be neurobiological? This might be true between humans and the great apes, but the brains of dolphins are vastly different in a number of important ways, both in terms of cortical cytoarchitecture and organization, perhaps reminding us that cetacean (dolphin, whale, and porpoise) and primate ancestral lines diverged at least 65 to 70 million years ago (see Reiss & Marino, 2001).

Despite these neurobiological differences, dolphins, great apes, and humans share some important similarities inasmuch as they all exhibit high levels of encephalization and neocortical expansion, neurological features that may give rise to between-species commonalities in some behavioral and social characteristics. For example, all three show sophisticated memory and classification skills, can learn symbol-based artificial codes, and exhibit complex social behaviors (Reiss et al., 1997). It may be that success on MSR tests is best understood as being mediated by high levels of encephalization as well as enhanced cognitive ability.

Indeed, all of these animals exhibit enhanced or complex cognitive abilities, including tool use. Tool use is well documented in chimpanzees, orangutans, and other primates (van Schaik et al., 1999), bottlenose dolphins (Krützen et al., 2005), and Asian elephants (Chevalier-Skolinikoff & Liska, 1993). In addition, recall that it has been speculated that corvidae (the family of birds that includes crows, ravens, rooks, and magpies) may be capable of MSR, and they, too, manipulate tools to obtain food (see Emery & Clayton, 2004). Other signs of complex cognition include the wild African elephants' ability to classify predators (e.g., the Maasai of Kenya who hunt them, from the Kamba who do not) by both visual and olfactory cues (Bates et al., 2007); and Asian elephants can make relative quantity judgments and understand means–ends relationships (Irie-Sugimoto et al., 2007, 2008). Similar sophisticated cognitive abilities are well documented in dolphins (for a review, see Reiss et al., 1997). Moreover, nonhuman primates and elephants recognize kin (Byrne et al., 2009; Parr & de Waal, 1999), and primates, elephants, and even western scrub-jays (*Aphelocoma californica*) exhibit prospective cognition (future planning) (Byrne et al., 2009; Clayton et al., 2006; Mulcahy & Call, 2006).

In addition to showing complex cognitive skills, it is well known that these same species also engage in sophisticated social relationships and even exhibit altruism (see de Waal, 2008; Payne, 2003; Warneken et al., 2007). Dolphins and elephants, like humans and nonhuman primates, are highly empathic animals and exhibit what has been termed "targeted helping"; that is, helping that takes into account the specific needs of others (e.g., de Waal, 2008). Like dolphins (e.g., Caldwell & Caldwell, 1966), elephants exhibit empathy. Indeed, there are numerous reports of elephants trying to assist injured, incapacitated, or dying conspecifics (e.g., Moss, 1988). Together, the species exhibiting MSR also share complex cognitive and social abilities.

Consistent with the idea that cognitive and social factors may be linked to MSR success, de Waal (2008) has proposed the hypothesis that *cognitive empathy* is key to self-recognition. Cognitive empathy has been defined as "empathy combined with contextual appraisal and understanding of what caused (an individual's) emotional state" (de Waal, 2008, p. 4.5). Humans, great apes, elephants, and dolphins are all thought to possess cognitive empathy and thus should and of course do pass the MSR test. To date, the cognitive empathy hypothesis has won considerable favor in the nonhuman animal literature when explaining MSR performance, but it is less well known when it comes to explaining human success on the MSR task.

More recently, Tannenbaum (2009) has argued that MSR success and its associated self-awareness is a "learned behavior, that emerges in organisms with a sufficiently complex and highly integrated ability for associative memory and learning" (p. 415). More specifically,

> The idea is that the organism's brain perceives the external world from a specific vantage point, and receives a continual set of inputs to the organism as a result of this vantage point. This continual set of inputs related to the organism leads to the formation of neural pathways that define a set of associations related to various aspects of the organism, resulting in behavior consistent with self-recognition. We call this set of associations the organismal self-image.
>
> (Tannenbaum, 2009, p. 415)

Essentially, the brain rewires itself based on inputs from its vantage point, forming associations between itself and the world as experienced. The "organismal self-image" develops automatically from this associative process. The resultant self-image is not necessarily localized in a well-defined set of neural pathways but is rather the set of associations between the organism and the environment.

The key to self-awareness, according to this model, is memory, and the larger the memory capacity of the organism, the more complex the self-image and the higher the level of self-awareness the organism can achieve. Although there are clear differences in the level of self-awareness achieved by human and non-human animals, ones that can be accounted for in this model, Tannebaum's approach does accommodate successful MSR performance across the species discussed in this section. Indeed, this model suggests that self-awareness should emerge in most, if not all, slowly replicating organisms. This is because, for these organisms, there is

> . . . a strong selection pressure to adopt a complex-brained survival strategy, in order to ensure organismal survival to allow for reproduction. Complex-brained organisms are likely also under selection pressures to evolve a brain topology that allows for the integration of many different sources of inputs together. This ensures that the brain operates as a unit, and not as several independent modules that can possibly engage in contradictory behaviors and thereby adversely affect fitness. In addition, an integrated brain topology allows for the co-processing of many different sources of information, which presumably leads to an improved ability to choose an optimal survival strategy.
>
> (Tannenbaum, 2009, p. 416)

Although there exist other, evolutionarily relevant ideas about the value of MSR performance and survival (e.g., Whishaw & Wallace, 2003), these ideas about the adaptive value of the self and autobiographical memory will be deferred until later in this volume (see Chapter 10). For now, the important point is that MSR is not unique to humans, having been observed in a number of nonhuman animals. That these other animals share many cognitive and social characteristics with us is more than mere coincidence. Moreover, these shared characteristics may provide a clue to the evolutionary significance of self-awareness, its link to memory, and the adaptive significance of autobiographical memory to survival.

THE IMPORTANCE OF SOCIAL COGNITION AND LANGUAGE

Alternative views of the onset and development of autobiographical memory set a somewhat different time course, one that is often at odds with the empirical research. For example, Nelson, Fivush, and their colleagues (e.g., Fivush, 2009; Fivush & Reese, 1992; Fivush et al., 1996; Nelson, 1996; Nelson & Fivush, 2004) have adopted a sociolinguistic perspective in which autobiographical memory is said to emerge when children are able to establish a "personal life story" in memory. This latter achievement comes about due in large part to conversations with adults and significant others in which personal experiences are shared. In essence, as young children learn to talk about the past with adults, who in turn help structure or scaffold memories about past experiences, they begin to organize these events along a timeline in their memory, making them autobiographical. Hence, the main function of autobiographical memory is to develop a life history, and this is accomplished by communicating with others about what one is like through narrating the events of the past. By doing this, children learn both how to report past experiences as well as about the social functions that talking about the past performs. This view of the emergence of autobiographical memory presupposes a level of linguistic and narrative competence that is immature until the preschool years, ruling out the emergence of autobiographical memory in the infant and toddler periods (see also Pillemer & White, 1989).

Another idea concerning the emergence of autobiographical memory links it to more general advances in metacognition, specifically to children's emerging theory of mind (see Perner & Ruffman, 1995). According to this approach, event memory in very young children is based on "noetic" awareness, or knowing that something happened, rather than on "autonoetic" awareness, or actually remembering that something happened (also see Tulving, 1984), a transition that does not occur until about the age of four years and heralds the beginning of autobiographical memory. Consistent with the sociolinguistic perspective, this proposal also suggests that the pivotal mechanism driving this transition is children's conversations with others (mothers in particular) suggesting that these conversations serve as important data for the development of their theory of the mind, and that this in turn promotes the establishment of autobiographical memory.

Examination of this approach has produced mixed findings, especially when it comes to demonstrating a link between theory of mind and autobiographical memory (evidence concerning assumptions about sociolinguistic variables will be discussed later in this chapter). For example, Perner and Ruffman (1995) found a correlation between children's theory of mind and free recall, even after removing the effects of receptive language. However, because the children's ages were not controlled in the study, this correlation could simply have been an artifact of the well-known age-related and independent increases in performance that occur on the different theory-of-mind and free-recall tests.

Other studies have similarly failed to demonstrate a direct link between theory of mind and autobiographical memory. For example, Reese and Cleveland (2007) found no evidence for this link in a longitudinal study once appropriate controls were put into place for children's language skills. Although correlations have been obtained between preschool children's theory of mind and their ability to retell a fictional story, these same children did not show any association between theory of mind development and autobiographical recollection of a trip to a museum (Kleinknecht & Beike, 2004). Thus, although theory of mind may be linked to improvements in source monitoring (remembering the *where* or *when* or *from whom* one learned something) or children's language skills, it does not appear to be linked to episodic memory or the emergence and early development of autobiographical memory. Indeed, "although source memory is an important part of episodic memory it should not be equated with it. The ability to recall the source of information does not require episodic memory, because it can be based on knowing and need not be remembered" (Perner et al., 2007, p. 473). Indeed, children can remember the source of information without being able to remember the information itself (Ceci et al., 2010).

Individual Differences in Autobiographical Memory

Because of the amount of research generated by these disparate but not mutually exclusive theoretical perspectives, it has become abundantly clear that the onset and early development of autobiographical memory involves a complex and extended interaction between the individual, their developing perceptual and cognitive systems, and influences in the social (e.g., familial, institutional, cultural) environment in which they are growing up. In this section, I focus primarily on variability in autobiographical remembering that emerges as a function of individual differences in the self, in sociolinguistic interactions between the child and significant others, and in their conjoint effects.

THE SELF

There has been little systematic investigation of individual differences in the onset of the self or studies of the implications of early versus late self-recognition for autobiographical memory. Although cross-sectional studies have shown that there are marked increases in children's success on the MSR task after about 18 months of age (e.g., Amsterdam, 1972; Asendorpf et al., 1996; Bullcock & Lutkenhaus, 1990; Lewis & Brooks-Gunn, 1979; Lewis et al., 1985), this research also underscores the high degree of individual variation in the age at which children exhibit stable responses on the MSR test (i.e., from 15 to 24 months; see Brooks-Gunn & Lewis, 1984). Although the origins of these individual differences have not been established, the onset of MSR has been related to mental age, attentiveness, and stress reactivity (e.g., Lewis & Brooks-Gunn, 1979; Lewis & Ramsay, 1997; Mans et al., 1978). Also, some factors, including socioeconomic status, maternal education, gender, birth order, and number of siblings, have been ruled out; and still other variables, such as attachment status, temperament, and general cognitive ability, where the evidence is still inconclusive (Brooks-Gunn & Lewis, 1984; DiBiase & Lewis, 1997; Lewis et al., 1985; Lewis et al., 1989; Lewis & Ramsay, 1997; Schneider-Rosen & Cicchetti, 1991).

More recent studies have used a microgenetic approach to assess the development of the cognitive self in toddlers from 15 to 23 months of age (Courage et al., 2004; Howe et al., 2003). Here, cross-sectional samples showed the usual pattern of the abrupt onset of MSR at about 18 months, with a range from 15 to 23 months. Although the longitudinal data were generally consistent with this trend, they also clearly showed that, for individual children, MSR emerged more gradually and exhibited greater variability in expression prior to becoming stable: findings that had been masked in the cross-sectional data. More interestingly, regardless of age, those infants who had achieved stable MSR performed better on a unique event-memory task than did those who had failed the MSR test. Consistent with these findings, Prudhomme (2005) reported that the emergence of the cognitive self was essential for early declarative, autobiographical memory. Indeed, she found that individuals with a stable cognitive self were not only better than those without a cognitive self on an elicited-memory task, but they were also considerably more flexible when retrieving information.

In another longitudinal study, Harley and Reese (1999) found that individual differences in self-recognition skill (early vs. late MSR) at 19 months of age predicted the toddlers' independent memory for autobiographical events at 2½ years. Interestingly, although parent–child conversational style was not as important initially, a follow-up study found that once children became language users themselves, the type of parent interaction (i.e., high vs. low elaborative conversational styles) and the child's language skill became increasingly important predictors of verbal memory reports (Reese, 2009). Recently, Reese and Newcombe (2007) found that training mothers in elaborative reminiscing with their children increased their children's recollection of those events, as anticipated. Of greater interest was the finding that by the age of 3½ years, the effect of this maternal elaboration training had extended to children's independent reminiscing, but did so only for the children who exhibited self-recognition at an early age, as measured at the beginning of the study. Clearly, what these studies demonstrate is that an early and stable self-identity provides the foundation for the development of autobiographical memory, and that autobiographical memory becomes better elaborated with advances in sociolinguistic skills.

SOCIOLINGUISTIC INTERACTIONS

As already mentioned, the sociolinguistic perspective concerning the onset of autobiographical memory sets a later beginning for this achievement than the cognitive self model does, as well as charting a different developmental course, one that is grounded in language and social cognition. The key role that social interaction plays in the emergence of autobiographical memory comes in the form of how experiences are shared with others linguistically (Fivush, 2009; Fivush & Reese, 1992; Fivush et al., 1996; Hudson, 1990). We have already seen that language plays a role in memory, whether that memory is autobiographical or not. However, theorists need to be careful not to confuse the functional aspects of memory with its representational structure. That is, although autobiographical memories are typically reported in a narrative format, their representation does not depend on language facility per se. Rather, memory representations are not simply verbal or lexical entries but contain a variety of features (perceptual, situational, conceptual, etc.) that are extracted during encoding, ones that are stored and later retrieved from autobiographical representations just as they are in memories more generally (e.g., see Damasio, 1999; Howe, 1998b; Paivio, 2007).

Studies of the emergence of linguistic communication have shown that by about 2½ years most children begin to talk about specific events, but that these early conversations are heavily "scaffolded" by adults (e.g., Hudson, 1990). By about three years, children assume more of the responsibility for talking about the past, rely less on parental scaffolding, and begin to use the story or narrative form in these conversational interactions. Although some of these advances begin to occur as early as three to four years of age, Nelson (1996) has maintained that "true" autobiographical memory develops late and may only be functional near the end of the preschool years. Here, autobiographical memory is predicated on the development of rather sophisticated language-based representational skills that do not emerge until around five or six years of age. It is only once these skills are established that autobiographical memories can be retained and organized around a life history, one that extends in time.

As already noted, there is research within this framework that has shown that individual differences in the ways parents talk about the past to their children can lead to individual differences in children's autobiographical reporting of their own experiences. Parents who are "high-elaborative" (i.e., those who provide a large amount of detailed information about past events and spend time elaborating and expanding on the child's partial recall) ask additional questions that elicit and enhance details of the event, and correct the child's memory when necessary. By contrast, parents who are "low-elaborative" (i.e., those who tend to simply repeat questions in order to elicit a specific answer from the child) do not seek elaborative details from their children's report. As might be anticipated, high-elaborative styles are associated with children's provision of more elaborate narratives, both initially as well as longitudinally (Haden et al., 1997;

Reese et al., 1993). There is strong evidence that this type of conversational style facilitates the richness and narrative organization of children's memory talk and plays a central role in the later development of children's ability to report autobiographical memories. However, high-elaborative conversational style does not determine the content or accuracy of children's memory reports (see Fivush, 1994; Goodman et al., 1994). Indeed, reconstruction of events through conversations with others is a technique that is known to lead to systematic distortions of memory details, ones that are congruent with the teller's current beliefs as well as with the expectations of the listener (e.g., Ross & Wilson, 2000). Thus, consistent with the memory literature more generally, verbal rehearsal (elaborative or otherwise) not only serves to potentially reinforce and reinstate memories, but also, equally important, can lead to some very fundamental errors in remembering.

THE SELF, SOCIOLINGUISTIC INTERACTIONS, AND CULTURE

Although the origin of the cognitive sense of self is primarily rooted in cognitive development, its subsequent maturation occurs in the context of family, society, and culture. Because these contexts can differ in their perspectives about the nature and importance of the self, they can have a considerable impact on the way that the self is viewed in the process of creating memories and hence in what is remembered (e.g., Mullen, 1994; Wang, 2001). For example, because many Western cultures place a considerable emphasis on individuality and personal achievement, this can promote the development and expression of an autonomous and independent self whose personal characteristics (beliefs, attitudes, and goals) are most important. By contrast, because many Asian cultures emphasize interpersonal connectedness, group solidarity, and achievement, the development of a relational or communal self is foremost. These latter individuals tend to define themselves in terms of their social roles, duties, and responsibilities, and these features come to make up their sense of self. These different cultural selves can have a profound impact on individuals' perceptions and emotions during an ongoing event, and consequently have a corresponding influence on the features of that event that get encoded and subsequently remembered and recounted. Predictably, these different self-constructs affect caregivers' interactions with their children, hence fostering more culturally appropriate self-systems that focus on autonomy or community as appropriate (e.g., see Wang & Conway, 2006).

Research on the impact of cultural differences in self-concept on the onset, form, and content of autobiographical memories has shown marked differences in the ages at which adults in certain Eastern and Western cultures can retrieve their earliest autobiographical memories. For example, those from

Western cultures (e.g., Americans and Europeans) date their earliest childhood memory about six months earlier than do Asians, and they also demonstrate greater age-linked increases in memory fluency (e.g., MacDonald et al., 2000; Mullen, 1994; Wang, 2001; Wang et al., 2004). What these findings suggest is that cultural differences in the early appearance of an autonomous self-construct (as seen in Western cultures) might facilitate the formation of a unique and detailed personal history, one that contributes to the organization of memories for early events as experiences that have happened "to me." Of course, the way the self is structured can also have an impact on how autobiographical memory is represented, evaluated, and reconstructed over time (e.g., see Conway & Pleydell-Pearce, 2000). For instance, individuals whose cultures focus on an autonomous self might be more likely to encode and retrieve information that is related to that self. Alternatively, those from cultures that view the self as part of a community of selves might be more likely to encode memories that focus on features relevant to the collective or group-centered aspects of events. This is exactly what the research by Wang and her colleagues has shown (e.g., Wang, 2001; Wang et al., 1998). Specifically, compared to Chinese college students, American college students report not only an earlier age of first memory, but also more self-focused, specific, and emotionally elaborate content in their autobiographical memories. In fact, Chinese students tended to provide briefer reports of routine collective events, reports that were also more emotionally neutral. Similar cultural variations in the content of autobiographical memories have been reported in preschool children (e.g., Han et al., 1998; Wang, 2004; Wang & Leichtman, 2000). Finally, culture affects not only the linguistic expression and content of event memories, but also the vantage point from which events are encoded and reported. For example, in a study with Asian and American adults, Cohen and Gunz (2002) found that memory content was influenced by the person's phenomenological experience as a member of these different cultures. That is, Asians were more likely than Americans to experience the self in memory from the perspective of the generalized other (e.g., to have more third-person memories).

The developmental literature also shows that children from other cultures who are exposed to different conversational styles also vary in important ways in the manner in which they report their memories. For example, American mothers who talk to their three-year-olds about past events more frequently (by as much as three times) than do their Korean counterparts, have children who talk about past events more than do Korean children (Han et al., 1998; Mullen, 1994; Mullen & Yi, 1995). Similar relationships have been observed when the comparison groups were Maori, Pakeha, and Asian adults living in New Zealand (MacDonald et al., 2000; Reese et al., 2008).

Interestingly, similar differences in autobiographical memory profiles have been observed as a function of gender. For example, it is well known that women have earlier first memories than men, although these differences can be small (e.g., Dudycha & Dudycha, 1933, 1941; Mullen 1994; Rubin, 2000). Women's autobiographical memory reports often contain longer, more detailed, and more vivid accounts of their childhood experiences than do those provided by men (e.g., see Bauer, 2007; Bauer et al., 2003; Fivush, 2009). Moreover, women and men express emotional content differently in their memory reports. Anger, shame, guilt, and attachment issues are more common themes among women, whereas for men, concerns about competence, performance, achievement, and identity are more commonly expressed (Cowan & Davidson, 1984; Dudycha & Dudycha, 1941). The origins of these gender differences have typically been interpreted in a sociocultural framework with a particular emphasis on dif-ferences in the ways boys and girls are socialized to talk about the past. As it turns out, parents talk to their daughters more frequently and at greater length about the past than they do with their sons. Moreover, parents place more emphasis on interpersonal and emotional components of experiences with their daughters compared to the individual, emotionally neutral aspects they tend to emphasize with sons (for discussions, see Bauer et al., 2003). By con-trast, there are very few gender differences in nonverbal recall of events in studies with infants and preverbal children. What this means is that these gender differences, ones that appear in later childhood and adulthood, are not a function of memory processes per se. Rather, they appear to be more a matter of the socialization of reminiscence and remembering, something that children learn through narrative interactions in their familial and cultural environments.

INDIVIDUAL DIFFERENCES IN AUTOBIOGRAPHICAL MEMORY FOR EMOTIONAL AND STRESSFUL EVENTS

Although I deal with the role of stress, emotion, and maltreatment and early memory in more depth later in this volume (see Chapters 7 and 8), it is impor-tant to introduce this topic in the current chapter. It is well known that stressful events lead to the release of adrenal stress hormones (e.g., catecholamines, glu-cocorticoids) that can have dramatic effects on memory and other cognitive processes (e.g., Cahill, 2000; Cahill & McGaugh, 1998). Although these hor-mones have different effects on the neural and neuroendocrine systems, they share an inverted-U shaped dose–response relationship, such that small amounts generally have modest effects on memory, moderate amounts can enhance memory, and large amounts can potentially impair memory. However, what the research has shown to date is that the effects of stress are not straightforward when it comes to predicting whether memory in (or for) any particular stressful situation is unaffected, enhanced, or diminished. As it turns out, the size and direction of these effects depends on a host of factors, including the chronicity of the stress, its intensity, and individual differences in reactivity to stress itself (see Howe, 1998a; Howe et al., 2006a, 2006b; Quas et al., 2004).

Despite considerable research, the nature of the relationship between stress and memory has eluded many theorists, and the theories that have been proposed have received mixed support at best. Whereas Christianson (1992) has suggested that during highly stressful events memory for the central features of the event is strengthened, but memory for peripheral details is impaired, others have concluded that memory is best for moderately arousing stimuli and becomes poorer when high stress activates defensive processes (e.g., Deffenbacher et al., 2004). What is known is that the release of stress-induced catecholamines and glucocorticoids, as well as the related changes in the delivery of oxygen to the brain that they precipitate, can modulate what gets stored in memory by altering (for better or worse) processes involved in encoding and consolidation of information as well as the effectiveness of subsequent retrieval processes (e.g., Cahill & McGaugh, 1996; Howe, 1997, 1998a; Howe et al., 2006a, 2006b; McGaugh, 2000). Moreover, nonhuman animal studies have shown that prolonged exposure to severe stress can precipitate damage to the developing brain, including dendritic atrophy, neuronal death, and hippocampal atrophy. This occurs across a variety of mammalian species and is suggestive of possible parallel effects in humans (see Howe et al., 2006a, 2006b).

As documented later in this book (Chapters 7 and 8), one difficulty in establishing the relationship between stress and memory in humans concerns disagreement among measures of behavioral, self-report, and physiological and autonomic measures of stress, especially in children (see Howe et al., 2006a, 2006b). A perhaps somewhat greater difficulty has to do with the multitude of individual differences in cognitive (e.g., knowledge), temperamental (e.g., reactivity), social (parent–child interactions), emotional (attachment), and situational (interviewer support) factors that also moderate the effects of stress (for reviews, see Chae et al., 2009; Christianson, 1992; Cordon et al., 2004; Deffenbacher et al., 2004).

Despite these difficulties, there is growing evidence that children's autobiographical memory for stressful events operates in much the same way as memory for non-stressful events. Across the wide range of methods, measures, situations, and ages that have been employed in this research, it is often found that children's recall of stressful events, at least after autobiographical memory has begun, can be quite accurate even after extended delays (e.g., see chapters in Howe et al., 2008). If an event, regardless of its valence or level of arousal, is personally salient to the child, that event will be better remembered than an event that is less distinctive (e.g., Howe, 2006a, 2006b; Howe et al., 2000). In general, emotional or stressful events are distinctive, although ironically, in cases of repeated maltreatment, individual instances may lose their salience and appear to be remembered more poorly (see Howe et al., 2006a, 2006b).

As noted, there is a multitude of parent–child interaction variables that can affect children's recall of emotional events in much the same way as they do for memory of non-emotional events. For example, parents who are highly elaborative in their conversational styles are likely to have children who provide more information in their autobiographical reports of both stressful and non-stressful events (Fivush & Reese, 2002; McGuigan & Salmon, 2004). These parent–child interactions do not just provide an opportunity for rehearsal of the event but, as detailed earlier in this chapter, they also provide children with information about how, what, and when to communicate about their emotions and experiences to others. Importantly, parents who are highly elaborative also tend to have more secure attachment relationships with their children than parents who are low-elaborative (e.g., Alexander et al., 2002; Fivush & Reese, 2002).

In fact, the quality of parent–child attachment has emerged as an important intervening variable that moderates the child's response to a stressful situation and in so doing may moderate the effects of stress on children's autobiographical memory (e.g., see Alexander et al., 2002; Chae et al., 2009). One reason for this can be found in Bowlby's (1969) attachment theory. Here, infants are said to form internal working models about themselves and their caregivers. These models emerge from the everyday dynamic interactions that occur between themselves and their caregivers very early in life. These representations of self and caregiver are then used to interpret the intentions and actions of others. This, in turn, leads to the formation of expectations of others' behavior in relation to them, and to the regulation of their own responses. Infants who experience secure attachment relationships, due to experiencing sensitive, responsive, and consistent caretaking, develop internal models that are coherent, organized, and facilitate the emerging sense of self. Those who develop insecure attachments usually form internal models that are disorganized, ones that tend to be disruptive to a coherent sense of self. Secure and insecure (avoidant, anxious, disorganized) attachments in infancy and their associated internal models are frequently carried into adulthood and can continue to characterize the person's affective relationships with others as well as the type of parenting behavior they themselves exhibit (e.g., see Fraley et al., 2002; Simpson & Rholes, 1998). Importantly, there is mounting evidence that children (and subsequently adults) who are the product of secure attachments have better access to autobiographical memories (especially those with negative emotional content) than those with insecure attachments (see Alexander et al., 2002; Chae et al., 2009).

You *Can* Take it With You: Redux

Recall from Chapter 4, the question arose as to whether memories formed during the infantile amnesia period, traumatic or not, can be remembered after the onset of autobiographical memory. It was concluded that although some vestiges of early experience may remain, they are fundamentally impervious to conscious inspection and remain, at best, as implicit memories. As noted at the beginning of this chapter, the remains of these experiences may form the basis of implicit semantic memories, ones that could still affect current behavior. However, more recently, studies have been conducted to test whether specific episodic components of early memories could be retained across the infantile amnesia barrier.

More specifically, the question addressed in this research was whether nonverbal experiences that were encoded during the period of infantile amnesia (i.e., before the age of two years) can be later translated into language and verbally remembered after the age of two years. If so, then perhaps infantile amnesia does not end abruptly as assumed in some theories, but rather gives way to auto-biographical memory as a function of more continuous changes in more basic memory processes (also see Courage & Howe, 2002). For example, Simcock and Hayne (2002) examined children's memory for events associated with a "magic shrinking machine." After a six- to 12-month delay interval they found that, despite improvement in children's language skills, preschoolers could not translate preverbal aspects of this experience into verbal recall. Similar findings have been obtained by Bauer and her associates (Bauer et al., 2004; Cheatham & Bauer, 2005) using imitation tasks. Here, only older children were able to provide verbal recall of earlier studied behaviors, with the best predictor of later verbal recall being children's verbal recall ability at the time of the original event. What these studies suggest is that only older children who are already able to express their memories using language can provide a verbal recollection of those events at some later time.

Finally, Morris and Baker-Ward (2007) examined children's memory for a unique event using a "bubble machine." Here, the machine only produced bubbles when the correctly chosen colored liquid was poured in the machine—that is, color was causally linked to the desired outcome. Children's color vocabulary was measured before the experiment, and training in color-naming was provided during the two-month retention interval for those colors children were naïve to (and had trouble correctly labelling) during training. When sufficient physical cuing was provided at this later test, some of the children (29%) were able to correctly remember the color of the liquid needed to obtain the desired outcome learned some two months earlier, even though they did not know that color name during training. What this finding indicates is that under some very rigorous training regimes, and with highly supportive conditions during testing, some children can provide verbal labels of what had been nonverbal experiences. However, as Simcock and Hayne (2003) caution, children only express a small fraction of the content of these memories through language, with much more being left unspoken than spoken. Indeed, consistent with what was concluded in the previous chapter, vestiges of early experiences are not easily translated across the infantile amnesia barrier, at least not as consciously available, autobiographical memories (also see Richardson & Hayne, 2007).

Summary and Conclusions

To summarize, I have provided an overview of the empirical literature on the onset and early development of autobiographical memory and related it to current theoretical perspectives that attempt to explain this achievement. One of these perspectives focused on the emergence of the cognitive sense of self (e.g., see Howe et al., 2003) and others on sociolinguistic and metacognitive interactions that occur when children share their personal memories with others. It is clear that the debate over the relative importance of the cognitive self versus sociolinguistic and metacognitive factors in the development of autobiographical memory deals with differences that are more apparent than real. Although I continue to maintain that it is the emergence of the cognitive self late in the second year of life that launches autobiographical memory, it is abundantly clear that coincident and subsequent achievements in language and social cognition affect its continued development throughout childhood.

More generally, subsequent to the advent of the cognitive self, developmental advances in memory (e.g., encoding, storage, and retrieval processes; knowledge acquisition and reorganization), language, and social cognition all assume increased importance as they provide for more stable memory representations as well as an expressive outlet for those recollections. As autobiographical memory matures, sociolinguistic theories make it clear, the language environment of the child, whether familial or cultural, serves to teach children that reporting memories is important, and that such reports have a particular narrative structure and content, and a particular social and cognitive function. In that capacity, conversational exchanges not only provide a narrative structure for reporting events, but also act to preserve (e.g., through rehearsal, reinstatement) or potentially alter (e.g., through reconstruction) memory records of personally experienced events.

I have also reviewed a number of individual differences in autobiographical memory and demonstrated that many of these are directly or indirectly related to individual differences in aspects of the self (e.g., early self-recognition, working self, cultural self) or to aspects of social cognition and socialization (e.g., parent conversational style, internal working models). These findings confirm that autobiographical memory emerges first from an early sense of self, one that begins in early infancy and becomes stabilized during the second postnatal year. Only at this time will familial, social, and cultural factors begin to influence the way the child perceives, thinks, and talks about themselves and in so doing, further shape the maturing self-concept and its expression in autobiographical memory.

Finally, I have pointed out that self-recognition is not uniquely human and is shared with nonhuman animals whose brains also share a number of similarities with our own, at least inasmuch as they, too, exhibit complex cognition as well as empathy and altruism. Indeed, it has been known for some time that the onset of mirror self-recognition in humans is associated with the appearance of empathy (Bischof-Kohler, 1994) and altruism (Zahn-Waxler et al., 1992). Additional similarities between ourselves and those nonhuman animals that do exhibit self-recognition include a reasonably well-developed long-term-memory capacity. Although it is not clear that these memory systems are, strictly speaking, autobiographical in nature, it is no stretch to state that they are indeed episodic-like. I will return to this issue in the later chapters of this volume when I articulate a more formal treatment of the adaptive nature of autobiographical memory.

6

Consciousness and Early Memory Development

Footfalls echo in the memory
down the passage which we did not take
towards the door we never opened.
—T.S. Eliot

One set of questions that have arisen throughout this book in a variety of guises concerns whether the residue of early experience continues to influence current and future behavior, and if so, whether the vestiges of these experiences persist in memory and, if so, whether they can be consciously recollected. There are really two questions here. First, can early experience affect our behavior regardless of whether we have a memory (conscious or not) of that experience? The answer would appear to be yes. Very early experiences can and do affect our development in a number of ways, not the least of which concerns neurobiological development, as outlined in the review of the experience-dependent and experience-expectant interactions in Chapter 3. In addition, as hypothesized elsewhere in this book (Chapters 2–5), some early experiences may lead to later preferences or to the development of phobias that can make us avoid certain stimuli (e.g., snakes, spiders, large dogs). Although all of these behaviors can be altered by subsequent experiences, the important point is that some behaviors may be shaped by early experiences even in the absence of any memory of the experiences themselves.

The second, and more relevant, question for the purposes of this book is whether some experiences do leave a memorial residue, and if so, can these memories be consciously accessed? Of course, if these memories can be consciously accessed, then there is the potential that we might be able to examine and modify them, perhaps leading to subsequent changes in the way they affect our behavior. As we have also seen, the main problem here is that early memories, if they do exist, are fragmentary at best prior to the onset of auto-biographical memory. Even after the advent of the "self in memory," experiences can be discarded, modified, and even forgotten over the years. Indeed, autobio-graphical memories are subject to the same factors that make memory fallible more generally (interference, disruption, decay, etc.). However, if we assume that some experiences survive unscathed and are not forgotten but are simply inaccessible to consciousness, might not these residues of early experiences still affect our current (and future) behaviors?

Although there is a distinct lack of empirical evidence on this matter (as noted, for example, in Chapters 2 and 4), there is no dearth of speculation and folk theories that either implicitly or explicitly claim that people are inexora-bly bound by their past regardless of whether they can or cannot consciously remember it. Indeed, it has been speculated not just that these experiences could lead to a change in one's behavior but that these experiences were some-how indelibly etched in one's mind (see Chapter 1). These ideas were further canonized in the writings of Freud and Erikson, both of whom embedded this fundamental notion in their theories about the influence and importance of experiences that occur very early in development. These ideas are also rampant in the popular press, where claims abound that memories, particularly those of abusive experiences, once locked in the unconscious can be subsequently recov-ered and consciously recollected (e.g., Pope & Brown, 1996). Although it is clear that children and adults can forget elements of their memories of experiences (see review by Ceci et al., 2010) and that these elements may come to mind later when the appropriate retrieval cues are present, there is no scientific evidence to suggest that wholesale repression of entire experiences is followed by subse-quent conscious recovery of the memory for that event (also see Chapters 7–9). While the jury may still be out when it comes to such possibilities as popularized in the media, the memory evidence is convincing in its indictment of such a phenomenon (for overviews, see Alpert et al., 1996; Brainerd & Reyna, 2005).

Consider a somewhat less controversial example. As already discussed, Bowlby's (1969) theory places considerable emphasis on early affective experi-ences as playing a key role in the development of attachment. That is, the bond of attachment is said to emerge following innumerable hours of infant–caregiver interaction. The record of these early interaction experiences, consciously recall-able or not, is said to be forever etched in the infant's memory. The persistence of this memory is what mediates people's attachment relationships throughout the rest of their life with peers and significant others (see Bretherton & Waters, 1985; Sroufe, 1983), as well as determining their psychological well-being in adulthood (Bowlby, 1980). Although it is clear that there are links between early and later behaviors within individuals, there is a paucity of scientific evidence to substantiate claims about the processes (including memories for these formative experiences) that mediate these outcomes. For example, insecure attachment, social isolation, institutionalization, and maltreatment, as well as a variety of other adverse rearing conditions, can produce deviant outcomes during infancy in both humans and nonhuman primates (e.g., Harlow & Harlow, 1966; Suomi & Harlow, 1972; also see Kagan, 1996). However, what has not been established is whether these behavioral, affective, and cognitive consequences persist or even remain stable indefinitely. Indeed, quite a different pattern has been frequently observed, with many children exhibiting considerable resiliency in their reactions to early adverse experiences (for a recent review of effects with institutionalized children, see Rutter et al., 2010; a more complete exegesis of this and other relevant work can be found in Chapter 8). Moreover, it has been well documented that the negative effects of early adverse experiences can be reversed. For example, some of the children who spent their first few years of life as orphans in concentration camps were, as adults, leading very productive lives (Moscovitz, 1983). Similar positive outcomes have been observed in children who were made homeless by war or who suffered severe malnutrition and emotional distress, once they were adopted into nurturing families (Clarke & Hanisee, 1982; Rathburn et al., 1958; Winick et al., 1975). Indeed, given the dire consequences anticipated by many theories dealing with early adverse experiences, many researchers have been surprised at these now well-documented accounts of resiliency following severe infantile trauma or deprivation (for reviews, see Emde, 1981; Kagan, 1984; Rutter, 1981). Of course, this does not mean that there are no consequences of early deprivation (see Rutter et al., 2010), but it does show that, for humans as well as nonhuman primates, the effects of early experience tend to diminish, and organisms tend to "right" themselves, even following extreme adversity (Cairns & Hood, 1983; Werner & Smith, 1982; Winick et al., 1975). Thus, in contrast to both theory and folk belief, the empirical facts overwhelmingly support the conclusion that early experiences do not indelibly fix behaviors, attachment, neurotic tendencies, or personality characteristics, particularly when subsequent experiences (e.g., moving into a nurturing environment) foster other, more positive adaptive responses.

Although the evidence is inconsistent with the strong version of early experiential determinism (where early experiences inexorably "fix" later behaviors; also see Kagan, 1996), it is possible that the vestiges of these early experiences remain in memory even in the absence of conspicuous behavioral expression. Despite the fact that the behaviors themselves can change in response to new and varied circumstances that accrue with development and experience, such behavioral discontinuities do not imply that the memorial vestiges of earlier experiences disappear or change along with alterations in behavior. In fact, these memories of earlier experiences might still guide the selection of newer, more adaptive responses. Indeed, the argument continues, if it were not for the memories of these earlier, formative experiences, these newer behaviors might not have been adopted.

Notwithstanding the circularity of these arguments, there is an important question that should concern us. Specifically, is there any scientific evidence that there exist memories of these early experiences, ones that continue to exert their influence on our behavior and development despite our inability to consciously remember them? The answer to this question is by no means simple. As already seen, it is extremely difficult, if not impossible, to unambiguously establish that a particular behavior exhibited by an individual (e.g., phobia, anxiety, food preference) is uniquely linked to a particular memory of a specific earlier experience, especially in the absence of conscious, verbal recall of that memory. Indeed, according to most theories, such memories are at best implicit (e.g., Newcombe et al., 2007) and hence impervious to conscious remembering (also see Chapter 2).

However, some say that simply because we cannot find unambiguous evidence for such memories does not mean that they do not exist. Indeed, they aver, it is possible that we simply need to devise a more sensitive test to detect the presence of such memories. Although arguments such as these may seem reasonable at first blush, they carry very little weight. This is because they are ubiquitous and have the dubious advantage of perpetually being in reserve to explain away failures to reject the null hypothesis, regardless of the circumstances in which these failures occur. That is, continued failures to confirm the existence of some hypothesized phenomenon do not rule out the possibility that it may exist, but repeated failures to substantiate its existence do call into question its authenticity. In what follows, I examine the types of tests that have been developed to evaluate hypotheses concerning the status of conscious and unconscious memories and then provide a critical examination of the empirical findings concerning what it is that might be developing early in childhood.

Testing the Development of Conscious and Unconscious Memory

Given we know that a variety of memory-relevant factors (e.g., distinctiveness, familiarity, similarity) influences people's performance despite their lack of awareness of those factors, there must also be some evidence for the existence of memories that affect people's behavior without their awareness of those memories (i.e., they are, therefore, unconscious memories). For example, concerning familiarity, people may vote for a particular political candidate for no other reason than the frequency with which they have been exposed to advertising for that candidate. Similar unconscious influences on behavior are equally well known, including the *sleeper effect*, where the influence of a persuasive message increases over time even though it has been presented by a discredited source (Pratkanis et al., 1988), and *becoming famous overnight* in which a previously non-famous name presented during an experiment is later, although not immediately, identified as someone who is famous (Jacoby et al., 1989).

Often, these effects have been interpreted as being mediated by unconscious memories. However, such an interpretation is not demanded by the data. That is, although the influence of memory-related variables may be outside of a person's conscious awareness, this does not mean that the memories themselves cannot be consciously remembered. In fact, all of these effects that are presumed to be due to the existence of unconscious memories can be explained using a combination of familiarity and misattribution effects. Simply being exposed to material (e.g., a person's name), even if it is only once, enhances its familiarity, making it easier to access in memory than material that people have not been exposed to. After a delay, the source of such information in memory (e.g., "it was told to me by the experimenter") is lost, and when later asked to use that information in a judgment task (e.g., assessing fame, voting for a political candidate), people can more easily retrieve this previously studied information (familiarity), can fail to recollect the original source of that information (presented during the experiment), and then can misattribute the source of that information to themselves (source-misattribution error). The effects of familiarity, along with the normal forgetting of source information, together serve as one basis for the "false memory effect" so frequently found in human memory (see Chapter 9). Indeed, younger children may be even more susceptible to some of these effects (specifically, misinformation effects due to suggestion; see Ceci & Bruck, 1995), particularly in light of their poorer source-monitoring skills, especially when it comes to discriminating between information that is self- versus other-generated (e.g., Lindsay et al., 1991; Roberts & Blades, 1998; Wimmer & Howe, 2009).

However, simply because the effects just discussed do not require unconscious memories as an explanation does not imply that conditions do not exist in which memories are unconscious. For example, if we define *consciousness* as a state of wakeful alertness, then, by definition, people's memories must exist in their unconscious during sleep, unless we care to entertain the unlikely notion that memories are reconstructed anew each morning. Although this definition may seem simpleminded—and, of course, there is evidence to indicate that sleep actually enhances memory, particularly explicit or declarative memory, in both adults (Diekelmann & Born, 2010) and children (Prehn-Kristensen et al., 2009)—there are two important points that can be taken from this example. First, we need to be extremely precise in how we define *conscious* and *unconscious* memories. Although preverbal infants and nonhuman animals are frequently wakeful and alert, there is still little agreement about how to measure their conscious awareness, or whether the memories they exhibit behaviorally should be properly classified as "conscious" (see Nelson, 1997; Rovee-Collier, 1997). As well, whereas conscious memories are usually identified with an explicit or declarative memory system and unconscious memories with an implicit or procedural memory system, there exists considerable debate as to whether this distinction is relevant to human developmental science (e.g., Rovee-Collier, 1997; Rovee-Collier & Cuevas, 2009a, 2009b).

Second, when we do come up with satisfactory definitions of what constitutes a conscious memory and how it differs from what it is that constitutes an unconscious memory, we must then establish that these memories differ in some meaningful way. That is, we must show that conscious and unconscious memories differ from each other in some fundamental manner, either structurally or functionally. More important, from a developmental perspective, we must show that conscious and unconscious memories have distinct age-related trajectories. If none of these differences pertains, then, at least from a memory theorist's point of view, there may be very little that is of any intrinsic interest to study. Indeed, as Rovee-Collier and her colleagues have maintained concerning the implicit-explicit memory distinction,

> Ontogenetic changes in infant memory have been attributed to the hierarchical emergence of dichotomous memory systems (implicit and explicit memory) during the first year of life. We propose that this division is both conceptually and empirically flawed on a number of counts. First, the conceptual basis of classifying memory systems as implicit or explicit is conceptually ambiguous. Second, conscious awareness is not an appropriate basis for classifying a preverbal infant's memory as implicit or explicit. Third, assumptions of a one-to-one mapping between processes and tests are wrong: No task is process pure. Fourth, classifying infant memory tasks as implicit and explicit is only descriptive and does not address the mechanism by which the memory is processed and extended. Fifth, the maturational status of the infants' brains is not the rate-limiting step in their ability to form, maintain, and retrieve long-term memories. Sixth, dichotomous memory systems cannot account for a large amount of learning and memory data from human and nonhuman infants.
>
> (Rovee-Collier & Cuevas, 2009b, p. 161)

According to this, there is little to gain and much to lose by aligning the conscious-unconscious memory distinction with the explicit-implicit memory dichotomy. Indeed, there would seem to be little currency to worrying about the conscious-unconscious distinction in early memory research and very little if anything to gain by way of theoretical advances in understanding very early memory development by adopting this distinction.

Can We Dissever Conscious and Unconscious Memories and Their Development?

THEORETICAL CONSIDERATIONS

Let us return to the earlier question; namely, are there unconscious memories of earlier experiences that still exert a powerful influence on our current and future behavior as some theorists would have us believe (e.g., Freud, 1916–1917/1963)? Can such memories exist, ones that are split off from consciousness; or is there a single memory system that develops and consciousness is simply that process by which memories come and go from our awareness? In this latter scenario, the dichotomy of conscious/unconscious is nonexistent, and memories simply exist in storage, with some being currently accessible and "in awareness" while others are not being accessed and are "outside of awareness." Indeed, it is quite plausible that much of what we have stored in memory is not conscious at any one time, although most of it is available to our consciousness "on demand" (depending on the current processing demands and its accessibility, which in turn depends on a host of storage and retrieval factors). This idea is not as strange as it might seem, once it is remembered that many of the behaviors we perform do not require conscious access to memories, that many aspects of our memory traces do not need to be consciously available at any one time, and that some aspects of our memories perhaps never become available to our conscious awareness (i.e., the actual representational nature of these traces, whether they consist of patterns of synaptic connectivity, distributed networks, etc.). Conscious recollection is not necessary for memories to guide behavior, as when a well-practiced driver does not need to consciously remember how to apply the brakes prior to stopping the car they are driving. Similarly, for a well-seasoned bicyclist to successfully ride a bicycle, it is not necessary to consciously remember memories of how to ride a bicycle (semantic/autobiographical memory) or memories of when, where, and with whom they learned how to ride a bicycle (episodic/ autobiographical memory).

Although such memories can be brought into conscious awareness as required, the critical point is that they are not necessary in order for those memories to affect behavior. Thus, memories can and do "drift" in and out of conscious awareness, depending on current processing demands, accessibility, and the cues (internal and external) available to elicit such memories. Once the appropriate demands and retrieval cues are in place, memories become conscious and can be easily remembered. Otherwise, such memories, although not disappearing, remain outside of conscious awareness and may differ in the ease with which they can be brought to mind, contingent on a host of well-known memory factors (e.g., the spontaneous or intentional use of retrieval cues, how recently they have been reinstated, and their representational strength, familiarity, and distinctiveness).

BEHAVIORAL AND NEUROPHYSIOLOGICAL INDICES

If we suspend our skepticism regarding the utility of the implicit-explicit memory distinction for a moment, there are both behavioral and neurophysiological indices that may be useful in examining the issue of conscious (explicit) memory and unconscious (implicit) memory in early memory development. For example, as seen in Chapter 2, there are a number of behavioral indices of early memory, including visual paired comparison, conjugate reinforcement, and various forms of imitation, all of which attest to the fact that infants possess remarkable memories. As we also saw, there is considerable debate about which procedures measure implicit memory and which ones measure explicit memory. If it can be assumed that this distinction tracks the debate about consciousness, then infants as young as one year of age (and perhaps even younger) apparently do exhibit conscious remembering. Although they cannot tell us verbally what they are remembering, they are conscious when remembering in these paradigms, and they may also be consciously aware of what it is they are remembering.

Recent studies have also examined early memory using event-related potentials (ERPs). ERPs are recordings of electrical oscillations associated with excitatory and inhibitory potentials as measured by electrodes on the surface of the scalp. Because these oscillations can be time-referenced to the presentation of specific stimuli, changes in the latency and amplitude of the response to different stimuli (reflecting familiarity or novelty) can be interpreted as evidence for differential neural processing. For example, in a series of studies by Bauer and her colleagues (Bauer et al., 2003; Carver et al., 2000), nine-month-old infants were exposed to a two-step imitation sequence. One week later, the infants' ERPs were recorded as they were exposed to pictures of the imitation sequences they had seen earlier, as well as to a sequence they had not been exposed to earlier. Following another delay of one month, these same infants were administered a standard imitation test to see whether they recalled the original sequences.

Interestingly, the size of the ERP response at one week predicted infants' recall performance at one month. That is, children who exhibited stronger recognition as indexed by their ERP response at one week also showed higher levels of deferred imitation one month later (also see Bauer et al., 2006). Although these findings were not interpreted within the conscious-unconscious memory debate, the use of ERPs may inform this debate. At the very least, this new exploratory tool gives researchers a window through which they can "look at" memories for stimuli that infants and toddlers are consciously aware of, as well as those that may be too weak for conscious remembering but are still present in storage and that can be subsequently reinstated or reactivated. However, to date, because ERPs following a one-week retention interval signal better conscious recall even after a further one-month delay, ERPs may be a better predictor of conscious than unconscious recollective processes.

Recall that earlier I focused on a distinction between semantic and episodic components of autobiographical memory. In semantic memories, traces of early experiences are retained without reference to the personal circumstances surrounding the memory for that event (e.g., learning about the properties of bananas); whereas with episodic memories, traces of early experiences do retain these personal circumstances (e.g., the first time I tasted a banana). Episodic and semantic components of autobiographical memory are said to be associated with two different states of awareness: *autonoetic* and *noetic* consciousness, respectively. Autonoetic consciousness is characterized by an awareness of the self in time and a mental reliving of the subjective experience being remembered. Noetic consciousness is characterized by the ability to be aware of information about the world in the absence of any specific remembering of experiences concerning this information. Subjective reports of both of these states of awareness are said to be reflected in two different types of memory judgments: *remember* and *know*. Specifically, following a recognition response, participants are asked to judge whether they remember that information (i.e., recollecting the encoding context) or know that information (i.e., recollect the information without remembering the encoding circumstances). The proportions of "remember" and "know" judgments are routinely interpreted as estimates of conscious and unconscious memory, respectively (also see Rajaram, 1996).

According to Tulving (2002), episodic memory develops later than semantic memory, a proposition that is consistent with Newcombe and colleagues' (2007) idea that memories for early experiences are stored semantically, not episodically. Although remember-know judgments are only meaningful somewhat later in childhood, the developmental evidence that does exist is consistent with these ontological assumptions. For example, Billingsley, Smith, and McAndrews (2002) examined remember-know responses in participants aged 8–10 years, 11–13 years, 14–16 years, and 17–19 years. They found that, whereas know responses did not vary with age, older children routinely gave more remember responses than younger children. Similar findings have been obtained by Lyons,

Ghetti, and Cornoldi (2010) with participants varying in age from six years to 18 years (also see Brainerd et al., 2004; Ghetti & Angelini, 2008). Using these measures, then, it would appear that conscious (episodic memory) recollective processes develop later than more automatic remembering processes (semantic memory).

Although this idea has considerable intuitive appeal, there are problems associated with this two-test method. First, it is not clear that the type of consciousness exploited in this paradigm maps well onto the conscious-unconscious continuum as originally envisaged in theories such as Freud's (1916–1917/1963). Second, Jacoby (1991) has pointed out that two-test methodologies are inadequate because direct and indirect tests of memory do not deliver pure measures of the various processes they are thought to be evaluating (also see Howe et al., 1993). In fact, Jacoby (1991) showed that measures of conscious recollection (direct tests of memory) are contaminated by unconscious memory, and unconscious memory measures (indirect tests of memory) are contaminated by conscious memory. Therefore, "remember judgments" do not deliver pure measures of conscious memory, because they can sometimes be based on unconscious memories; and "know judgments" do not deliver pure measures of unconscious memory, because they can sometimes be based on conscious memories (also see Strack & Forster, 1995). Although there are some ways that these problems can be addressed, they bring with them significant changes in methodology, ones that do not permit testing of very young children (see Brainerd et al., 1998).

A final line of research has focused on more circumscribed questions with somewhat older children. Here, some researchers have examined whether better-than-chance performance on unconscious memory tests can be seen in young children after long delays (e.g., Drummey & Newcombe, 1995; Newcombe & Fox, 1994); others have explored how to dissociate performance on conscious and unconscious memory tests (Newcombe & Lie, 1995); and still others have examined age trends in performance on unconscious memory tests (Russo et al., 1995). To dissever unconscious and conscious memories, respectively, these researchers have focused on measures of picture recognition under blurred versus intact conditions (Drummey & Newcombe, 1995), skin conductance responses to pictures of classmates versus picture recognition (Newcombe & Fox, 1994), covert versus overt recognition (Newcombe & Lie, 1995), and picture completion versus picture recall (Russo et al., 1995). For example, Newcombe and Fox (1994) showed children, now eight to 11 years of age, photographs of their classmates from the preschool they attended some two to four years earlier, when they were five to six years of age. The photographs of their classmates were interspersed with pictures of other children who were unknown to the participants. Two measures were used to index memory—conscious recollection (an overt-recognition response) and an index of unconscious memory (changes in skin conductance)—both of which showed that children recognized their preschool classmates. That is, above-chance levels of overt recognition and changes in skin conductance were observed for faces of classmates but not for unfamiliar faces. More important, measures of unconscious memory (changes in skin conductance) for familiar faces revealed indications of such memories regardless of whether overt recognition responses occurred. According to the authors, this result suggests that unconscious memory may still be active even though children cannot consciously access those memories.

Although such a conclusion is intuitively appealing, as already noted, there are several methodological concerns with studies that use different tests to evaluate conscious and unconscious memory. Moreover, it is always difficult to evaluate the retention of memories when their initial strength at acquisition was never measured (e.g., whether children were friends and played together at the preschool, were simply acquaintances, or had few, if any, interactions). This same criticism applies to many tests of children's retention. That is, if we do not know the strength of information in memory following initial acquisition, then later differences that are measured at retention could be due to these initial strength differences at acquisition, differences in rates of forgetting across the retention interval, or both. This criticism applies more generally to many, if not all, studies involving the retention of preverbal memories in the absence of measures of initial memory strength (for a more detailed discussion, see Howe, 2000, Chapter 7).

Perhaps as a consequence of these measurement issues, results from studies like those just discussed have produced conflicting findings concerning whether there are developmental differences between conscious and unconscious memory. For example, developmental differences are often nonexistent on measures of implicit memory, due perhaps to ceiling effects, whereas measures of explicit memory frequently show standard age-related improvements (Drummey & Newcombe, 1995; Russo et al., 1995). Moreover, using two different tasks to separate conscious from unconscious memory is less than satisfactory because the type of task is confounded with the type of memory. That is, it is not clear whether any differences in performance are due to variation in conscious and unconscious memory processes or simply the use of different tasks, a problem that also plagues the study of implicit and explicit memory more generally. This is because there is no assurance that the tasks are equivalent on all dimensions except the one of interest; namely, the conscious (explicit) versus unconscious (implicit) status of the memory being measured. What this means is that results from studies such as these fail to provide convincing evidence for the existence of dissociable conscious and unconscious memories and may, in fact, simply provide evidence that different tasks provide different access routes to the same memory trace (see Brainerd et al., 1998; Howe et al., 1993).

Despite other attempts at dissevering conscious and unconscious memory in adults, and to a lesser degree in children, much of this research has failed to provide convincing evidence that these are different memory systems or that they exhibit distinct developmental trajectories (e.g., see Howe, 2000). Indeed, a reasonable conclusion from this research might be that, if there are different conscious and unconscious memory processes, they operate in a very similar manner, exist very early in life, and continue to be refined even into adulthood. As already seen, tests of implicit and explicit memory are inconclusive for a plethora of reasons. Similarly, the use of different memory measures to distinguish between conscious (e.g., a "yes–no" recognition response) and unconscious (e.g., skin conductance) memories also has serious drawbacks. However, regardless of which procedure has been used, the evidence is clear that implicit and explicit, or unconscious and conscious, memory processes must be operating in a very similar fashion very early in life.

If there are no differences in the onset or developmental trajectory of these allegedly different memory processes, then one has to question the utility of such a distinction. What this suggests is that there is little explanatory gain by postulating separate conscious and unconscious memory systems. Perhaps the most parsimonious explanation is the one given earlier: that is, that there is a single memory system in which stored information passes in and out of conscious awareness as a consequence of need and circumstance. As others have suggested, perhaps both implicit learning (i.e., acquiring information without the awareness that one is learning) and implicit memory (i.e., remembering information without awareness), differ from explicit learning and memory simply because these measures "reflect differences in the retrieval cues and processing operations used for two kinds of tasks, rather than the operation of conscious and unconscious forms of information processing" (Neal & Hesketh, 1997, p. 34). That is, these task differences are just that and do not signal differences in fundamentally distinct memory systems. In fact, these differences may have more to do with the flexibility, and variety of ways, with which people can access memories and not with differences between types of memories.

Summary and Conclusions

I began this chapter by asking whether memories that are conscious are somehow different from those that are not; whether conscious and unconscious memories have distinct developmental trajectories; and whether people's current and future behaviors are influenced by memories for early experiences, even if they did not have conscious access to them. What research exists shows that there need not be any association between early experience and subsequent behavior. This was especially true when earlier experiences were supplanted by additional, perhaps more adaptive, experiences later in childhood. Although this evidence does not rule out the possibility that memories for early experiences that were initially associated with these behaviors are not still somewhere in storage, this evidence is not consistent with such claims either.

In a similar vein, the literature on dissevering conscious and unconscious memories is fraught with methodological problems. Indeed, researchers have frequently confounded the type of task (or type of test) with the type of memory being measured, making it difficult to know whether performance differences were due to different kinds of memories being accessed or differential task difficulty. Even if these tasks did discriminate conscious from unconscious memories, because performance differences tend to be similar across age from infancy through adulthood (see Howe, 2000), studying their developmental trends does not provide theorists with any new insights into the nature of early memory. Indeed, most if not all studies have shown few or no differences between measures of conscious and unconscious memories, with developmental studies showing that, even if we were to assume that there were two types of memories, they both started early in life and had similar if not identical developmental trajectories.

Overall, then, there is little or no support for the hypothesis that there are separate conscious and unconscious memory systems, at least not early in life. Although there is little doubt that memories can inhabit both conscious (as when we remember a specific autobiographical experience when awake) and unconscious (when we are asleep) states, this does not mean that these memories are somehow fundamentally different when they occur during these different states. Similarly, simply because we may not be aware of the fact that we are learning certain types of information (i.e., as in an incidental-memory task) or that we are using that information to perform a task at some later date (e.g., riding a bicycle) does not mean that these memory traces are fundamentally different from the times when we are aware that we are trying to learn information (i.e., as in intentional-memory tasks), or mean that we need to recollect specific memories in order to perform a task at some later date (e.g., solving a crossword puzzle). In fact, there is little or no empirical evidence that indicates that there exist separable types of conscious and unconscious memories, whose properties or age of onset differ reliably. Although the various measures used to examine unconscious and conscious memory (implicit versus explicit tasks, changes in skin conductance versus picture recognition, changes in ERP versus recall of the sequence to be imitated) may make very different demands on access to memory traces themselves, these task demands should not be confused with the idea that there are separable and distinct memory systems.

Thus, the current reasoning and the scientific evidence it is based upon leave little doubt that there is no foundation for the idea that unconscious memory should be accorded any special status, even when it comes to retaining the vestiges of early (or any) experiences. Indeed, the argument here is that because it is the same trace that is in memory when the person is conscious as it is when this same person is unconscious, there is little reason to ascribe different properties to this trace (e.g., longevity; resistance to forgetting, interference, or suggestion; reinstatement and recoding) contingent on the state of the rememberer. In fact, it seems that theorists would be hard-pressed to justify the evolution of different memory systems based on an organism's state of consciousness. That is, there does not appear to be any adaptive advantage associated with having one set of memories that are relegated to the unconscious and another set that are available to consciousness, when a single, awareness-invariant system will suffice. Thus, despite potential differences in the retrieval demands associated with the various tasks used to "dissever" conscious and unconscious memories, such differences should not be confused with separate memory systems. Instead, they should be properly assigned to variations in how easily memory traces are accessed in the presence of differentially effective retrieval cues.

PART III

THE ROLE OF DISTINCTIVENESS, EMOTION, STRESS, AND TRAUMA IN MEMORY DEVELOPMENT

7

Distinctiveness and Emotion in Early Memory Development

> Canst thou not minister to a mind diseased, Pluck from the memory a
> rooted sorrow, Raze out the written troubles of the brain?
> —William Shakespeare (from *Macbeth*, Act 5, scene 3)

> Memory is a very amorphous thing. It is selective and shaped by
> emotion ... people are constantly in pursuit of the details of their past
> because it is from that they determine their own identity upon which
> they can base their strategy of survival.
> —Will Eisner (American cartoonist)

Unusual or unique information tends to be easier to learn and better remembered than more routine or commonplace information. This so-called distinctiveness effect holds for children (for a review, see Howe, 2006c) as well as adults (for a review, see Hunt, 2006). Of course what we mean by *distinctiveness* is quite frequently defined in a relative sense (see Hunt, 2006): as something that exists in information (memory lists, pictures, events, etc.) that is unusual or unique in a specified context. Generally, two types of contexts are defined: The immediate, or *primary*, context, in which the distinctive information exists; and the more global, or *secondary*, context, in which the individual's knowledge base in memory serves as the backdrop against which uniqueness occurs. In *primary distinctiveness*, "unusualness" occurs when there is a contrast between the features of information currently being processed and the features in other recently processed information. For example, if you are reading a list of animal names and the word "turnip" appears, it is distinctive (a vegetable) relative to the local context (animals) provided by the other items. In general, the word "turnip" will be better remembered subsequently than the animal terms. In *secondary distinctiveness*, unusualness occurs when there is a contrast between the features of information currently being processed and information that is already stored in long-term memory derived from the larger context of our previous experiences.

For example, for most of us, if we were shown a picture of a dog riding a bicycle, this would stand out against our previous experiences with dogs and with bicycles. Such distinctive information will be remembered better than the more commonplace pictures of people riding bicycles.

Although secondary distinctiveness is often viewed as being independent from primary distinctiveness, the reverse does not hold. This is because distinctiveness in the local context depends on the more global context of one's past experience. Thus, a vegetable among a list of animals is only distinctive if we have already learned about, and stored in memory, exemplars that belong to these different categories. This is a particularly important consideration when examining distinctiveness effects in children. This is because, in order for distinctiveness effects to be observed in memory, children must have the requisite knowledge base with the appropriate conceptual distinctions before the unusualness in the immediate or local context can be apprehended.

Extant research that has implemented these definitions has developed a diverse array of tasks to examine distinctiveness effects in memory. Included among them are tasks examining episodic memory by varying the semantic attributes of lists (as in the earlier example), presenting bizarre images (as in the dog riding a bicycle), and using humorous text (for recent reviews of this research, see chapters in Hunt & Worthen, 2006). As already seen (see Chapter 5), this operational definition of distinctiveness has also been useful in the study of autobiographical memory, where particularly well-remembered events are those that are distinctive—that is, they are personally consequential events (e.g., marriage), change points or formative periods in one's life (e.g., moving to a different country), or are unique with respect to the self (e.g., being a prisoner of war). Indeed, *distinctiveness* as defined here has also been useful when trying to understand the role of emotion and trauma in children's and adults' memory, something reviewed later in this chapter (also see Schmidt, 2006).

Before we examine the effects of emotion and trauma, it is important to establish the fact that children's pattern of distinctiveness effects, given that the appropriate knowledge base has been formed, parallel those effects found for adults. For example, even in infancy, children, like adults, focus on elements of experience that are novel, surprising, and unique, elements that violate their expectations, expectations that must be stored in memory (see Howe, 2006c). It is not just children's attention and encoding of uniqueness and novelty that is present relatively early in life, but also the changes in memory performance per se. Although these memory performance differences tend to be larger in older children, all children can remember atypical information better than information that conforms to their current expectations. Indeed, atypical information is especially well remembered if it disrupts current expectations or if it is implausible and not simply irrelevant. This is what has been called the *disruption effect* (e.g., Hudson, 1988).

Secondary distinctiveness effects in children's memory have also been examined using bizarre-imagery techniques (Howe et al., 2000). Here, children were presented with pairs of toys (e.g., dog, bicycle) and the experimenter either enacted a common (e.g., the dog running behind the bicycle) or bizarre (e.g., the dog riding the bicycle) interaction. When tested immediately and after a three-week retention interval, older children remembered more than younger children, and all children remembered more bizarre than common interactions. Thus, the distinctiveness of bizarre interactions among common objects facilitates children's immediate and long-term retention of information about those objects.

Similar effects have been found for primary distinctiveness in children's memory using the isolation or von Restorff procedure. Here, a prevailing context is established by presenting a homogeneous list of items (e.g., animals). Embedded in this list is an item or items that do not fit the prevailing context (e.g., hammer, television). Although again, older children remember more than younger children, these latter, distinctive items were better remembered than the items that served to set the context by children of all ages (Howe et al., 2000).

Another interesting property of distinctiveness effects is whether we use item-specific or relational processing when encoding information from an event. It has been argued that distinctiveness recruits item-specific processing at encoding in the sense that the object or objects that are distinctive may receive more "in-depth" encoding than items with which we are more familiar. Indeed, information we are very familiar with may receive little or no processing at all except confirmation that it is as we expected (i.e., a quick comparison with what is already in memory). If that comparison results in a high degree of familiarity, the item or object may not be processed further. However, if the item or object is not highly familiar, it may receive additional item-specific attention in order to interpret its meaning. This additional item-specific processing increases that item's memorability, perhaps because of this additional processing. Thus, although relational processing (e.g., all of these words refer to animals) can also facilitate remembering, particularly when we are trying to retrieve that information (e.g., try to remember all of the animals on the list), item-specific encoding facilitates discrimination of information in memory.

To illustrate, consider an experiment in which children (seven-year-olds and nine-year-olds) learn two lists of toys in succession. After learning the second list, some of the children are told that, despite the fact that all of the words they learned referred to toys, the words on the second list were also vehicles (e.g., truck, car, bus). Normally, when we learn two lists one right after the other, information from the second list will interfere with our memory for the first list, particularly when there is a high degree of similarity between the two lists.

So although such relational properties can facilitate some types of memory performance (e.g., if we were simply interested in having children remember all of the toy names they heard), memory performance is impaired when a more precise memory question is asked (i.e., tell me all of the items from the first list only). Here, relational processing produces high rates of retroactive interference, such that children will tend to remember toys from the second list as well as those from the first list. However, when given the vehicle-recoding instruction, retroactive interference almost disappears. That is, children, like adults, can discriminate among items in memory and edit them at the time of retrieval so that items from second list are not recalled along with the ones from the first list (see Howe, 2004b).

Similar effects have been established using directed forgetting of stories in children's recall (Howe, 2002). Children (four-year-olds and six-year-olds) were read two stories that were very similar (e.g., going to a store to buy candy, and going to a store to buy a birthday present for a friend). For some of the children, the experimenter said that she had made a mistake and was not supposed to have read them a second story. Children were told to simply forget that second story. Later, when asked to remember the first story, children in the directed forgetting condition were able to edit out any interference from the second story, whereas children who did not receive that instruction experienced considerable retroactive interference (i.e., confused the two stories when trying to remember only the first one). It seems that directed forgetting also acts to recode information in memory, making the second story distinct from the first story, as it is the one to be "forgotten."

Finally, the role of similarity (relational processing) and distinctiveness (item-specific processing) was examined in children's (five-year-olds and seven-year-olds) immediate and long-term retention of semantically related concepts (Howe, 2006a). Children were given related pairs of words (e.g., *dog* and *cat*) and given their categorical relationship (e.g., *animals*). This was done in order to ensure that all children knew the semantic relationship between the presented items, and so that in those conditions in which children were asked to generate a way in which the items were similar, they would not simply rely on the category itself. In the first experiment, children in the similarity condition were given a concrete property that the items shared (e.g., *both cats and dogs have four legs*) and children in the difference condition were given concrete properties that items differed on (e.g., *cats meow, dogs bark*). In the second experiment, children were asked to generate these similarities and differences themselves. The results showed that both similarities and differences were important when learning the pairs (i.e., learning took fewer trials), regardless of whether they were experimenter- or self-generated. Later, during a test of retention (three weeks after learning), self-generated pairs were easier to remember than those generated by the experimenter. However, regardless of who generated them, pairs in which additional differences were generated were better remembered than pairs for which additional similarities were generated.

Although the role of both relational and item-specific processing will be discussed again in Chapter 9 when memory illusions in children's recollections are examined, the studies reviewed here illustrate the importance of distinctiveness in memory. That is, making information distinctive either at the time it is encoded (e.g., isolation effects, bizarre imagery, learning of similarities or differences) or after it is in storage (e.g., directed forgetting, recoding) increases the durability of information in memory even over relatively protracted retention intervals. As we will see as this chapter unfolds, these effects hold across development, affecting infants, toddlers, older children, and adults.

This preservation of distinctive information in memory may have a particularly important adaptive significance. If memory is useful as a way of understanding the world we live in, predicting outcomes of various behaviors, and guiding future behaviors, then it is important to develop schemas or memory-based expectations about the world. Equally important is when such expectations are violated—these exceptions to the rule must be noted and understood. If they recur, then the schema needs modification. If they are rare events, then they need to be stored in order to have some sort of "record" of when and how these expectations are violated. As shown later in this chapter, this may be especially important for events that are emotional, particularly for those that may be life-threatening.

Building on the differences between item-specific and relational processing, we can make another distinction, one between *novelty* and *significance*. As mentioned, infants, children, and adults are all drawn to novelty—that is, novel stimuli attract attention and recruit additional cognitive resources that may lead to richer encoding of that information. Although novel experiences are quite often significant, and significant experiences are quite often novel, the two should not be confused or confounded in research (also see a review by Schmidt, 2006). "Novelty" refers primarily to a difference between information that is currently being processed and what is stored in memory that forms the basis for what to expect. As Gati and Ben-Shakhar (1990) have shown, the novelty of information is a positive monotonic function of the number of new features and a negative monotonic function of the number of shared features of the information currently being processed relative to what has just been processed or with what is stored in memory (also see Hunt, 2006). "Significance," on the other hand, does not refer to feature overlap in a strict sense but rather to the meaning or relevance of the information to the individual. According to Gati and Bar-Shakhar (1990; also see Bar-Shakhar, 1995), each individual stores representations that are significant to them, and significance of the current information is assessed as a linear combination of the number of features shared and the number of features not shared by this current information and the significant representations stored in memory. Thus, according to these definitions, increasing novelty is defined by decreasing feature overlap with prior experiences stored in memory, whereas increasing significance is defined as increasing feature overlap with representations of particular significance to the individual.

As Schmidt (2006) has pointed out, "if novelty is defined relative to a lifetime of experience, then a truly novel stimulus cannot be significant" (p. 48). This is because there will never be any feature overlap between anything already stored in memory and a truly novel event, something that the definition of significance just articulated relies on. One way around this is to relax the definition of significance and simply suggest that, although a significant event may have some novel components, it must also share features with other important experiences we have stored in long-term memory. Also, novelty can be defined both more and less inclusively than simply in the context of the information accumulated over an individual's lifetime.

> We can reasonably assume that we are prepared, because of a lengthy evolutionary process, to find some stimuli significant. The sucking and startle reflexes exhibited in newborns come to mind as examples. Thus, certain stimuli unknown in the life of an individual are not novel with respect to our genetic heritage, and these stimuli match information genetically coded as significant.
>
> (Schmidt, 2006, p. 48)

This suggestion is consistent with some recent research showing that the detection of threatening stimuli occurs more efficiently and more quickly than detection of neutral stimuli. Obviously the detection of threatening stimuli in the environment is an important survival mechanism, one that both human and nonhuman animals alike possess. For example, both human and nonhuman primates evolved an innate predisposition to rapidly form fear associations with certain potentially threatening stimuli, including snakes and spiders, stimuli that were omnipresent throughout human evolution (e.g., Ohman & Mineka, 2001; Seligman, 1970). In humans, because it is important to respond rapidly in the presence of such life-threatening stimuli, the visual system gives priority to such stimuli (see Isbell, 2006). Indeed, Ohman, Flykt, and Esteves (2001) tested this idea in an experiment in which participants were asked to identify a discrepant stimulus in a 3 x 3 matrix of pictures. The discrepant picture was either a threat-producing stimulus (a snake or a spider) or a neutral stimulus (a flower or a mushroom), and the background pictures were either fearful or neutral. The results showed that participants were faster at detecting the discrepancy when the picture was of a fearful object than a neutral one. Moreover, search times for fearful, but not neutral, stimuli were independent of where the stimulus was located in the matrix. These findings with adults have been replicated (e.g., Blanchette, 2006; Brosch & Sharma, 2005; Flykt, 2005) and extended to children (e.g., LoBue, 2009; LoBue & DeLoache, 2008), making it clear that being distinctive is simply not enough. Rather, being distinctive and potentially life-threatening permits such stimuli to "pop out" of a visual display.

More recently, similar findings have been demonstrated in infants (DeLoache & LoBue, 2009; LoBue & DeLoache, 2010). DeLoache and LoBue (2009) found that infants (seven- to 18-month-olds) demonstrated a fear of snakes, but only when movement was involved (e.g., when shown on a film) and not when motion was absent (e.g., when shown in a photograph). Although not arguing that such fears are innate, they did suggest that humans are predisposed to learn to associate snakes with fear. This was further confirmed in a subsequent set of two experiments in which infants (eight- to 14-month-olds) responded more rapidly to the presentation of threatening stimuli (e.g., snakes, angry faces) than nonthreatening stimuli (e.g., flowers, happy faces) (LoBue & DeLoache, 2010). Together, these studies confirm that even in infancy, there is an evolved bias toward detecting and processing threat-relevant stimuli (I return to this issue and the role of early experience, specifically maltreatment, in the next chapter).

Emotion frequently conveys significance. Emotional events contain important information, and oftentimes that information is survival-relevant, as in the threatening stimuli just discussed. But what is emotion and how does it influence memory? Emotion can be divided into at least two major components, *valence* (positive or negative) and *arousal* (low or high). Emotional experiences that are arousing, whether negative or positive, may be more memorable simply because high arousal is often associated with the distinctiveness of the experience. Aspects of experiences that are (relatively) novel and significant tend to be better remembered, perhaps because they are correlated with higher levels of arousal. These higher levels of arousal in turn may direct more cognitive resources that are deployed for attending to and encoding such experiences. For example, if one is walking to work and witnesses a tragic car accident, one in which people are seriously injured, such an experience (if it is atypical for that person—i.e., they do not work in an emergency room or for an ambulance company) will be better remembered than a more commonplace experience (e.g., seeing a blue car drive past). Similarly, if one were walking to work and a car pulled up beside someone who was walking ahead of you and a clown jumped out with a bouquet of balloons and started singing "happy birthday" to that person, such an event would also be remembered better than a more commonplace one. Thus, to some extent, arousal and distinctiveness are correlated.

However, distinctiveness is not the whole story, and it cannot explain all of the observed effects of emotion on memory (also see Schmidt, 2006). Arousal functions independently of distinctiveness, as, for example, when arousal occurs to a frequently witnessed event (e.g., an EMS worker witnessing a tragic car accident). Such arousal may be more often correlated with negative emotional experiences than positive ones. What this means is that arousal is frequently associated with stress, something that affects memory and whose effects on the brain are reasonably well understood.

In what follows, I outline the impact of stress and trauma on memory and its development. I begin by reviewing the relevant neural substrates related to the impact of stress and trauma on memory processing. I then review the literature on children's true memory for emotional information (the discussion of false memory for emotional events will be deferred until Chapter 9), both as it has been studied in relatively controlled situations (e.g., laboratory experiments) as well as in more naturalistic settings (e.g., medical experiences, hurricanes). Although this latter discussion will be restricted to typically developing children who experience a single traumatic or stressful event, it turns out that memory for emotional information behaves pretty much the same regardless of the venue (laboratory or naturalistic) it occurs in (discussion of children experiencing chronic stress and trauma is deferred until Chapter 8).

Neural Substrates of Stress, Emotion, and Memory

Stressful events (i.e., events that are negative and high-arousal) frequently lead to the release of adrenal stress hormones, including catecholamines and glucocorticoids (see McGaugh, 2000, 2003; Sapolsky et al., 2000). Endogenous glucocorticoids impact declarative memory by altering the morphology and functioning of the brain, alterations that are correlated with changes in memory and cognition (Cahill & McGaugh, 1998; Lupien & McEwen, 1997; McEwen & Sapolsky, 1995; McGaugh et al., 1996). Exposure to acute stressors can enhance memory storage and consolidation by facilitating synaptic plasticity (for reviews, see Howe, 1998a; Wolf, 2009) whereas more chronic exposure to stress can lead to memory impairment (McEwen & Sapolsky, 1995). Of course, whether an acute or chronic stressor enhances or impairs memory functioning depends on a number of factors, including the intensity of the stressor (see Howe, 1998a) as well as individual differences in stress reactivity (see Quas et al., 2004).

To see how these variables impact memory, a brief overview follows that outlines the neurobiological mechanisms involved in the biopsychological reactivity to stressors. I begin by reviewing studies concerning neuroendocrine-induced changes that affect memory. I then turn to a more general discussion of how these and other effects impact the brain and how these translate into changes that impact memory encoding, storage, and retrieval during stressful and emotional experiences.

GLUCOCORTICOIDS AND CATECHOLAMINES

Stress provokes an integrated response that involves both neural (including sympathetic and parasympathetic responses) and neuroendocrine (including the hypothalamic-pituitary-adrenocortical [HPA] axis) systems. The neural (sympathetic) contribution involves the secretion of catecholamines (epinephrine and norepinephrine) and the neuroendocrine contribution includes secretion of glucocorticoids by the adrenal gland. Both catecholamines and glucocorticoids exhibit an inverted U-shaped function with respect to the amount secreted and memory. That is, small amounts have little effect on memory, moderate amounts can enhance memory, and extreme amounts can impair memory (Gold & McCarty, 1995; Izquierdo & Medina, 1997; Korneyev, 1997; McGaugh, 1995). Although it is not clear what constitutes "extreme levels" in terms of children's real-world experiences (see discussion in Chen et al., 2000; Howe et al., 2006b), experimental studies have shown that high levels can be deleterious to memory and can even lead to cell death in the hippocampus (see Sapolsky et al., 2000, and later discussion in this chapter).

Thus, stress can have opposite effects on memory, depending, as mentioned, on a number of factors (e.g., an individual's stress reactivity) that modulate the intensity of the neural and neuroendocrine responses. Moreover, these differences can either be specific and experience-contingent, influencing only the particular episodic trace related to a specific event, or general and experience-independent, affecting basic memory functioning more generally and having structural as well as functional consequences (e.g., hippocampal cell loss, elevated levels of circulating catecholamines). Although both effects will be outlined in this section, it is the former experience-specific effects that will dominate the rest of the coverage in this chapter as it pertains to issues concerning memory for single stressful experiences. The latter coverage of more long-lasting effects of stress on memory is pertinent to the next chapter, where the effects of chronic stress (e.g., maltreatment) are discussed in greater detail.

Of course, there are key differences between how catecholamines and glucocorticoids function. Catecholamines (a) do not enter the brain directly, exerting their influence indirectly through second-messenger cascades at postsynaptic sites; (b) exert their effects quickly, usually within seconds; and (c) primarily influence the amygdaloid complex. Glucocorticoids, on the other hand, (a) directly influence the brain, especially the hippocampus, a structure rich in glucocorticoid receptors; (b) exert their effects slowly over a matter of minutes, and their impact may not be apparent for hours; and (c) primarily influence the hippocampal complex. Of particular interest are the differences in the time course of these effects (points b). That is, because catecholamines act quickly, their impact may be felt earlier (perhaps even during encoding and trace registration) in the consolidation process, whereas the more protracted course of the effects due to glucocortioids may mean these latter hormones have their impact much later (during trace stabilization) in the consolidation process.

In fact, the different loci of their effects (amygdaloid complex versus the hippocampal complex) would also suggest that they play different roles in the establishment of memory traces. It is well established that the amygdaloid complex plays a key role in modulating (either enhancing or impairing) memories of stressful experiences (see Cahill, 2000; Cahill & McGaugh, 1996; McGaugh, 2000, 2003; Pelletier & Pare, 2004). Similar memory-enhancing and memory-impairing effects are well known during the presence of stress-induced release of the endogenous glucocorticoids in animals such as rats (i.e., corticosterone) as well as in humans (i.e., cortisol) (Diamond et al., 1996; Newcomer et al., 1994; Oades, 1979; Pugh et al., 1997). Regardless of the loci of their effects, both catecholamines and glucocorticoids modulate what is in storage and probably do so by affecting consolidation processes (Abel et al., 1995; Cahill & McGaugh, 1996; Izquierdo & Medina, 1997). Recall from Chapter 3 that consolidation is that period of time in which the memory trace is most vulnerable to interference and distortion. In its original conception, stabilization of the memory trace (consolidation) was thought to take only a few hours following encoding, although as we saw, current theorists suggest that this process may take days, months, or even years. However, given the time course of the effects of catecholamines and glucocorticoids, it is thought that the modulatory effects of stress on memory occur over a shorter period, one that more closely maps onto the original time frame for consolidation and consists of hours, not weeks, months, or years (e.g., Abel et al., 1995; Izquierdo & Medina, 1997; Richter-Levin & Akirav, 2003).

OXYGENATION AND GLUCOSE

There are additional mechanisms that mediate the effects of stress on memory. For example, catecholamine release may affect changes in the delivery of oxygen and glucose to the brain. Specifically, epinephrine (a catecholamine) may affect memory due to its well-known effects on blood glucose. Such modulatory effects of glucose on memory are dependent on a central cholinergic mechanism (e.g., Kopf & Baratti, 1995) and may be specific to the learning situation itself (Cahill & McGaugh, 1996). Even when the release of epinephrine is blocked during an emotional event (meaning that glucose levels are not modified), β-adrenergic receptor activation (via norepinephrine) may enhance memory for that episode. Indeed, the neurotransmitter norepinephrine is also important to memory as it enhances the activity of neurons that encode significant events (see Kety, 1970). In fact, novelty is directly linked to the release of norepinephrine in some animals, with the consequence being enhanced retention (Kitchigina et al., 1997). When the release of norepinephrne is blocked in humans, the normal memory-enhancing effect of surprise is reduced (Cahill et al., 1994; Nielson & Jensen, 1994). Interestingly, when propanolol is used to block β-adrenergic receptors, memory for emotional, but not neutral, information from stories is selectively impaired (Cahill et al., 1994).

BRAIN STRUCTURES AND SYSTEMS

Limbic and Hippocampal Structures

Limbic and frontal structures that are important to the proper functioning of declarative memory are particularly vulnerable to the effects of chronic or prolonged stress. The structure, neurochemistry, and function of the hippocampus, amygdala, and PFC are all affected by both acute and chronic stress (e.g., Brown et al., 2005; Murmu et al., 2006; Schin et al., 2006; for recent reviews, see Bremner, 2008, Navalta et al., 2008, and Chapter 8). As just discussed, this is largely due to the fact that the hippocampus, with its high density of glucocorticoid receptors, is subject to damage in the presence of high levels of corticosterone (cortisol in humans) (see Akirav & Richter-Levin, 2002). Interestingly, moderate levels of glucocorticoids are critical to the health of the hippocampus, and their absence can cause atrophy (and even death) of the dentate gyrus (see Sloviter et al., 1993), an area that we saw from Chapter 3 is key to consolidating memories. The damage caused by excess levels of glucocorticoids to hippocampal areas includes morphological changes such as decreased size of cells, decreased neuronal connectivity, changes to the structure of synapses themselves (Watanabe et al., 1992), and decreased neurogenesis (Tanapat et al., 2001). Importantly, reduced neurogenesis occurs with acute stress, whereas hippocampal atrophy is seen in chronic stress (McLaughlin et al., 2007; Tanapat et al., 2001; Vyas et al., 2002). A more complete discussion of the effects of chronic stress can be found in Chapter 8.

Amygdala

A limbic area critical to processing emotional information, the amygdala, is also affected by corticosterone. Specifically, the basolateral nucleus of the amygdala (BLA) plays an important modulatory role in the synaptic activity in the hippocampus and related structures, influencing consolidation (Kim et al., 2001; McGaugh et al., 2002). That is, the BLA can either facilitate or inhibit long-term potentiation (LTP), a form of synaptic plasticity critical to memory formation. As arousal increases in response to emotional events and stress, so, too, does the activity of the BLA, increasing hippocampal plasticity (Cahill & van Steegeren, 2003). Indeed, Cahill and van Steegeren (2003) demonstrated that increased arousal during the encoding of an emotional event, as well as the post-event stress associated with the event, interact to affect consolidation. Of particular interest is the finding that whereas short-term stress increases the activity of the BLA, synaptic plasticity can be inhibited in response to stress and the corresponding rise in corticosterone levels (Kavushansky & Richter-Levin, 2006).

Prefrontal Cortex
The effects of stress on the PFC are not as well understood, although the PFC is involved in the regulation of negative feedback in the HPA axis (Mizoguchi et al., 2003). Like other neural structures important for memory (e.g., the hippocampus), chronic stress can also lead to the death of pyramidal neurons in areas of the PFC (Radley et al., 2004). Importantly, chronic stress that leads to post-traumatic stress disorder (see Chapter 8) is associated with smaller PFC volumes and lower activity when processing affective information (e.g., faces; see Shin et al., 2005). These findings suggest that prolonged stress may impact the processing of fearful and threatening stimuli.

THE EFFECTS OF STRESS ON THE DEVELOPING BRAIN

Although arousal and stress affect brain structures and function throughout the lifespan, they can also have particularly important consequences for the developing brain. Because of the developing brain's high degree of plasticity, it may be particularly susceptible to the potentially harmful effects of high levels of glucocorticoids associated with stress and arousal. However, this is a double-edged sword. On the one hand, the young brain may be particularly at risk of sustaining severe and long-standing damage in response to adverse experience. On the other hand, it may be because of this high degree of early plasticity that the immature brain can adapt and recover from these adverse experiences (also see Chapter 8). Of course, the effects of stress on brain maturation, like its effects at other points in life, depend on the severity and chronicity of the stressor(s) and on the developmental stage(s) at which they appear (also see Vallee et al., 1999). In what follows, I document what is known about the effects of stress on the developing brain prenatally and then postnatally.

Prenatal Effects of Stress

There are two primary ways in which the fetus can be exposed to increased glucocorticoid levels. Maternal stress can lead to elevated levels of endogenous glucocorticoids (e.g., Huizink et al., 2003; Weinstock, 2001). The fetus can also be exposed when mothers at risk for preterm labor are administered synthetic corticosteroids (e.g., betamethasone, dexamethasone). These latter synthetic glucocorticoids, particularly when administered repeatedly, can lead to subsequent negative effects on cognitive, physiological, and behavioral development (Schoener et al., 2006; Spinillo et al., 2004). Of course, much of what is known about the effects of prenatal stress on brain mechanisms that subserve memory comes from studies involving nonhuman animals (i.e., rats, nonhuman primates) whose brain maturation timetables differ from that of humans. However, there is evidence to suggest that there are sufficient similarities in neurological development between nonhuman and human animals that reasonable parallels can be drawn between species, and effective models of outcomes concerning the impact of prenatal elevations of glucocorticoids can be constructed (see Lupien & McEwen, 1997; Zola-Morgan & Squire, 1990).

Not surprisingly, the hippocampal complex is perhaps the most sensitive to, and negatively affected by, prenatal increases in glucocorticoids (e.g., Vallee et al., 1999). These effects include decreases in neurogenesis, proliferation, and differentiation of cells in the hippocampus, changes that affect, at the very least, synaptic plasticity by attenuating LTP (see Coe et al., 1988; Lemaire et al., 2006). In humans, prenatal exposure to elevated levels of glucocorticoids, whether they result from endogenous or synthetic sources, tends to increase the risk of learning impairments, hyperactivity, attentional deficits, and emotional problems, as well as changes in the functioning of the HPA axis (Gutteling et al., 2005, 2006; Huizink et al., 2007; Yeh et al., 2004). Many of these effects can appear regardless of which trimester these increases in maternal stress occur, including the first trimester (see Schneider et al., 1999). However, increased levels of glucocorticoids may be particularly detrimental during the last trimester, as this is the time during which there is considerable brain development involving neural proliferation, synapse formation, and myelination (see Chapter 3). Thus, the presence of stressors may not be as important as the timing of the stressors when it comes to their effects on early memory and the development of brain mechanisms that serve them.

Finally, the effects of prenatal stress on memory may be avoided or reversed, depending on postnatal variables. For example, Brabham and colleagues (2000) found that memory impairments due to prenatal stress were not permanent and could be prevented when appropriate postnatal care was provided by a non-stressed mother. This latter finding is also important when considering postnatal stress (see next section), as there is evidence that postnatal care can affect synaptic plasticity in the hippocampal dentate gyrus (Bagot et al., 2009). Also, there is some evidence that mild, short-term prenatal stress during the last trimester can actually result in improved learning (Fujioka et al., 2001). Unfortunately, more severe stress does lead to permanent changes, ones that result in learning difficulties as well as an increased responsiveness to stress (Szuran et al., 2000). As discussed next, under some circumstances, an increased responsiveness to stress may be quite adaptive (Bagot et al., 2009).

Postnatal Effects of Stress

The first postnatal year (in humans, and the first few weeks of life in rats) is referred to as the *stress hyporesponsive period,* during which concentrations of glucocorticoids are low and are not elevated in the presence of mild stressors (Gunnar & Donzella, 2002). These low concentrations of glucocorticoids may be important for early postnatal brain development (de Kloet & Oitzl, 2003). As it turns out, maternal behavior may be critical in the maintenance of this stress hyporesponsive period (Bagot et al., 2009; Levy et al., 2003). Although this period may act to protect organisms from minor fluctuations in stress hormones early in life, it cannot protect against more extreme changes in glucocorticoids that may result from more potent environmental stressors (or the administration of large doses of synthetic glucocorticoids). In such circumstances, permanent damage may occur, damage that can include neural cell death (e.g., Roskoden et al., 2005).

The earlier these stressors are experienced, the more detrimental the effects on brain morphology and behavior. Early maternal deprivation is extremely stressful (in humans and rats) and is associated with raised levels of endogenous glucocorticoids (e.g., Ladd et al., 1996). These experiences not only elevate stress responsiveness later in life (Becker et al., 2007), they may also have life-long effects on learning and memory (Oitzl et al., 2000).

In general, proper maternal care of the infant early in the postnatal period is associated with enhanced hippocampal development and better learning and memory, and poor maternal care with increases in responsiveness to stress and decreases in learning and memory (Liu et al., 2000; Toki et al., 2007). Importantly, the news is not all bad when it comes to early postnatal stress and brain development (see Bagot et al., 2009; Blaise et al., 2008; Faure et al., 2007). What this research has shown is that the effects of stress hormones on early plasticity in the dentate gyrus, although contingent on postnatal maternal care, may differ as a function of the type of learning under consideration. For example, variations in maternal care were associated with differences in learning under stress in a hippocampal-dependent task—that is, rats receiving poor maternal care (i.e., low levels of maternal pup licking/grooming) showed higher levels of fear conditioning than rats receiving good maternal care (Bagot et al., 2009). As these authors and others (e.g., Meaney, 2001; Zhang et al., 2005) have pointed out,

> a shift towards enhanced hippocampal learning under conditions of stress might indeed be adaptive for individuals living under persistent and severe adversity. . . . Thus, such phenotypic variation is neither inherently beneficial nor detrimental. Rather, the adaptive virtue of any specific phenotypic variant is determined by the demands of the specific context.
>
> (Bagot et al., 2009, p. 299).

Although there is considerable research ahead of us before we will know all of the neurobiological effects of stress and emotion on infants' and children's learning and memory, it is clear that stress can alter the functioning of the neural mechanisms that "create" declarative memories. These effects can begin prenatally and can have a long-lasting impact on the neural systems that encode, store, and retrieve memories for events, stressful or not. Research on individual differences in stress reactivity (see Quas et al., 2004; Wallin et al., 2009) and the role of the appraisal of discrete emotional responses (see Davis et al., 2008) is providing a much-needed insight into mechanisms that might modulate the impact of stress and trauma on memory. A review of this research, along with work concerning the impact of chronic and prolonged stress in childhood, will be deferred until the next chapter. In the remainder of the current chapter, I review what is known about otherwise normally developing children's memory for stressful experiences, ones that may be experimentally contrived (e.g., memory for events when a fire alarm is intentionally set off) and others that are the result of more naturally occurring events (e.g., medical procedures and emergencies; hurricanes).

Remembering Stressful and Emotional Experiences

The preceding review of the neural mechanisms recruited when stressful and emotional events confront us provides a critical backdrop for understanding how children's memory for such experiences might be enhanced or impaired. However, although it is clear theoretically that stress, even acute stress, should have an impact on how we encode, store, and retrieve information about emotional and traumatic experiences, it may be difficult to directly measure these effects on children's memory performance. Indeed, for the most part, research concerning children's recollection of stressful experiences has not measured stress directly. Instead, researchers have simply assumed that the event being measured was stressful to the child in question. Although oftentimes such assumptions may be valid (as in the case of children who receive emergency medical treatment for accidental injuries), there are large individual and developmental differences in children's physiological reactivity to the same emotional or traumatic event. Therefore, before turning to a consideration of children's memory for stressful events, I examine the impact of individual and developmental differences in children's stress reactivity.

DEVELOPMENTAL AND INDIVIDUAL DIFFERENCES IN STRESS REACTIVITY

To begin, the literature is very clear that traumatic experiences can elicit high levels of stress hormones. Indeed, traumatized individuals may exhibit an exaggerated tonic level of arousal (e.g., elevated heart rate, hypersensitive startle response), something that may affect attention, compromising information processing and the encoding of information into memory. If the information that does get encoded is somewhat limited, later retrieval may also be constrained (see Howe, 1997, 1998a).

More generally, there is a negative relationship between physiological arousal and attention, particularly in children (Richards & Casey, 1991; Suess et al., 1994). High stress-reactive children have difficulty attending to information when they are experiencing stress. This phenomenon necessarily limits what gets encoded into memory, leading to more impoverished memory traces that are not only less durable, but also may be harder to retrieve. In addition, stress can impact a child's ability to recollect information. That is, arousal levels may be so high that children have difficulty utilizing memory search cues (internal or external) effectively. This turns out to be particularly problematic when high stress-reactive children are being queried about stressful experiences or when the process of being questioned about an event is itself stressful (see Quas et al., 2004).

Variations in stress and stress reactivity have been measured using a variety of techniques. Some researchers have examined changes in the autonomic nervous system, including alterations in heart rate, respiratory sinus arrhythmia (an index of parasympathetic activity on the cardiac cycle), and the pre-ejection period (an index of sympathetic activity on the cardiac cycle). Measures of increased heart rate during encoding are *negatively* related to children's subsequent recollection of those events (Bugental et al., 1992; Stein & Boyce, 1995). It appears that increased heart rate interferes with encoding leading to impoverished representations of events in memory. Although there are many limitations when using autonomic measures with children (see Quas et al., 2004), additional work using heart rate variability during retrieval might prove useful.

A second series of measures are related to the HPA axis, which is most frequently indexed by salivary cortisol. Unfortunately, a number of studies have failed to find a relationship between elevations in children's cortisol levels and their memory for a stressful experience. For example, Merritt, Ornstein, and Spicker (1994) used salivary cortisol to index the amount of stress children experienced during a medical procedure. However, these researchers found no association between levels of cortisol and memory for the medical event. Chen, Zeltzer, Craske, and Katz (2000) also failed to find a relationship between cortisol levels and children's memory for lumbar punctures. However, the results of these studies are difficult to interpret because of relatively small sample sizes, the manner in which cortisol levels were calculated (Merritt et al., 1994), and the presence of memory-relevant medications prior to the stressful procedure (Chen et al., 2000).

Other research has provided some confirmation of a link between physiological reactivity (both autonomic responses and cortisol) and children's memory (Quas et al., 2004). Children's physiological reactivity was measured at encoding. Social support was explicitly manipulated at retrieval (supportive versus non-supportive interviewer) while children were attempting to remember a stressful event (memory involving a fire alarm incident), both immediately after the event as well as after a long-term retention interval. Although few relationships emerged during the immediate-retention test, cortisol reactivity was associated with poorer long-term retention. Interestingly, autonomic reactivity was related to greater accuracy during a supportive interview but with lower accuracy during a non-supportive interview. Apparently, autonomic and HPA-axis reactivity tap different components of memory processing for stressful events, although both are related to retrieval components of long-term retention.

Although stress should, theoretically at least, affect children's encoding, storage, and retrieval of an event, what this research shows is that it is been difficult to demonstrate this connection at the level of memory performance. This is true regardless of whether stress is acute or chronic (see Chapter 8) and may have something to do with how stress is being measured, at least in children. In fact, when it comes to assessing stress in children, there is little or no consensus on how stress can best be measured. This is not for the lack of alternative measures. Indeed, stress in children has been measured using subjective self-ratings (where children judge their own subjective state of stress); behavioral and objective scales (where parents, teachers, or other objective observers deduce children's stress levels); physiological indices (e.g., heart rate, blood pressure); and neuroendocrine measures (salivary cortisol).

Unfortunately, each measure has its own weakness, and together they have faired poorly when it comes to predicting children's memory for a stressful event. For example, Howe, Courage, and Peterson (1994, 1995) found no relationship between children's memory for an emergency-room treatment and their or their parent's ratings of the child's stress. This was true for immediate recollection as well as when children were asked to remember the events one year later. Similarly, Goodman and Quas (1997) found no relationship between subjective and behavioral measures of stress and children's memory for a stressful medical procedure, the voiding cystourethrogram (VCUG). Of course, the failure to find relationships between children's memory performance and their levels of stress as measured by subjective and behavioral scales may not be too surprising. Indeed, not only do these measures make serious (and perhaps unrealistic) demands on the observers' ability to translate perceived stress onto an "objective" scale, a task that may be particularly difficult for children who are judging their own subjective stress, but such indices may simply be insensitive to the actual underlying physiological changes that occur during a stressful experience (see Howe, 1997, 1998a). Thus, like other measures used to index stress (autonomic and neuroendocrine measures of stress reactivity), subjective, objective, and behavioral scales do not unambiguously associate changes in children's stress levels with subsequent memory for the stressful events themselves (similar problems exist for linking measures of chronic stress and subsequent event memory: see Chapter 8).

Another reason that these measures, particularly salivary cortisol, may not predict memory performance in children is that there is considerable variability in stress reactivity, variability that exists both developmentally as well as at an individual level (also see Wallin et al., 2009). Indeed, there are marked developmental and individual differences in cortisol responses to stress (for a review, see Gunnar et al., 1997) and neuroendocrine reactivity can fluctuate not only with age but also as a function of attachment style (Nachmias et al., 1996), temperament (Boyce et al., 1992; Kagan, 1994), stress reactivity (Gunnar et al., 1997), and knowledge (Stein & Liwag, 1997; for a review, see Howe, 1998a). Recall that individual differences in these same variables have been linked to differences in children's memory performance more generally (see earlier chapters in this volume). Perhaps it is only when we measure these individual difference variables together with a variety of indices of physiological reactivity that we will get a better understanding of what is looking to be a very complex relationship between underlying stress and children's memory performance.

Given these difficulties in establishing a direct link between measures of stress and children's memory performance, many researchers have used the emotional or traumatic nature of the stimulus or the event itself as a proxy for indexing stress. Although these are crude measures by comparison, ones that often ignore developmental and individual differences, they do provide us with some insight into children's ability to recollect emotional experiences and how those recollections differ from those of more mundane events. In what follows, I review laboratory-based studies of children's memory for emotional stimuli first, and then turn to children's recollections based on field studies of more naturalistic, traumatic experiences.

CHILDREN'S MEMORY OF EMOTIONAL AND TRAUMATIC EVENTS: A LABORATORY PERSPECTIVE

The advantage of laboratory-based research is that the experimenter has control over a number of extraneous variables that can influence children's memory other than the one of interest; namely, emotion. As we saw in earlier chapters, developmental differences in children's memory can be influenced by variables such as concept frequency and familiarity, meaningfulness, concreteness-abstractness, and so forth. In natural settings, it is not clear that these variables are sufficiently known (or controlled) that we can separate out their different influences, limiting our examination to only those effects that are of direct interest (i.e., emotion).

Of course, the advantage of exercising control comes at the cost of only being able to manipulate emotion within a modest range and in a relatively mild manner. For obvious ethical reasons, researchers cannot duplicate the effects of child maltreatment or mimic the devastation caused by war, floods, hurricanes, and other natural disasters. Instead, they must rely on manipulating the valence and arousal of verbal (e.g., word lists, stories) or visual (e.g., pictures, videotaped or live staged events) stimuli. In these instances, children do not actually experience the stressful incident themselves but are simply witnesses to the event being staged. As it turns out, despite not being able to duplicate the extremes of emotions in the laboratory that we see in more natural stressful experiences, the basic memory principles that are uncovered in the laboratory are the same as those seen in the field.

In order to determine whether emotion effects children's memory, researchers will frequently vary valence (positive or negative) and contrast this with so-called non-emotional or neutral stimuli. Of course, such neutral stimuli are not really devoid of emotion, rather, they simply tend to be rather low in arousal and neither very positive or very negative. For example, children might hear statements such as "Maria's dad gave her a beautiful present," representing positive emotion; "That night Maria dropped a carton of eggs in the kitchen and her parents got mad at her," representing negative emotion; or "After dinner, Maria and her brothers did their homework together," representing neutral or non-emotional stimuli. Across two experiments using statements of this sort, Davidson, Luo, and Burden (2001) found that although older children (e.g., 11-year-olds) recalled more information than younger children (e.g., six-year-olds), regardless of age, children remembered more emotional (both positive and negative) than unemotional information.

This advantage for remembering emotional information regardless of valence is not universal. In fact, when word lists are used rather than stories, children frequently remember neutral lists better than negatively valenced lists. For example, Howe (2007) had children (eight- and 12-year-olds) study lists that were either neutral (e.g., words such as *table, sit, couch, apple, basket, tooth*) or negative (e.g., words such as *mad, fear, hate, sad, frown, cheat*). When these materials were controlled for other between-list word features that affect children's memory performance (e.g., word frequency, word length), neutral items were better recalled and recognized than negative items regardless of age. The same neutral over negative list advantage has been found in a subsequent series of five experiments, and holds not just for children but also for adults (Howe et al., 2010b). Thus, for word lists, although older children and adults recall and recognize more items than younger children, regardless of age, neutral information is better remembered than negative information (for additional discussion of these and other findings concerning the role of emotion in both true and false memory, see Chapter 9).

Of course, one reason for these contradictory findings might be that both the story and word list studies confound valence and arousal. Recall that "emotion" refers to both the direction of the emotion or *valence* (positive or negative) as well as the strength of the emotion or *arousal* (low or high). As we have already seen, neurobiological reactivity to emotional or stressful information is usually studied with respect to arousal, not valence, although there, too, they have frequently been confounded (i.e., valence is usually set to negative and arousal is then varied). If it really is arousal that causes neurobiological changes in acute stressful or emotional situations that affect memory, then perhaps we should examine arousal independently of valence. Only when these two variables are separated and made orthogonal (i.e., where there are positive and negative items that have similar high and low values on an arousal scale) can we extract separate measures of the role of valence and arousal on children's memory.

Recently, Brainerd and his colleagues (Brainerd et al., 2008b, 2010) have done just that in a series of experiments with adults and children. These researchers used word lists where both positive and negative items were presented, half of which were high in arousal (e.g., highly positive terms such as *kiss, caress, beautiful, baby,* and highly negative terms such as *funeral, grave, gun, jail*), and the other half were low in arousal (e.g., mildly positive terms such as *lawn, sea, robin, dream* and mildly negative items such as *mud, break, flu, bashful*). Somewhat surprisingly, regardless of whether the participants were children (Brainerd et al., 2010) or adults (Brainerd et al., 2008b), valence was more important than arousal for remembering the words that had been presented. That is, regardless of the subjects' age, they remembered positive items better than negative items. Although high-arousal words were better remembered than low-arousal words, the magnitude of this effect was smaller than that for valence. Moreover, this effect interacted with valence such that arousal effects were smaller for negative than positive words. So, although arousal is an important component of emotion that can and does influence children's memory, valence, particularly positive valence, plays a more important role in determining what children remember.

Although the results concerning arousal are in line with what might be anticipated on the basis of previous neurobiological research, the findings concerning valence are somewhat puzzling. Indeed, the finding that positive and neutral information is better remembered than negative information runs counter to the traditional belief that negative information should be better remembered by both children and adults. To resolve this conundrum, we need to consider a third variable in addition to valence and arousal, one that I began this chapter with: namely, distinctiveness.

It is often the case that differences in valence are confounded with differences in content. For example, in the story-memory study, dropping a carton of eggs on the floor might be more distinctive (e.g., occur less frequently) than getting a present or doing one's homework. Perhaps the same can be said for concepts such as *kiss, caress, beautiful,* and *baby,* compared to concepts such as *lawn, sea, robin,* and *dream.* That is, the former terms may appear less often in one's day-to-day life than the latter terms, making them much more distinctive and hence, more memorable. Thus, although we may expect negative information to be better remembered than neutral or positive information, such a result might not always be obtained as it may depend on how distinctive the negative information is relative to other information being processed, or information that is already in memory. I extend this line of reasoning in Chapter 9 when I review research on the role of emotion in false recollection of words as well as entire events.

Other laboratory-based research on emotion and memory concerns children's eyewitness testimony. Here, children are either shown a videotape of a staged event or watch a staged event performed live. Importantly, the child does not usually participate in the event itself, but rather, passively watches the event as an impartial witness. These events are usually emotional in content, being both arousing and differing in valence. For example, in a study by Roebers and Schneider (2002), children (six- to 10-year-olds) might be shown a video-tape of a staged robbery (negative valence) or a treasure hunt (positive valence). Following a delay, they were asked to remember the event using free recall (e.g., "Tell me everything you can remember about the video"), cued recall (e.g., "How much money was in the wallet?," "What did they find on the treasure hunt?"), and misleading questions (e.g., "The boy had blond hair, didn't he?"). For both free and unbiased cued recall, although older children recalled more than younger children, there were no differences due to the valence of the video. For biased cued recall, or the misleading questions, children were more accurate with the negative or theft video than with the more positive or treasure hunt video. As in the story recall and word list studies, it is not clear whether this greater resistance to suggestion when misleading questions were used was due strictly to valence, as arousal was not measured separately, or due to other, correlated differences in event distinctiveness.

What these laboratory-based studies show is that, at a behavioral level, the link between emotion and children's memory may not be as direct and straightforward as the underlying neuroscience research might have us believe. Indeed, whether negative or positive information is better remembered depends to some extent on the arousing potential of that information (with arousal having larger effects on positively valenced than negatively valenced information, at least for word lists), as well as on how distinctive that information is to the individual child. This latter point gets us back to the earlier discussion of the importance of considering a person's knowledge base when making predictions about what will and what will not be encoded, stored, and subsequently retrieved (this chapter as well as Chapter 5). This is important, not only with laboratory-based research, but also with more naturalistic studies, which are reviewed next.

CHILDREN'S MEMORY OF EMOTIONAL AND TRAUMATIC EVENTS: A FIELD PERSPECTIVE

The advantage of field-based research is that the researcher can study the impact of emotion in situations that occur naturally, events that cannot, for ethical reasons, be reproduced in the laboratory. This provides a greater insight into the complexity of traumatic events, a richness that is not easily duplicated in the laboratory. Indeed, it is this very confluence of situational, individual, and developmental variables that allows the researcher a unique perspective on the richness of children's recollection of emotional experiences.

Of course, this, too, comes at a cost. In particular, although one can determine the valence of an event retrospectively, it is difficult to obtain "on-line" measures of arousal. As noted earlier, even if one were at the event as it was occurring, it is not clear what measurement of stress or arousal would be most appropriate. Like the laboratory-based studies, it is also difficult to deduce the distinctiveness of the event, although as we will see later, attempts to assess the frequency of event occurrence have been made. As a result, it is often found that the more unusual the event in an individual's history, the more likely it is to be remembered. However, this, too, is tempered by a host of other variables, including the personal significance of the event both at the time it was encoded as well as later when it is being retrieved.

A number of reviews concerning children's recollection of stressful and traumatic experiences (Cordon et al., 2004; Howe, 1997, 1998a, 2000; Howe et al., 2006a, 2006b; Paz-Alonso et al., 2009) agree that, barring cerebral insult, children can and do remember many of the central elements of traumatic events. For example, Howe et al. (1994, 1995) reported that many young children (18 months old up to five years old) could remember core features of both the accidents and subsequent emergency room treatments on tests of immediate, six-month, and one-year retention. Despite being able to remember the central features of these events over time, peripheral elements were frequently forgotten or later blended with similar experiences (Howe et al., 1995).

An important feature of this research is that the accidents and subsequent emergency-room treatment were unanticipated. However, these results are not confined to conditions in which the experience was unexpected. Indeed, similar findings have been reported for script-like medical examinations (Bruck et al., 1995; Ornstein et al., 1997, 2006) and anticipated painful medical experiences such as the VCUG (Goodman et al., 1994; Merritt et al., 1994), lumbar punctures (Chen et al., 2000), and bone marrow transplants (Stuber et al., 1991). Together, studies such as these converge on the conclusion that at least the core of emotional and traumatic experiences is remembered reasonably well, even over intervals of one year or more. Of course, there is considerable survival value in remembering these core features as they may help us anticipate and, hopefully, avoid similar incidents in the future. However, to the extent that memory for traumatic experiences is reconstructive and prone to the same errors as memory for more mundane events (Howe et al., 2006a, 2006b), one does need to be cautious, as even emotional memories can contain errors (see Chapter 9).

These conclusions (and caveats) have been further substantiated by research on children's memory for other, naturally occurring events that are both unanticipated and traumatic. For example, children's recollections of sniper attacks (Pynoos & Nader, 1989; Schwartz & Kowalski, 1991), hurricanes (Ackil et al., 2003; Bahrick et al., 1998; Shaw et al., 1996), tornados (Bauer et al., 2008), earthquakes (Najarian et al., 1996), a fatal bus-train collision (Tyano et al., 1996), attacks during the Gulf War (Dyregov et al., 2002; Laor et al., 1997), and imprisonment in Cambodia (Kinzie et al., 1986), although they were accurate in terms of central or core features, were also subject to reconstructive errors. Children who watched the explosion of the *Challenger* space shuttle provided clearer, more consistent, and more detailed accounts of the event than children who simply heard about the event, both immediately (i.e., five to seven weeks after the explosion) as well as 14 months later (Terr et al., 1996). Importantly, for the children who misunderstood at least one or more details of the event (and at least 30% of the children did), these misunderstandings were incorporated into their memory reports both immediately as well as 14 months later.

Similarly, Terr (1981) examined children's memories for a highly publicized crime, the Chowchilla school bus kidnapping in which five- to 14-year-old children were abducted and subsequently buried alive. Approximately five to 23 months after the event, the child victims received clinical interviews as part of their psychological treatment. During these interviews, children provided very vivid accounts of the incident, and they retained the core of the event up to five years later (Terr, 1983). However, these reports also contained some important inaccuracies involving peripheral details associated with the incident, including the date, time, and duration of the event. Again, like more mundane events, the central components of traumatic events can be remembered, but reconstructive processes can and do create key inaccuracies in children's memories for even the most horrific experiences.

Finally, consider one study of a natural disaster in which the researchers tried to estimate different levels of stress children experienced during the event. Bahrick et al. (1998) examined the memories of three- and four-year-old children who experienced a Category 4 storm, Hurricane Andrew, that devastated Florida's coast in 1992. The key to this study was that the children were grouped into low-, medium-, and high-stress groups according the severity of the storm damage they experienced. Although all of the children provided detailed accounts of their experiences during the storm when interviewed a few weeks after the event, children classified as high-stress remembered more than those classified as low-stress. When interviewed six years later, children were still able to recount their experiences, but there were no differences in the amount recalled as a function of stress classification (Fivush et al., 2004). Interestingly, children in the high-stress group required more prompting than children in the other groups when recalling the event six years later. Thus, although stress may have had an impact immediately after the event, these effects dissipated with time.

The literature reviewed so far suggests that stressful events can be remembered reasonably well immediately as well as five or six years later. This overview has also shown that like non-traumatic memories, recollections of traumatic experiences are reconstructive and can contain errors. However, the question remains, are stressful events remembered any better than other, more mundane experiences? Overall, the literature shows that stressful events are remembered at least as well as, and in some cases better than, more benign experiences (Fivush, 2002; Ornstein, 1995). In some studies, children who experience high levels of stress produce more memory errors than children who were not as stressed (e.g., Goodman & Quas, 1997). One limitation of these studies is that they have examined traumatic and non-traumatic event memory in different, rather than the same, children. What this means is that individual differences (e.g., in stress reactivity), as well as developmental differences, are confounded with event type. What is needed is research that compares the recollection of both traumatic and non-traumatic experiences in the same child.

Fortunately, there are some studies that have examined recall of both traumatic and non-traumatic events in the same children. For example, Fivush and colleagues (2003) examined five- to 12-year-old children's recollection of non-traumatic (and perhaps positively valenced) events such as parties and holidays, as well as traumatic (and negatively valenced) events such as parental separation, serious illness, and death. The results showed that children's recall of events, whether traumatic or non-traumatic, was quantitatively similar in terms of the amount of detail remembered. Although as expected, these narratives differed qualitatively in terms of the type of information remembered (e.g., more emotional states concerning the self or others with traumatic events), it would seem that when individual differences are controlled for, traumatic events are no better remembered than more positive and possibly less emotional events.

More recently, Bauer and colleagues (2008) examined children's memory for non-traumatic experiences as well as for a traumatic experience. The traumatic event was a series of tornados with winds in excess of 200 miles per hour that devastated a small rural town, St. Peter, in Minnesota. In two interviews, one four months after the tornados hit and the other one ten months after they hit, narrative length was approximately twice as long for the tornados as for either of the two non-traumatic events. These results are similar to those obtained by Sales, Fivush, and Peterson (2003), who found longer conversational length between mothers and their three- to five-year-olds for traumatic (medical emergencies) than non-traumatic experiences.

Although this was interesting, Bauer et al. (2008) are quick to point out that conversation or narrative length is not necessarily monotonically related to the amount remembered. That is, there may be more redundancies in narratives concerning traumatic experiences or discussion of emotional states (see earlier comment concerning the Fivush et al., 2003, study), information that is not necessarily directly related to differences in the amount recalled. Another reason for differences in narrative length, unrelated to what is represented in memory about an event, is that there may simply have been more to talk about (or more that had been discussed with parents and peers) concerning the devastation brought by the tornados than about the non-traumatic events. This may be because the tornados represented an extremely consequential event, both to the individuals in the study, but also to the town itself. Indeed, the devastation caused by the tornados impacted many aspects of the resident's lives (e.g., work, school) for some time after the event itself. Finally, it is also possible that these differences are related to what we know about distinctiveness effects in memory. Hopefully, events such as these (medical emergencies, devastating tornados) are rare in one's lifetime and hence constitute a relatively unique experience.

Together, the results from more naturalistic research endeavors confirm the laboratory-based findings reviewed earlier. That is, despite speculation based on some very solid neuroscience research suggesting that stressful and arousing events should be remembered better than more benign events, the behavioral evidence is found wanting. Although there are some reports showing that traumatic events are remembered better than other events, there are an equivalent number of reports showing no differences. Although the type of information recalled may differ between traumatic and non-traumatic events, the accuracy of what is remembered, the amount that is remembered, and the longevity of these memories may not differ as a function of stress or arousal. Indeed, although the amount of stress may have an impact on children's recollection in an immediate timeframe, such effects apparently dissipate over time. Thus, amount of stress or arousal is not as good a predictor of children's memory performance as our developmental neuroscience might have us believe.

Perhaps, like the laboratory-based findings, distinctiveness of the event is a better predictor of long-term retention of experiences. Although certainly short-term arousal is frequently associated with unique events, positive or negative, if that event no longer has personal significance, memory for that event may be no better than memory for other events that carry less emotion. As we saw with autobiographical memory, events that are critical to the self are typically the ones that are best retained, although they, too, like all memories, are reconstructive and prone to error. These are the experiences that are unique and hence distinctive in the course of an individual's lifetime, the core of which will be retained for some time.

Summary and Conclusions

The evidence reviewed in this chapter shows that children's memory for traumatic events, like their memory for more mundane experiences, is reasonably good for the core or central details, even though such recollections are reconstructive in nature. When recollections of traumatic memories are contrasted with non-traumatic memories in the same individuals, there is some evidence that traumatic events may be retained for relatively long periods of time (e.g., six years or more), but so, too, are non-traumatic events, especially if they are of positive experiences (e.g., holidays, parties). Perhaps short-term arousal, regardless of valence, enhances the memorability of events. Indeed, evidence from laboratory studies would suggest that arousal is particularly important for retaining information that is positive in both children and adults.

To the extent that stressful and traumatic experiences enjoy increased longevity in memory may be indicative of their adaptive significance. Indeed, from a purely adaptive point of view, it would make sense that we should remember negative and traumatic experiences better than more benign ones, particularly as memories of these former experiences should aid our future survival. That is, to the extent that we can avoid similar experiences in the future, our likelihood of survival is enhanced. Stressful or traumatic memories can signal impending danger when appropriate cues are present in the environment (e.g., Ehlers et al., 2002; Foa & Rothbaum, 1998). Indeed, the preservation of stressful and traumatic memories helps the survival of the organism by assisting in the avoidance of similar dangerous or threatening events (also see Wiedenmayer, 2004). The research reviewed in this chapter on the neuroscience of the effects of acute stress and arousal on memory would also seem to support this view. Indeed, time and time again, neuroscience research has shown that stress and arousal can have a beneficial effect on the brain structures and systems that mediate declarative memory.

Of course, the same could be said for positive experiences, as they, too, carry adaptive significance (e.g., finding a partner may be related reproductive success). These experiences are also arousing, and the same neural structures and systems that can enhance memories of traumatic experiences can also enhance memories of positive experiences. That these two seemingly opposite types of experience (at least in terms of valence) may be better encoded, stored, and retrieved in children's and adults' long-term memory may signal, not just the adaptive significance of acute stress and arousal, but also the key role that distinctiveness plays in memory formation and retention. These experiences tend to be distinctive and personally significant, qualities that are well known to enhance the longevity of autobiographical memories (see Chapter 5). As outlined at the beginning of this chapter, there is considerable evidence attesting to the fact that naturally occurring distinctive experiences, as well as those created in the laboratory, tend to be better remembered than less distinct events, both by children and by adults.

Like other aspects of memory, age differences exist in children's ability to recall stressful events, with older children and adults often remembering more than younger children. The literature reviewed in this chapter suggests that there might not only be age differences in the amount of information that is recollected, but perhaps, too, in the type of information that is remembered. However, these qualitative age differences in the content of what is remembered are not always obtained, and there is reason to suspect that individual differences in what is remembered outweigh any developmental differences.

Of course, as we have seen throughout this book, what is remembered is to a large extent contingent on one's knowledge base. Although there are well-documented individual differences in knowledge base, there are equally well-documented developmental differences in children's knowledge structures. Indeed, what is distinctive to each individual is determined by that individual's knowledge base, including both semantic and episodic components of autobiographical memory. Perhaps because of these links between autobiographical memory, the knowledge base, and distinctiveness, a developmentally invariant phenomenon also exists in this literature. That is, despite age differences in the amount of information that can be remembered, as well as the types of information that can be remembered, distinctive events are nonetheless remembered better than less consequential ones, regardless of age.

Finally, it is important to remember that like memory for non-traumatic experiences, memory for traumatic experiences is reconstructive and error-prone. Although stressful events may be better retained than more benign events, especially if they are personally consequential, they are still subject to the same laws of memory. That is, memory traces become weaker (e.g., less integrated) over time, becoming not only less accessible (retrieval failures) with time, but also less available (storage failures). Also, they are subject to interference and distortion from new experiences, from misinformation effects, as well as when they are recoded (reconsolidated) in memory following reinstatement or reactivation. Although oftentimes these alterations to memory are confined to peripheral details, there is evidence that even extremely important components of the core of a life-changing experience (e.g., events in a concentration camp) can be misremembered or even forgotten (see Wagenaar & Groeneweg, 1990; and Chapter 9).

Overall, the evidence concerning the neurobiologically based, memory-enhancing effects of acute stress and arousal on children's memory performance is not as straightforward as might have been thought at first blush. That these effects are contingent on a number of other, cognitive factors (e.g., distinctiveness in relation to both the semantic and episodic components of autobiographical memory) may be somewhat surprising. However, this is not the entire story, because these effects pertain to children who, other than during the traumatic experience itself, are living what would otherwise be called a typical life. The question remains, are the general processes that govern memory and memory development altered in children whose lives are not so typical? In particular, if stress is severe and chronic, do the neural structures and systems underlying memory become altered in some fundamental manner that causes memory development to go askew, affecting children's memory performance? Perhaps the effects of traumatic experiences are only apparent at the behavioral level when chronic stress is an everyday event, as it is in child maltreatment. To answer this question, the next chapter considers what is known about the effects of chronic stress and child maltreatment on memory and its development in childhood.

8

Chronic Stress and Maltreatment in Early Memory Development

> I was brought up in a very poor and very violent household. I spent
> much of my childhood being afraid.
> —Patrick Stewart, Actor

> As a child, I was never drawn toward depraved or extreme
> situations; I really wanted a normal little childhood.
> Unfortunately, that's just not what happened.
> —Augusten Burroughs, Writer/Author

In Chapter 7 we saw that children's memory for emotional stimuli and events can differ from that for stimuli and events that are more neutral or mundane, although perhaps not quite as much as some might expect. Despite providing some insight into the effects of stress and emotion on memory development with otherwise typically developing children, the question addressed in this chapter is whether childhood trauma, especially that associated with the more prolonged and severe stress of maltreatment, alters the normal course of memory development. This question is not easily answered, although there are several ongoing research programs that are guiding our current knowledge in this matter. These programs include work with maltreated (including physically and sexually abused) and orphaned (and neglected) children. Before reviewing this research, I provide a brief digression on the neurobiological consequences of severe and chronic stress on mechanisms related to memory and its development.

Neurobiological Consequences of Severe and Chronic Stress

As briefly outlined in Chapter 7, even acute short-term stress can lead to morphological changes in the brain regions that are responsible for declarative memory. Severe and prolonged stress can produce even more dire consequences, particularly if children also develop post-traumatic stress disorder (PTSD) (see review by Bremner, 2008). In this section, I provide an overview of the consequences of chronic stress early in life, specifically maltreatment (neglect and abuse), on the neural structures and systems related to memory performance. I begin with a review of the neurohormonal effects of chronic stress on memory and then turn to a discussion of how severe and chronic stress can affect neural structures and systems specific to memory.

NEUROHORMONAL EFFECTS OF CHRONIC STRESS ON MEMORY

Recall from the last chapter that hormones released during stress (catecholamines, glucocorticoids) modulate the encoding, storage, and retrieval of memories. Changes in memory performance can occur as a function of chronic stress, with poorer performance often being more pronounced with chronic than with acute stress (Jelicic & Bonke, 2004). This can also occur when children are experiencing more, rather than less, severe levels of stress (Anda et al., 2006; Bremner et al., 2004). One hypothesis about this relationship between chronic or severe stress and memory is that such stress is associated with the atrophy of synapses (specifically, dendritic branches in the pyramidal neurons of the Cornu Ammonis area 3 [CA3] region) of the hippocampus (Wantanabe et al., 1992; Woolley et al., 1990). Although some (perhaps most) of this loss is reversible, more permanent losses of hippocampal synapses have been reported when stress is prolonged and exposure to glucocorticoids is elevated (Kerr et al., 1991; Mizoguchi et al., 1992; Sapolsky et al., 1985; Uno et al., 1989). Although there is some evidence for greater deficits occurring in younger than in older individuals, these deficits may be secondary to normal age-related reductions in glucocorticoid receptor density found in the hippocampus (Newcomer et al., 1995).

That prolonged exposure to stress-induced glucocorticoids first affects dendritic branching, followed by neuron loss, may not be something that is species-specific, having been observed in animals as diverse as rats, tree shrews, and monkeys (see McEwen & Sapolsky, 1995). Studies with humans, although less well controlled, also suggest that similar patterns of hippocampal atrophy are associated with sustained exposure to glucocorticoids (Axelson et al., 1993; Starkman et al., 1992). In fact, it has been known for some time that sustained exposure to high levels of glucocortioids is associated with specific impairments in declarative memory (Nasrallah et al., 1989). Although many of these findings with human participants are confounded by coincident disease, there is some evidence that even healthy adults can exhibit compromised declarative memory performance when increases in glucocorticoid levels are sustained for long periods of time (Lupien et al., 1994; Newcomer et al., 1994; Wolkowitz et al., 1990).

Most of the studies conducted with human populations use adult participants; very few studies have been conducted with children. However, as in the research with adults, there is evidence that declarative memory performance in children is similarly compromised. For example, asthmatic children who have been prescribed high-dose prednisone treatment evidence lower verbal memory scores than do children with asthma who are taking a low-dose treatment (Bender et al., 1991). Moreover, children who are maltreated and whose abuse is associated with chronic stress exhibit altered patterns of diurnal cortisol activity. That is, compared to non-maltreated children, maltreated children who are depressed have lower concentrations of cortisol in the morning and exhibit an increase instead of the normal decrease in cortisol across the day (i.e., from morning through to afternoon) (Cicchetti & Rogosch, 2001; Hart et al., 1996). Differences in neuroendocrine regulation between maltreated and non-maltreated children have recently been linked to changes in susceptibility to false memories (Cicchetti et al., 2010; see Chapter 9). Additional evidence has shown that children who have been abused, including sexually abused girls (DeBellis et al., 1994), or have been exposed to prolonged stress, exhibit deficits on declarative memory tasks, although it is not always clear that these deficits are associated solely with stress (e.g., Schacter et al., 1996). In addition to exhibiting transient amnesia for the abuse itself, the participants in these studies also have many more global memory deficits, including difficulties with autobiographical memory (Kuyken & Brewin, 1995; Parks & Balon, 1995; see later discussion in this chapter on autobiographical memory and stress).

THE EFFECTS OF CHRONIC STRESS ON NEURAL STRUCTURES AND SYSTEMS RELATED TO MEMORY

Now that we have examined the effects of chronic and severe stress on the neurohormonal system, we can turn our attention to neural structures, systems, and their development. In particular, what are the consequences of severe or prolonged stress, especially that associated with maltreatment, on the development of neural systems specific to declarative memory? Before examining the individual structures and systems in isolation, consider the effects of maltreatment at a more global level. Here, childhood physical and sexual abuse has been associated with decreased cortical integration (Schiffer et al., 1995; Teicher, 1994). There is even some evidence of abnormal connectivity among brain regions involved in the recall of traumatic events in individuals who develop

PTSD but not in those who do not (Lanius et al., 2001, 2003, 2004). Such dysregulation may be responsible for changes in the way in which individuals with PTSD access and retrieve traumatic experiences, but it does not change the fact that such experiences still exist in memory (see later discussion in the current chapter).

Childhood maltreatment has also been associated with increased electroencephalogram abnormalities (Ito et al., 1993 1998; Teicher et al., 1997) and diminished size of the corpus callosum (DeBellis et al., 1999; Jackowski et al., 2008; Teicher et al., 2004). Not only is maltreatment associated with attenuated maturation of the corpus callosum (Teicher et al., 2004), but there are gender differences such that there is a greater negative impact on the developing corpus callosum of males than females (DeBellis & Keshaven, 2003; Teicher et al., 2004). In fact, these gender differences in the development of the corpus callosum were more important (i.e., accounted for more of the variance) than whether maltreated children had developed PTSD. Finally, traumatized children who have been exposed to prolonged stress and who do develop PTSD exhibit greater differences in pituitary volume with age than control children (Thomas & DeBellis, 2004).

It is not clear what the consequences of these neurological differences are when it comes to memory and its development in maltreated children. Indeed, recent reviews of this literature have revealed surprisingly few, if any, differences in memory performance between maltreated and non-maltreated children (Goodman et al., 2010; Howe et al., 2006a, 2006b). In fact, maltreatment-related PTSD (Beers & DeBellis, 2002; Moradi et al., 1999), dissociation (Cicchetti et al., 2010; Eisen et al., 2002), and depression (Orbach et al., 2001) are not always associated with memory deficits. Although some studies have found that children with greater dissociative tendencies and higher cortisol levels made more memory errors than children without these symptoms (Eisen et al., 2007), others have failed to do so (Howe et al., in press) (see Chapter 9 for some additional exceptions). Perhaps differences in memory performance are only seen when maltreatment-related changes target memory-specific areas and systems of the brain. An overview of the effects of prolonged and severe stress on the limbic and hippocampal structures, amygdala, and prefrontal cortex is given next.

Limbic and Hippocampal Structures
There are some findings concerning maltreatment-related changes in hippocampal development that may be suggestive of corresponding changes in declarative memory performance. For example, physical and sexual abuse during childhood has been associated with diminished hippocampal development in adulthood (Bremner et al., 1997; Ito et al., 1998; Stein, 1997), and this change

is particularly marked when it is comorbid with PTSD (Bremner et al., 2003a, 2003b). Such findings are consistent with evidence that prolonged and severe stress can lead to atrophy of the hippocampus, where this atrophy is more pronounced in people following the experience of particularly tragic events and whose consequences include PTSD (Bremner et al., 1995). Other consequences include morphological changes in limbic structures that have more indirect effects on memory, including alteration in the functioning of the HPA axis. For example, adaptation to uncontrollable and prolonged stress may lead to what is called "down-regulation" of glucocorticoid receptors in the hippocampus (e.g., Kanitz et al., 2003). This, in turn, can result in impairments in the HPA axis as glucocorticoid receptors are involved in negative feedback within this axis (see Jacobson & Sapolsky, 1991). Therefore, the effects of prolonged and severe stress have both structural and functional consequences on the hippocampus and related structures, ones that may have additional consequences at the level of memory, affecting performance in both human and nonhuman animals (Becker et al., 2007; Bremner, 2008; Buss et al., 2004).

However, not all studies have found differences in hippocampal volume as a function of maltreatment. For example, Bonne et al. (2001) found no differences in hippocampal volume as a function of trauma, even in individuals who developed PTSD. Similarly, other researchers found no support for the claim that hippocampal development differs between maltreated and non-maltreated populations (DeBellis et al., 2001; Pederson et al., 2004). In general, studies with children have provided mixed results concerning changes to the hippocampus, where some researchers have found decreases in hippocampal volume in children diagnosed with PTSD (Carrion et al., 2007) and still others have found increases (Tupler & DeBellis, 2006). Such contradictory findings may be the consequence of differences in the timing of measurements in these studies. Depending on when measurements were taken, changes in the developing hippocampus may be such that growth itself outstrips any measurable decline that may be associated with maltreatment, hence masking any potential impairment associated with prolonged and severe stress. For example, participants in the Bremner et al. (1997) study were adults who retrospectively reported childhood abuse, whereas participants in the DeBellis et al. (2001) study were children whose abuse was documented. Moreover, caution is needed when interpreting results from studies whose participants are adults, because childhood maltreatment (if and when it is substantiated) is often confounded with later substance (drug, alcohol) abuse, the negative effects of which can also target memory-sensitive areas of the brain, particularly the hippocampus (among other neural structures). Finally, although statistical significance is important, results of imaging studies must be gauged against sample size. Outcomes may need to be interpreted more cautiously with smaller samples (e.g., in the DeBellis et al. [2001] study, Ns were 9 maltreated and 9 control participants) than with larger ones (e.g., in the Bremner et al. [1997] study, Ns were almost double, with 17 maltreated and 17 control participants).

Again, like the discussion of more global changes in neural connectivity between different brain regions, although there exists some evidence of maltreatment-related changes to the hippocampus and surrounding structures, the empirical evidence is mixed at best. Moreover, despite there being sound theoretical reasons for concluding that these neurological substrates should be altered as a consequence of early stressful experiences, there is no conclusive evidence that they are, and even if such evidence were found, there is little or no research demonstrating that these effects alter memory performance. In fact, as shown later in this chapter, researchers are hard-pressed to find stable differences in memory performance between maltreated and non-maltreated children.

Amygdala

In addition to the hippocampus and related structures, the amygdala is critical to the establishment of memories of stressful experiences. Recall that the amygdala is viewed as a key structure in threat detection and the regulation of vigilance (Phelps & LeDoux, 2005). During acute stress, the amygdala may be in a heightened state of vigilance, one that has considerable survival value for the organism (van Marle et al., 2009). Although heightened sensitivity to environmental threat is associated with acute stress, because such processing is relatively fast and automatic, there is a higher rate of false positives (Ohman & Mineka, 2001). Moreover, acute stress might cause a reduction in control of the amygdala by the prefrontal cortex, a finding reported in the neuroimaging literature for individuals with PTSD (Etkin & Wager, 2007; Shin et al., 2005).

As reviewed in the previous chapter, short-term or acute stress may also enhance the establishment of emotional memories. This may be due, in part, to the increased activation of the basolateral nucleus of the amygdala (BLA), something that can facilitate consolidation via its impact on long-term potentiation. Perhaps because research on the effects of prolonged and severe stress on the amygdala is not as rich as that concerning these effects on the hippocampus, much less is known. However, like the hippocampus, the BLA is rich with glucocorticoid receptors. It may be, then, that sustained, increased levels of glucocorticoids may result in structural and functional changes in the BLA, something that in turn may affect consolidation of emotional memories (see Roozendaal et al., 2008).

Prefrontal Cortex

Like the amygdala, less is known about the effects of chronic and severe stress on the prefrontal cortex (PFC) than about these same effects on the hippocampus. Like the hippocampus, atrophy of pyramidal neurons in the PFC may occur due to chronic or prolonged stress (Radley et al., 2004). As it turns out, individuals with PTSD have smaller PFC volumes then healthy controls (DeBellis et al., 2002; Kitayama et al., 2005; Shin et al., 2005).

Limitations and Caveats

As already noted in the section concerning the hippocampus, there are several potential problems associated with the study of traumatized individuals when understanding the neurobiological consequences of prolonged and severe stress. Indeed, exposure to abuse or neglect is a major risk factor for psychopathology (Lange et al., 1999). Like the study of other atypical groups (e.g., participants with amnesia) or nonhuman animals, when trying to understand the neurobiological consequences of some phenomenon, the interpretation of outcomes is not straightforward. This is because the participants in these studies—maltreated individuals—frequently come with related psychopathologies (e.g., dissociation) or drug and alcohol dependencies. Indeed, the most common psychopathology associated with the detection of neurobiological differences between maltreated and non-maltreated individuals is PTSD. As a consequence, these studies may (a) overestimate the impact of abuse by selecting individuals who have been most adversely affected by maltreatment, (b) confound maltreatment-related changes with those that are actually psychopathology-related, and (c) identify preexisting brain abnormalities that are risk factors for developing a particular disorder when exposed to trauma but mistakenly attribute alterations in these brain regions to maltreatment (also see Gilbertson et al., 2002). Because of these problems, it may not be that unusual to find that, across studies, there are differences in the degree and direction of maltreatment-related changes in the brain.

An alternative strategy to participant selection might be to sample only maltreated individuals without psychopathology. The problem with this approach is that such a biased selection may underestimate the effects of childhood maltreatment-related brain changes. In addition, sampling only participants without psychopathology might lead to the mistaken identification of preexisting brain differences that are related to resilience with maltreatment-related changes in the brain. An obvious way around such a dilemma is to recruit participants regardless of additional psychopathology. Although this avoids problems associated with preexisting brain anomalies as well as issues associated with over- and underestimation of the consequences of maltreatment, it may not be ideal, as there may be important individual differences that are obscured when comorbidity is ignored. Ideally, researchers would be able to recruit enough participants with and without different maltreatment-related psychopathologies, although such samples are difficult to achieve in a single study.

A final problem with the study of maltreatment-related changes in neural structure and function is that it is often difficult to get participants whose abusive experiences are limited to a single type of abuse. In almost all studies, the maltreatment experienced by most participants has occurred on multiple occasions and is varied (e.g., emotional, physical, and sexual). Moreover, age of onset of the abuse and the severity of abuse are rarely measured systematically. Although consistency is a tall order, when left unchecked, these variables represent potentially serious threats to the validity of any conclusions about maltreatment-related changes in brain structure and function.

These problems do not just haunt research on maltreatment-related brain changes, but are also relevant to the study of differences between maltreated and non-maltreated children's declarative memory performance. As shown in the next section, few differences emerge between these populations. However, when differences are obtained, they are often confounded with comorbid psychopathology or other factors that may be the more likely source of memory differences rather than maltreatment per se. In what follows, I provide a review of these studies concerning true memories of events (false memories are reviewed later, in Chapter 9) and point out whether differences that are obtained are related to maltreatment or to other factors known to influence declarative memory.

Declarative Memory in Children Who Have Experienced Prolonged or Severe Stress

There are two questions I will attempt to answer in this section. The first question has to do with what children remember about their abusive experiences. With Chapter 7 as a relevant backdrop concerning children's memory for events involving acute stress, the current chapter examines what children remember of events involving severe and chronic stress, including neglect and emotional, physical, and sexual abuse. The second question concerns whether the prolonged exposure to stress due to child maltreatment somehow alters the course of memory development. That is, are the neural structures and systems that support memory and its development somehow changed by the maltreatment experiences these children have endured, changed in ways that may affect these children's ability to encode, store, and retrieve information about experiences more generally?

MEMORY OF TRAUMATIC EXPERIENCES UNDER CONDITIONS OF SEVERE AND CHRONIC STRESS

As noted in Chapter 5, the necessary, although perhaps not sufficient, conditions for the beginnings of autobiographical memory occur as early as 18 to 24 months of age. In the clinical literature, there are numerous reports of traumatic memories from this age range, if not earlier, in infants who have been traumatized (see Gaensbauer, 1995, 2002; Paley & Alpert, 2003; Terr, 1988, 1994). As noted in Chapter 2, the majority of these infant memories were elicited nonverbally during play therapy, and caution should therefore be exercised when interpreting these behaviors as memories per se. It is not clear whether nonverbal play behaviors represent memories because they normally require considerable prompting when elicited, are heavily reliant on contextual cues (e.g., events, places, people), and may simply be a reflection of the demand characteristics of the props themselves or the context in which the play therapy is being conducted (e.g., Cordon et al., 2004; see Howe et al., 1994, for a case study). Although the nonhuman animal literature suggests that vestiges of early traumatic experiences may still be present in implicit memories (including phobias), the literature reviewed in this book shows that there is little evidence to suggest the same exists in humans. Moreover, there is good evidence that explicit memories, even for traumatic episodes, formed before the age of two years are not retained and do not become part of our consciously accessible, autobiographical memory as adults (also see Williams, 1994). Although child maltreatment has been associated with later psychopathology in childhood and adulthood (including depression and PTSD; see later in this chapter), it is not clear that such psychiatric disturbances are contingent on the individual's being able to consciously remember the early maltreating events.

As demonstrated in Chapter 5, even after the age of two years, most autobiographical memories tend to be very fragmentary, and this is true regardless of the nature of the event. As autobiographical memory continues to develop, children are able to store more and more information about experiences, linking those events with their sense of self. Children, regardless of maltreatment status, encode and store information in the context of what they already know (e.g., their knowledge base), something that develops as a consequence of the experiences they have had to date. Although the processes used to form, retain, and retrieve memories are the same regardless of maltreatment status, because maltreated children have had considerably different experiences than non-maltreated children, one might expect that these maltreated children would tend to focus on and encode different cues in the environment than children who have not been maltreated.

That maltreated children attend to different features in the environment than non-maltreated children may, perhaps, be a given. Indeed, Pollak (2003;

Pollak & Kistler, 2002) has proposed that maltreated children process emotional cues differently than non-maltreated children, particularly when it comes to negative emotions. Such emotions may be heightened in maltreated children because negative emotions may be frequent in the home environment and may signal potential threats to survival. Indeed, maltreated children are quick to recognize angry facial expressions (Pollak & Kistler, 2002) and remain aroused for longer periods of time by anger in background situations (Pollak et al., 2005). As we saw in Chapter 7, there is considerable adaptive currency in the detection of threat, something that even very young infants do automatically (LoBue & DeLoache, 2010). This currency is increased manyfold in environments in which threat is an everyday occurrence.

The question remains, do these differences in attention to environmental threat cues translate into differences in the content of maltreated children's memories? Although the answer to this question with adults is a resounding yes (e.g., Golier et al., 2003; McNally et al., 1990, 1994, 1998, 2000) the jury may still out when it comes to children's memories. However, Moradi and colleagues (2000) did find that children and adolescents (ages varied from nine to 17 years) with PTSD resulting from either traffic accidents or exposure to violence exhibited a memory bias for negative information relative to a control group. That is, the PTSD participants remembered more negative and trauma-related words than neutral and positive words.

It might be more likely that we would observe trauma-related memory biases in children's autobiographical memory. Unfortunately, here again, there is very little research on this topic, although the literature is just witnessing an increase in the number of studies on autobiographical memory in maltreated children. Fortunately, much of this research involves attempts to recollect *documented* cases of abuse, so the accuracy of these recollections can be examined. What these studies have shown is that child maltreatment victims are no more (or less) accurate in their memories of childhood, and their narratives are no more (or less) devoid of detail, than non-maltreated control children. This finding holds even when children and adolescents (ages varied from three to 17 years) are the participants (Eisen et al., 2002; Eisen et al., 2007). Interestingly, although there was a tendency for children who had suffered neglect to be somewhat less accurate than children who had been physically and sexually abused, a diagnosis of PTSD did not predict memory accuracy.

Although accuracy may not differ as a consequence of maltreatment, the question is whether the content differs. One approach to this question has been to examine the consistency of traumatic versus other non-traumatic (and often positive) memories over time. For example, Porter and Peace (2007) compared adults' memories of trauma and their memories of highly positive events over time. They found that while positive memories deteriorated over time both in quality and vividness, traumatic memories did not change. Of course such findings may simply indicate that participants rehearsed (e.g., ruminated about) traumatic memories more than positive ones, but these results do hint at a memory bias for trauma-related experiences in maltreated individuals.

Other research with child participants confirms the longevity of autobiographical memories of abuse. For example, Alexander and colleagues (2005) examined child sexual abuse victims' memory for documented sexual abuse that had occurred 12 to 21 years before the interview. They found that memories of the abuse were relatively detailed and reasonably accurate. Thus, child maltreatment does not seem to lead to problems when it comes to remembering the abuse. Indeed, the accuracy of such memories is consistent with potential biases that occur during the original encoding of these events during childhood in addition to any rehearsal such memories might receive.

The studies reviewed up to this point demonstrate that maltreated children can clearly and accurately remember much of the trauma they have experienced, and that their memory for past events may be dominated by more vivid traumatic than positive experiences. This is consistent with the idea that abused children are more sensitive to threats in the environment and that these experiences are the ones that may be better encoded, stored, and later retrieved. Additional evidence consistent with this hypothesis comes from a recent longitudinal study on family violence (Greenhoot et al., 2008) as well as a recent study that examined the link between maltreated children's negative self-schema and autobiographical memories of abuse (Valentino et al., 2009). This latter study provides a more direct link between children's more negative view of themselves and their environment (including their caregivers) and what is encoded, stored, and retrieved in autobiographical memory.

Valentino et al. (2009) examined autobiographical memory in maltreated ($N = 77$) and non-maltreated ($N = 115$) children between the ages of seven and 13 years. Participants were administered the Autobiographical Memory Test (AMT; Williams & Broadbent, 1986) which consists of 10 emotional cue words: five negative (e.g., *sorry, angry, clumsy, hurt, lonely*) and five positive (*happy, safe, interested, successful, surprised*). Cue words were presented in alternating order as a function of valence, and children were asked to generate a specific memory for each word given a prompt such as, "Tell me about a time when you felt _____." Tests such as this often produce what has been termed the over-general memory (OGM) effect in participants suffering from depression and other psychopathologies. That is, rather than recalling a specific episode, depressed individuals remember repeated experiences (e.g., "Every day when I was at school. . .") or events that last for a long period of time (e.g., "When I was a teenager. . ."). Such effects are somewhat reminiscent of the earlier discussion in this book about the use of schemas in autobiographical memory. That is, for events that are repeated, individual episodes can become integrated into a single pattern that is representative of those events as a whole, and hence lose their individual distinctiveness. Individuals with repeated episodes of depression or who experience similar chronic and severe maltreating events may similarly develop schemas for these events, ones that blend the separate episodes into a single representation. It may be then that the findings concerning OGM are simply a result of individuals recalling schemas rather than specific episodes. Indeed, when cued to give specific episodes, the OGM effect can disappear and specific events can be remembered (see Howe et al., 2006b).

However, it may turn out that the OGM effect is not necessarily a memory-based phenomenon at all, as it may simply represent a reporting bias. That is, individuals with depression may be simply less motivated to reveal to others, or talk to others about, specific memories, not that they are unable to access specific episodes in memory. Indeed, they may simply report the schematized memory and not wish to reveal (to others and perhaps not even to themselves) the individual episodes; something that may serve to regulate emotion (see later in this section). That participants with depression can recall specific episodes is supported by research that shows that when they are queried about specific memories, they are able to access them and report them in considerable detail (for recent review, see Howe et al., 2006b).

Interestingly, although the OGM effect has been reported for affective disorders, there are mixed results concerning exposure to trauma and maltreatment (for a review, see Moore & Zoellner, 2007). For example, adults who experienced childhood trauma have difficulty with specific memory retrieval even when controlling for depression (e.g., DeDecker et al., 2003; Henderson et al., 2002; Kuyken & Brewin, 1995). Others have found no effects of maltreatment on the retrieval of specific autobiographical memories (e.g., Orbach et al., 2001; Wessel et al., 2001), or fewer OGMs in adolescents with depression and exposure to trauma than in adolescents with depression without trauma exposure (Kuyken et al., 2006). These contradictory findings may have arisen because, in all of these studies, the evidence for the traumatic events that were experienced was provided in the form of retrospective reports without additional, documented measures of the abuse itself. As Valentino and colleagues (2009) point out, such an approach is inherently flawed inasmuch as the investigators are relying on participants' memories both to identify the abuse and to provide evidence of a memory deficit.

Valentino and colleagues (2009) found that abused children (those who experienced physical or sexual abuse in addition to any emotional abuse and neglect) exhibited more OGMs than either the non-maltreated children or the children who suffered neglect. Moreover, abused children's memories contained more negative self-representations than those of the non-maltreated children, with the neglected children falling somewhere in between these two groups. These effects were still reliable when depression was controlled for and clearly show that abuse is related to both a more general reporting style, and a more negative self-representation, in children's autobiographical memory. Thus, when objective measures of maltreatment are in place, as they were in the Valentino et al. (2009) study, it appears that abuse does lead to the encoding, storage, and retrieval of negative aspects of the environment, including negative self-attributes, in children's autobiographical memory.

Similar findings have been reported from a longitudinal study of memory in children and adolescents exposed to family violence (for a summary, see Greenhoot et al., 2008). These researchers were able to document individual participants' abuse exposure prospectively and found that both early experience with abuse (during childhood) and recent or concurrent stressors both predicted performance on the AMT. Specifically, the children whose abuse experiences started early and whose abuse was ongoing demonstrated an unwillingness to report specific childhood memories. Childhood abuse was also correlated with lower levels of emotional language use and fewer references to emotion in the events that were recollected. These trends were observed not only on the AMT but also on children's and adolescents' untimed answers to questions about past experiences. Of course, reluctance to talk about the past and the frequent omission of emotional components of these memories do not mean that these autobiographical memories do not contain that information. Indeed, when specific probes that elicit emotional information are used as part of a memory interview, maltreated children can and do talk about more negative aspects of their past (e.g., Valentino et al., 2009). Instead, children's reluctance to spontaneously report these aspects of their memories may be more an attempt to regulate their current emotional state than an index of a memory failure.

To summarize, it is clear that the chronic and severe stress associated with childhood maltreatment sets the stage for hypersensitivity to threat and anger cues in the environment, the development of more negative self-schemas, and a reluctance to spontaneously report specific memories of the past in an interview setting. That children exposed to chronic and severe stress do encode, store, and retrieve these traumatic experiences along with all of their emotional overtones is not in question, as plenty of evidence (reviewed in this chapter) exists attesting to their ability to recall such information when asked to do so or when the appropriate cues are provided. That these "deficits" are in reporting and not in memory per se is further substantiated by evidence that there are no differences between maltreated and non-maltreated children when it comes to standard episodic memory tasks. Indeed, Greenhoot et al. (2008) found no differences in performance on a standard paired-associate memory task between children exposed to family violence and non-traumatized children (also see the research reviewed next section in this chapter). These studies also suggest that whatever the effects of chronic and severe stress are on the neural structures and systems underlying declarative memory, they do not translate into differences at the level of memory performance. In the next section, additional studies will be reviewed that demonstrate the resilience of children's memory development even under conditions of being exposed to the chronic and severe stress associated with maltreatment.

BASIC MEMORY PROCESSES AND THEIR DEVELOPMENT UNDER CONDITIONS OF SEVERE AND CHRONIC STRESS

When differences are observed between maltreated and non-maltreated children's general memory functioning, they tend to be limited to comparisons involving maltreated children who have also developed PTSD (e.g., Yasik et al., 2007). As noted earlier in this chapter, research has shown that smaller hippocampal volumes are associated with maltreatment that is comorbid with the development of PTSD; however, this finding has not always been obtained (e.g., DeBellis et al., 2001; Pederson et al., 2004), and even when it is obtained, it is not universally associated with impaired memory (e.g., Gurvits et al., 1996; Neylan et al., 2004). Furthermore, it is not clear whether exposure to severe and chronic stress is the source of smaller hippocampal volumes or whether smaller hippocampal volumes predispose individuals who experience trauma to develop pathological stress reactions such as PTSD (Gilbertson et al., 2002).

Laboratory-based research has shown that when socioeconomic status is controlled for, there are few if any differences between maltreated and non-maltreated children's memories for word lists. For example, Howe et al. (2004) compared maltreated (sexual abuse, physical abuse, emotional abuse, neglect, or any combination of these abusive experiences) and non-maltreated children's memory for lists of semantically related words. Although older children remembered more words than younger children, no differences emerged as a function of maltreatment status.

Howe, Toth, and Cicchetti (in press) wondered whether the absence of differences due to maltreatment status in the Howe et al. (2004) study was an artifact of the type of material (standard, neutral word lists) children were asked to remember. Indeed, if maltreated children are hypersensitive to emotional information, perhaps differences might emerge when children are asked to memorize word lists that are emotionally arousing. Using a similar word-learning procedure, children in the Howe et al. (in press) study were required to remember either emotionally arousing negative words or words that were less arousing, and neutral. Children either learned a single word list (control group) or two lists, one after the other. Half of the children who learned two lists were asked to continue remembering the first list while they also learned the second list (directed-remembering condition). The other half of the group who learned two lists were asked to forget the first list while they tried to learn the second list (directed-forgetting condition). The question of interest that sparked this manipulation was whether maltreated children were as able as non-maltreated children to suppress emotional information. Thus, Howe et al. (in press) examined not only whether emotional information was remembered differently as a function of maltreatment status, but also whether maltreated children could suppress the output of emotional information as easily as non-maltreated children when required to do so.

The findings again revealed the usual age differences in children's memory. More important, regardless of age and maltreatment status, all children were able to inhibit the output of emotional information to the same extent, although the suppression of emotional information was less effective than the suppression of neutral information. Although verbal IQ was positively correlated with children's memory, dissociative symptoms were not related to the amount children recollected or to their ability to suppress the output of emotional or neutral information. Consistent with these findings, Porter, Lawson, and Bigler (2005) have also found that there were no reliable differences in basic memory functioning between sexually abused and non-abused children, despite there being considerable differences in psychopathology and lower performance on measures of attention and executive function for the maltreated than non-maltreated children.

In a final laboratory-based study, Cicchetti and colleagues (2010) administered a standardized test of children's memory, the California Verbal Learning Test–Children (CVLT-C; Delis et al., 1994), to both maltreated and non-maltreated children who were participating in a summer camp. This test provides an evaluation of the strategies and processes children (normed for ages from five through 16 years) use when memorizing and recalling or recognizing verbal material. It is frequently used as a diagnostic tool for the presence of impairments in children's memory functioning. In addition to measuring IQ and dissociation as in the Howe et al. (in press) study, Cicchetti et al. (2010) were also able to collect salivary cortisol over the one-week testing interval. This, of course, is key to examining the link between chronic and severe stress, neurohormonal changes, and children's basic memory processes. For example, hypocortisolism frequently occurs in individuals who have experienced chronic stress (including ongoing maltreatment) and can result in reduced adrenocortical reactivity and secretion as well as an enhanced negative feedback inhibition of the HPA axis (Gunnar & Vazquez, 2001; Heim et al., 2000; Miller et al., 2007). The flattening of the normal diurnal decrease that occurs in cortisol may result in an increased risk for cardiovascular impairment as well as a reduction in the functioning of the immune system (Heim et al., 2008). The negative effects of hypocortisolism may also extend to areas of the brain that are responsible for both memory and cognitive functioning and hence may alter the developmental course of these processes.

Like the other laboratory-based studies of memory, Cicchetti and colleagues (2010) found that child maltreatment by itself neither enhanced nor adversely affected basic memory processes. That is, maltreated children's recall and recognition scores on the CVLT-C did not differ from those of non-maltreated children. Moreover, correct recall and recognition did not fluctuate as a function of differences in dissociation or hypocortisolism (however, cortisol-related differences were found for false memories, and these will be discussed in Chapter 9).

Together, these studies are in agreement that childhood maltreatment does not have negative (or positive) consequences on the development of basic memory processes. Moreover, there is no link between children's memory performance and associated psychopathology, at least as measured in terms of dissociation. Finally, these conclusions do not differ when children are learning neutral stimuli or emotionally arousing stimuli. Thus, although there is little doubt that the neural structures and systems that mediate declarative memory can be affected by severe and chronic stress, the effects do not give rise to changes in maltreated children's memory performance.

Perhaps such differences are not apparent on simple list-learning tasks and only arise in more natural circumstances. To explore this, Eisen and colleagues (2002) investigated maltreated and non-maltreated children's memory and suggestibility concerning an anogenital examination and clinical assessment. Children aged three to 17 years who had been referred to an inpatient hospital unit specialized in the assessment of child abuse and neglect were divided into three groups: (1) an abuse group (children whose sexual and physical abuse was substantiated); (2) a neglect group (children who experienced neglect or whose parents had documented addictions); and (3) a non-abused group (children referred to the clinic but no evidence of abuse was found). Children were administered a standardized sequence of tests of general psychological functioning, stress, memory, and dissociation as well as a questionnaire concerning their memory of the psychological consultation (including a photo-identification test about the clinician who administered the interview).

The results showed the usual age effects, where older children remembered more than younger children. More important, like the laboratory-based research, Eisen and colleagues (2002) found that maltreated children's memory performance was as good as that of the non-maltreated children. Similar follow-up studies have replicated these findings and have also found that maltreated children who scored high in dissociation and whose cortisol levels were higher than non-maltreated children's were more prone to memory errors (Eisen et al., 2007). Although I defer discussion of these and other memory errors, including false memories, until Chapter 9, it is clear from the research reviewed here that the developmental course of basic memory processes is similar in maltreated and non-maltreated children. Furthermore, this conclusion holds even when the memory being studied involves remembering in more natural settings, something that has been confirmed in a variety of different studies (for a recent review, also see Goodman et al., 2010).

EARLY DEPRIVATION AND MEMORY DEVELOPMENT

Finally, an area of childhood maltreatment that has witnessed a recent increase in scientific scrutiny has been the effect of early institutionalization on later cognitive functioning. Because early deprivation may impact plasticity-related processes, including memory and its development (e.g., see Nelson, 2000), it is important to understand the effect of extreme neglect on experience-dependent and experience-expectant processes early in development (Greenough et al., 1987). In addition, we can ask the question as to whether these effects are long-lasting and whether they can be modulated by intervention.

Although a number of projects have looked at the effects of early deprivation on subsequent development, I am going to focus on the two major research studies that have examined these issues in the context of Romanian orphanages. In the first of these, Rutter and his colleagues (e.g., Rutter, 1998, 2006; Rutter et al., 2007a, 2007b, 2010) have monitored the development of children who were adopted from Romania into homes in the United Kingdom (the English and Romanian Adoptees, or ERA, study). In this study, retrospective reports about the children's abilities upon entry into the United Kingdom indicated a significant degree of cognitive impairment at the time of adoption (Rutter et al., 2004). In a follow-up measurement study, most children showed dramatic improvement after adoption, even in the most severely impaired children (Beckett et al., 2006). Later assessments at four, six, and 11 years showed that some cognitive impairment still persisted for a significant number of children, but that children adopted before the age of six months showed the best recovery compared to children adopted later than this age (Beckett et al., 2006; Rutter, 2006; Rutter et al., 2004, 2007a, 2010).

The second research program also concerns the Romanian orphanage children and is known as the Bucharest Early Intervention Project (BEIP; see Zeanah et al., 2003). Unlike the ERA study, BEIP researchers randomly assigned young children living in orphanages (average age 21 months; range seven to 33 months) to one of two conditions—moving to foster care provided by BEIP, or "care as usual" in the Romanian orphanages. Children in this latter group did not all remain in the orphanage for the entire study, with many being adopted within Romania, returned to their biological parents, or placed in government foster care. In essence, then, the comparison was between the effects of high-quality intervention (the BEIP foster care) with the natural course of institutionalized living.

Prior to randomization, institutionalized children showed moderate levels of cognitive impairment compared to control children living in the community, as measured by the Bayley Scales of Infant Development (Smyke et al., 2007). On a follow-up test, children placed in foster care showed higher overall cognitive functioning than those in the "care as usual" group (Nelson et al., 2007). Like the ERA results, the BEIP study showed that the earlier the intervention, the more the improvement, but that even children whose intervention came early still lagged behind a typically developing community sample.

Although these studies examined general cognitive functioning, these tests do include a memory component. From this research, it is clear that early experience is important to both memory and cognition, and that early deprivation due to institutionalization results in lower performance on tests of global cognitive functioning. Although the earlier the intervention the better the outcome, the findings also indicate that not all of the effects of deprivation can be ameliorated, even in the presence of high-quality intervention.

A key to understanding the effects of neglect and abuse on children's memory concerns the age at which the abuse started, the severity of the abuse, and whether and when interventions were instituted that might remediate the impact of maltreatment. Results such as the ones reviewed in this section are highly suggestive that many of the effects of early abuse, in this case neglect, can be remediated if intervention occurs relatively early. Although it is clear that additional research on the effects of early deprivation (neglect) will be critical to understanding the role of experience-dependent and experience-expectant processes in the development of declarative memory, these findings provide some of the first evidence concerning the resilience of memory and cognitive function in the face of neglect and deprivation.

Summary and Conclusions

The evidence reviewed in this chapter, like that in the previous chapter on the effects of acute stress and memory, show that the development of children's basic memory processes is not affected, at least not at the level of performance, by the experience of maltreatment. Although few studies have been published, those that do exist show that regardless of whether maltreated children are given standardized memory tests (e.g., Cicchetti et al., 2010), standard laboratory-based list-learning tasks (Howe et al., 2004, in press), or are tested in more natural settings (Eisen et al., 2002, 2007), their memory performance is essentially no different from that of non-maltreated children. Whatever neurobiological changes have been brought about by the severe and chronic stress that is associated with ongoing maltreatment, these changes do not appear to have affected (enhanced or diminished) maltreated children's declarative memory abilities. This holds true regardless of the nature of the material being remembered, whether it is emotionally arousing or more mundane.

The evidence is also clear that maltreated children can and do remember their abusive experiences. Indeed, like acute stressful and traumatic experiences, children remember the core details of their abusive experiences quite well over time, but not the more peripheral aspects of these experiences (also see Goodman et al., 2003). As Alexander and colleagues (2005) documented in their prospective study of childhood sexual abuse and subsequent memory, despite the passage of some 12 to 21 years since the abuse, most victim's memories were extraordinarily accurate (72% correct with only a 14% rate for errors of commission and the same 14% rate for errors of omission). In fact, the more traumatic the childhood sexual abuse had been, the more accurate the memory was for that abuse. That is, for participants who rated the abuse as the worst thing that happened to them or who had developed PTSD, their memories were among the most accurate.

Of course, the experience of maltreatment, although perhaps not affecting basic memory processes, does affect the content of memory. That abused children can have a more negative self-representation is reflected in what they remember about their experiences (e.g., Valentino et al., 2009). We also saw that maltreated children are often much more sensitive to threatening and fearful stimuli in the environment than are non-maltreated children (Pollak, 2003; Pollak & Kistler, 2002). This differential sensitivity to emotional cues and negative emotions may have considerable adaptive value, as they signal potential threats to survival. Thus, although maltreatment may not adversely affect how memory operates, it can influence the content of abused and neglected children's memories inasmuch as it directs attention to threat-relevant cues in the environment and biases the type of information that is stored by favoring information that is congruent with the children's negative evaluation of themselves.

Although these findings show accurate recollection of traumatic events, perhaps more accurate than memories of more mundane experiences, they also caution that traumatic memory, like all memory, is subject to error (both commission and omission). This will be amply demonstrated in the next chapter, where I consider children's false memory, suggestibility, and susceptibility to misleading information. As it turns out, having experienced childhood maltreatment does not make one any more (or less) vulnerable to memory errors. Indeed, as we will see, maltreated children are no more susceptible to misinformation and suggestion than non-maltreated children, nor are they any more prone to false-memory illusions.

9

Children's False-Memory Illusions

> Memory is a complicated thing, a relative to truth, but not its twin.
> —Barbara Kingsolver, *Animal Dreams*

> The difference between false memories and true ones is
> the same as for jewels: it is always the false ones that look
> the most real, the most brilliant.
> —Salvador Dali

As we have seen throughout this book, memory is a powerful and flexible system that is essential to the young organism's ability to adapt to the environment in which it finds itself. This representational flexibility is something that allows the organism to restructure its knowledge base and update what is in memory, a critical feature linked to its survival. This representational flexibility is accomplished by combining, rewriting, and blending incoming information with information that already exists in storage. However, because memory representation is so flexible, remembering is more a matter of reconstruction than of reproduction, a process that is not completely infallible, and at times can go horribly wrong.

But just how fallible can memory be? At one extreme, people can simply be mistaken about some peripheral aspects of events, either by confusing two similar experiences (e.g., whether they were eating a popsicle or an ice cream cone) or by inferring that something must have happened because it is consistent with their expectations, schemas, or scripts (e.g., inferring but not directly remembering that the bill had been paid at the restaurant they ate at last week). At the other extreme, people can come to believe that entire events have occurred, when in fact they never took place. As we will see, even young children (seven- and eight-year-olds) can come to believe, and later falsely remember, that they had been abducted by aliens (Otgaar et al., 2009).

As mentioned, false recollection is a natural consequence of the reconstructive nature of memory as well as the way in which knowledge (e.g., semantic relations) is structured in the memory system. In particular, because information in memory is organized associatively (Roediger et al., 2001b), containing many different types of semantic relationships (e.g., antonymity, entity, situational, synonymity, taxonomic; see Wu & Barsalou, 2009), once activated, individual concepts can activate other, related concepts. Frequently people have difficulty discriminating information that actually occurred from information they only thought about, including concepts that are activated automatically in the presence of actual information. Subsequently, this related but not presented information comes to be part of one's memory of things that actually happened.

This process is captured in the popular Deese/Roediger-McDermott (DRM) paradigm (Deese, 1959; Roediger & McDermott, 1995) and is part of a more general phenomenon termed *spontaneous false memories*. Here, participants are either shown or read a list of words (e.g., *nap, rest, doze, dream, pillow, bed*) each of which is related to an unpresented word or "critical lure," *sleep*. When later asked to recollect (i.e., recall, recognize) the words that were presented, participants not only remember many of the words that were actually presented, but they also falsely remember the unpresented critical lure. In fact, participants are often more confident that the critical lure was among the presented items than they are about the actual words that were presented. These spontaneous false memories arise because of relatively automatic associative processes, ones that occur as a normal consequence of the way memory operates.

In contrast, *implanted false memories* occur as a consequence of suggestion, and can involve falsely remembering only a part of an autobiographical experience (e.g., actually having been in hospital as a young child, but coming to believe you suffered a broken leg rather than having tonsillitis) or creating an entirely new autobiographical recollection (e.g., coming to believe that as a young child, you had taken a ride in a hot air balloon). Such suggestions can come from others in the form of misinformation (e.g., "Remember when you took a ride in a hot air balloon?" when in fact you have never been in one) or they can be auto-suggested—for example, reading a newspaper report about people who believed they were abducted by a UFO and then ruminating about one's own past to see if anything like that ever happened to you. Although similar associative processes may mediate false recollections in both spontaneous and implanted memory illusions, their developmental courses are very different. That is, in most cases, spontaneous false memories tend to increase with age, so that older children and adults are more prone to this type of false memory illusion than younger children. Implanted false memories, on the other hand, tend to decline with age, as older children and adults are less susceptible to *suggestion* than younger children. However, as we will also see, there are age-related increases in children's ability to construct elaborate implanted memories, ones that, like spontaneous false memories, are contingent on corresponding developments in their knowledge base. Although these age effects are robust, it should be remembered that under the right circumstances, both children and adults can and do form false memories and do so both spontaneously or through implantation.

In what follows, I first review theory and evidence concerning the development of spontaneous false memories in childhood, including some recent developmental research that examines the neural correlates of true and false memory in children (eight- and 12-year-olds). Next, I review the literature on children's implanted false memories of autobiographical events. In both sections, I will first trace the developmental course of memory illusions in typically developing children and then review the evidence for children growing up in stressful and maltreating environments. In the penultimate section of this chapter, I will examine the idea that false memories can also play a positive role in human cognition, having potentially adaptive significance in related tasks (e.g., problem solving), tasks that may be relevant to survival.

Development of Children's Spontaneous False Memories

THE BASIC PHENOMENON AND THEORETICAL ACCOUNTS

The DRM paradigm has figured prominently in research on the development of children's spontaneous false memories. A key finding, and one that runs contrary to what intuition might predict, is that younger children are *less* susceptible to these types of memory illusions than older children and adults. Indeed, younger children (e.g., five-year-olds and younger) are less likely to recall or recognize the critical lure than somewhat older children (e.g., seven-year-olds) who, in turn, are less susceptible to spontaneous false-memory illusions than older children (e.g., 11-year-olds) and adults. Interestingly, then, the course of true memory development and that of the development of susceptibility to spontaneous false memories both increase monotonically with age.

One obvious reason for this developmental increase in spontaneous false memories is that these illusions are contingent on having a well-developed knowledge base, one that contains the associations necessary to generate the critical lure, given presentation of the concepts on the list. Like true recollection, false recollection is contingent on the presence of these concepts in associative memory, as well as on how well integrated and organized these concepts are into cohesive structures in children's declarative memory. If these associations are absent in children's memory or they are poorly organized, then there is no reason to suppose that false memories will arise. As we have already seen, research concerning children's knowledge base shows that, although concepts and the associative links between them may be present at a relatively young age, additional learning and experience further strengthen these associations and refine the memory structure they are embedded in (also see Bjorklund, 1987, 2005; Ceci et al., 2007). This may have been a problem early in this research, because some of the original findings on DRM effects in children used associations that were derived from norms provided by adults and not those for children (for a review, see Brainerd et al., 2008a). This does not mean that adult associations (e.g., *nap* and *sleep*) are not seen in children's knowledge bases, but rather that they are more likely to be present and better structured in older, not younger, children's free associations. If so, then it may not be that younger children are any less susceptible to spontaneous false-memory illusions than older children, it is simply that they do not have the same associative networks in memory as older children and adults.

In order to test this idea, three separate studies were conducted in which children's word-association norms were used to construct DRM lists (Anastasi & Rhodes, 2008; Carneiro et al., 2007; Metzger et al., 2008). In each study, age differences in children's false memories were attenuated, due primarily to younger children's exhibiting more false memories with child-friendly lists than with adult lists. Importantly, despite this attenuated age trend, younger children still produced reliably fewer false memories than older children and adults. So, although the concepts themselves, as well as the links between them, certainly play an important role in the development of false-memory illusions, because age-related differences were not entirely eliminated, this cannot be the whole story.

These outcomes are consistent with two theories concerning the development of children's false-memory illusions: fuzzy-trace theory (FTT; Brainerd & Reyna, 2005; Brainerd et al., 2008a) and associative-activation theory (AAT; Howe, 2005, 2008c; Howe et al., 2009b, 2009c). In FTT, children's memory is organized in terms of two different memory traces—*verbatim* traces that encode the surface features of what has been presented (e.g., phonological, orthographic), and *gist* traces that encode the meaning or thematic structure of what has been presented. Although the ability to extract both traces improves with age in childhood, the improved ability to extract gist is what is mainly responsible for increases in children's false memories. Because the critical lure is related to the general theme of the other list members, it becomes active as part of the gist-extraction process. If child-friendly lists allow children to access the gist more readily than adult lists, then the findings reviewed earlier can be predicted using FTT.

Alternatively, AAT acknowledges the importance of, not only the content and structure of children's developing knowledge base when explaining age-related changes in false-memory illusions (including the number and strength of associative relations), but also changes in how fast and how automatically these associative relations are accessed and activated (Howe & Wilkinson, 2011; Knott et al., in press; Wimmer & Howe, 2009, 2010). Indeed, it has been shown that children's false memories occur less automatically than adults' false memories (e.g., Howe, 2005; Knott et al., in press). For example, when children were instructed to "forget" items on a list that had been studied (Howe, 2005), they, like adults (Kimball & Bjork, 2002), showed decreased recall of items that had actually been presented, relative to children's performance in relevant control conditions (either presentation of a single list with only standard memory instructions, or when two lists were presented and children were instructed to remember both lists). For adults, because false-memory production is thought to be relatively automatic in semantic memory, false-memory rates remained relatively high and comparable to those in the control conditions. However, for children, because false memories are not generated as automatically and are treated like items that appeared on the episodic list, they can be edited when directed-forgetting instructions require them to, and false-memory rates declined like they did for true memories. Thus, children, unlike adults, can suppress the output of false memories when *intentionally* asked to do so during *retrieval*, an indication that their false memories are not as automatic as those of adults (Howe, 2005; Kimball & Bjork, 2002; Knott et al., in press). As noted, this is consistent with AAT, whereas FTT makes no predictions about the development of automaticity and children's false memories.

Perhaps children's, but not adults', false memories can be inhibited when *explicitly instructed to do so during retrieval*, but this does not answer the question of whether children's false memories, like adults', are *automatically generated during encoding*. Research with adults has demonstrated that false memories are produced not only automatically during retrieval, but also during the encoding or generation phase. For example, Dodd and MacLeod (2004), using a Stroop-like DRM task (Stroop, 1935), presented participants with words of different colors, and they were to indicate the color of each word as quickly as possible rather than read the word itself. Unbeknownst to the participants, they were later given a recognition test for the words themselves (an incidental memory test). The result of this test was that true recognition scores were reduced, a finding that is common when incidental memory tests are employed following processing of surface information (color of the word) rather than meaning (the word itself). Critically, there was no reduction in the rate at which adults produced false memories. Additional evidence of the automaticity of false memories during encoding comes from studies in which adults are warned about the false-memory phenomenon before studying DRM lists. Despite being forewarned, adults still falsely remember the critical lure as having been part of the presented list (Gallo et al., 1997, 2001; McDermott & Roediger, 1998). What both of these results show is that adults both *generate* and *retrieve* false memories automatically.

Recently, we have explored these same questions about children's ability to automatically *generate* false memories. For example, Wimmer and Howe (2009; Experiment 1) asked five-, seven-, and 11-year-old children to give a word that was associated with each of the 20 child-friendly words they were given (e.g., *rabbit, wash, long*). Children were given some examples (e.g., "If I say *doctor* you might say *nurse* because they both work in a hospital" or "If I say *cow* you might say *milk* because cows give milk") prior to test in order to ensure that they were familiar with the procedure. The words provided and the times to produce each of the words (generation times) were recorded. Following a brief distraction period, children were given a recognition test that consisted of the 20 items presented to the child (other-generated information), the 20 items each child gave in response to these cue words (self-generated information), and 20 unrelated and unpresented words. For each word on the recognition test, children were to say "no" if the word had not appeared earlier and to say "yes" if the word had appeared earlier. For every "yes" response, children were then asked to indicate whether they had said the word (self-generated information) or whether the experimenter had said the word (other-generated information).

The results showed several important and hitherto unreported findings concerning the growth and restructuring of children's knowledge base as well as changes in the automaticity with which concepts in this knowledge base can be accessed and activated. First, concerning the knowledge base itself, the results showed that, not only did the number of semantically relevant associations increase with age (growth in knowledge base) but the type of association also changed with age. That is, younger children were more likely to produce *syntagmatic* associations (e.g., *dog-bark*) whereas older children were more likely to produce *paradigmatic* associations (e.g., *dog-cat*). This shift in the number and type of associations shows that children's knowledge base is not only growing from five to seven years, but is also being reorganized.

Second, concerning the growth of automaticity, there were two findings that showed that automatic access to and activation of concepts in the knowledge base increased with age. To begin with, across all three age groups, children were better able to correctly recognize and identify the source of other-generated information than information they generated themselves. More important, the speed with which word associates were generated increased significantly with age. In fact, 11-year-olds accessed and activated word associates three times faster than five-year-olds.

In a second experiment, Wimmer and Howe (2009) used a modified DRM paradigm in which children (five-, seven-, and 11-year-olds) were asked to provide the first word that came to mind following the presentation of a list (five-item DRM lists) of associated words (note that, unlike the first experiment, they were not explicitly asked to provide an associate, just the first word that came to mind). The important question here was whether children would spontaneously produce the critical lure and whether this tendency would be stronger for older children who produce false memories with greater frequency. In addition to examining how long it took to generate the first word that came to mind, we also examined children's ability to discriminate between items that were self-generated and those that were other-generated on a later recognition test. Therefore, a second important question in this experiment was whether children's self-generated words became part of the episodic list, making it more difficult for children to discriminate them from the list members actually presented by the experimenter.

The results showed that children's ability to generate meaningful associations and, more importantly, the critical lures, in response to DRM-like lists spontaneously increased with age. In addition, the speed with which these associates were generated increased with age by a factor of three. Interestingly, when children did recognize the critical lure on the recognition test, older children were more likely than younger children to have correctly identified it as something they had generated rather than something that had been presented by the experimenter. Because related research on metamemory has shown that older children (eight-year-olds and older) can reflect on and use source information to edit memory (e.g., Ghetti, 2003), it is not surprising that our older children (11-year-olds) were more likely to correctly identify themselves as the source of the critical lure and not confuse it with the episodically presented information by the experimenter.

Together, these experiments demonstrate that (a) the ability to spontaneously generate meaningful associations increases with age in childhood, (b) the type of associations change with age, and (c) the speed with which meaningful associations are produced increases with age. Thus, not only do the numbers and types of associations change with age in children's knowledge base, but so, too, does the speed with which they are accessed and activated in memory. Consistent with the predictions of AAT, it is not simply the quantitative and qualitative aspects of one's knowledge base that change with age, but also the automaticity with which it can be used. These different aspects of memory development, including increases in false memories, represent both a *domain-specific trajectory* (the concepts themselves that are contained in the knowledge base as well as the way they are organized) and a *domain-general trajectory* (global increases in speed-of-processing regardless of what is being processed). Clearly, the individual concepts, their associative links, and the manner in which they are organized and integrated in memory are domain-specific and depend on a child's experience and exposure to information (e.g., learning in school) (e.g., Bjorklund, 2005; Howe, 2000). What the research has shown is that some of the age differences in children's false memory production are attenuated when the knowledge base for associations is made more child-friendly (Anastasi & Rhodes, 2008; Carneiro et al., 2007; Metzger et al., 2008). What the research by Wimmer and Howe (2009, 2010; also see Howe, 2005; Knott et al., in press) has shown is that these domain-specific changes are not sufficient by themselves to account for all of these age differences. Instead, one must also consider a more global, domain-general change in speed-of-processing and automaticity that occurs as children develop.

There is plenty of evidence supporting the existence of a domain-general component in children's development. For example, children's performance on any number of tasks (e.g., verbal memory, visual search, memory search, mental addition, mental rotation, and mental imagery) improves, and much or all of this improvement can be attributed to increases in speed of processing (e.g., Kail, 1988, 1997). As memory search becomes faster and more automatic, there is every reason to believe that, not only will more correct information be produced during this search, but also more semantically related and active, but unpresented, information will be produced (e.g., false memories). Unless there is an additional filtering mechanism that can edit these false memories from the output queue (e.g., via source monitoring), children's false memory production should increase with age.

There is also neurodevelopmental evidence that supports this distinction between domain-specific and domain-general processing. Concerning domain-general processing, recall from Chapter 3 that the frontal and associative areas of the brain (specifically the prefrontal and lateral temporal areas) are later-maturing, suggesting that higher-order executive and associative functions should show delayed development. These executive control functions are used across a number of different cognitive processing tasks, including memory and, potentially, in the inhibition of false memories. Specifically, these immaturities in the medial temporal lobe (resulting in reduced processing of associative information) and the prefrontal cortex (reduced strategic control during episodic retrieval) may explain age differences in false recollection (Paz-Alonso et al., 2008). Thus, although many of these important domain-general functions may not come online until somewhat later in development, the neurological evidence also clearly shows that children's domain-specific knowledge and associative memory representations develop from birth and mature gradually throughout childhood. In fact, there are clear differences in lifespan neurodevelopment trajectories for domain-specific (e.g., cognitive representation) and domain-general (e.g., cognitive control) functions (see Craik & Bialystok, 2006).

So far, I have discussed three lines of evidence that support AAT's assumption that increases in children's spontaneous false memories are due to both a domain-specific change and a domain-general change: neurodevelopmental findings, children's false memories when child-friendly lists are used, and speed of generating associates in a DRM-like task. Additional evidence comes from two other lines of research. The first of these has investigated the automaticity of children's false memories at *encoding* using a levels-of-processing paradigm and a divided-attention paradigm (Wimmer & Howe, 2010). The second of these concerns a series of three experiments that investigated the automatic inhibition of children's false memories at *retrieval* using a part-set cuing and a retrieval practice procedure, as well as examining controlled inhibition of false memories at retrieval using a directed-forgetting paradigm similar to the one used by Howe (2005) (Knott et al., in press).

Concerning *encoding*, we (Wimmer & Howe, 2010) speculated that if children's generation of false memories occurs automatically during encoding, then disrupting the encoding process, although reducing true recollection, should have little or no impact on false recollection. Using a levels-of-processing manipulation (Experiment 1), we asked children (seven- and 11-year-olds) and adults to either encode DRM lists using deep or meaningful processing (e.g., studying the words themselves as in the standard DRM paradigm or as presented in a meaningful sentence) or using shallow processing of details unrelated to meaning (e.g., color of the list word or counting the number of words in the sentence containing the DRM word). The results showed that these levels-of-processing manipulations had different effects on true and false memory on a subsequent test of recognition. Specifically, whereas true recognition was lower for information that was processed in a shallow context than for that same information processed in a meaningful one, there were no differences for false recognition. Moreover, this basic pattern of results held true regardless of the age of the participant. In other words, children, like adults, generate false memories automatically during the encoding process.

In order to examine the automaticity with which false memories are generated during encoding using a different procedure, we (Wimmer & Howe 2010, Experiment 2) examined the effects of divided attention on children's (seven- and 11-year-olds) and adults' true and false memory rates. Research by Dewhurst and his colleagues (Dewhurst et al., 2005, 2007b; Knott & Dewhurst, 2007) showed that for adults, any secondary task that is resource-consuming during encoding can prevent associative processing and hence may affect false-memory production. Of course, divided-attention tasks used with adults are too demanding for children, so we used a secondary task that required inhibitory processes (Wimmer & Howe, 2010). It is known that younger children have greater difficulty than older children and adults when trying to inhibit irrelevant information (Bjorklund & Harnishfeger, 1995). Hence, the use of an inhibition task should directly interfere with memory processes. What this means is that if children's and adults' false memories are derived from automatic associative processes, whereas true memories are a product of conscious processing, then the divided-attention manipulation should affect true but not false memories.

In our second experiment, children and adults were required to perform the Day-Night Stroop task (Gerstadt et al., 1994; Simpson & Riggs, 2005) on half of the DRM study trials. Here, while studying words on DRM lists, participants also had to press a dark blue button on a keyboard in response to a daytime scenario that appeared on a computer screen (yellow sun and white background), and press a yellow button in response to a night scenario that appeared on the screen (white stars and moon with a dark blue background). This requires participants to inhibit a prepotent response. The results showed that dividing attention decreased true recognition but had no effect of false recognition, and these effects were age-invariant. These results, together with those from Experiment 1, provide strong evidence that despite age differences in the number of false memories generated by children and adults, that when false memories are produced, they are generated automatically during encoding for both children and adults.

Although these experiments demonstrate that the processing leading to the *generation* of false memories is relatively automatic in children and adults, there are developmental differences in automatic processing after false memories have been created (recall the studies by Howe, 2005, and by Kimball & Bjork, 2002). These latter results indicate that children, unlike adults, treat related but unpresented information as part of the episodic list and can intentionally suppress their output like they can with items that had actually been presented. Thus, despite children's false-memory generation being automatic, the outputs of this process may be subject to later conscious control.

However, automaticity at retrieval may depend on whether incidental or intentional inhibitory processes are activated during testing. Specifically, when retrieval inhibition occurs incidentally without a person's awareness (e.g., as in part-set cuing and retrieval practice paradigms), then both children's and adults' false memory rates should decline. For intentional inhibition (i.e., as in the directed-forgetting paradigm), because adults' semantic activation of information during retrieval occurs more automatically than it does in children, only children's false memory rates should be affected by intentional attempts to inhibit recall (Howe, 2005; Kimball & Bjork, 2002).

In order to examine this idea in more detail, Knott et al. (in press, Experiment 2) used the part-set cuing procedure. Here, participants studied DRM lists, and later during testing were either given some of the words on the list before being asked to recall the rest of the words, or were simply allowed to recall each list without the part-set cues. This procedure was developed, in part, based on the observation that participants often falsely remember the critical lure near the end of their output stream. What this suggests is that false memories can be induced at test—that is, the act of recalling items that were presented on a DRM list may in itself activate the critical lure during the recall process and cause it to be falsely remembered during the test session itself (presumably even if it was not automatically generated during encoding). However, the part-set cuing procedure has produced the opposite effects with adults. That is, rather than facilitating the production of false memories, part-set cuing led to a decrease in false recall (Dewhurst et al., 2009; Reysen & Nairne, 2002). Knott and colleagues (in press, Experiment 2) used the part-set cuing procedure with children (five-, seven-, and 11-year-olds) and adults and varied the type of associations across lists. Some lists were associative (DRM lists) and some were taxonomic (categorized lists). The results showed the same outcome as previous research. Regardless of age or list type, part-set cuing reduced the amount of false recall. Although adults falsely recalled more than children, the reduction in false recollection due to the part-set cuing was the same regardless of age.

In a follow-up experiment, Knott et al. (in press, Experiment 3) used a different technique to investigate the effects of testing on false memories in both children's (five-, seven-, and 11-year-olds) and adults' false recall rates. In this retrieval-practice paradigm, participants were shown a series of DRM lists and were then given either free recall instructions with no cues, part-set cues prior to recall, or a word-stem completion task for some of the items to be retrieved (in a manner similar to the part-list cues) prior to recall. Word stems consisted of the first two or three letters of each word, depending on word length. After hearing the word stem, participants were asked to complete the stem using a word from the list they had just heard. Like the part-list cue procedure, cuing remembering with word stems reduced the amount of false recall relative to the free recall control condition. Indeed, this reduction in false recall was similar in magnitude for both children and adults. Thus, when retrieval inhibition occurs *incidentally* (outside of a person's awareness and conscious control) due to cuing during the test phase, children's and adults' false memories are reduced. The question that was addressed in our next experiment was whether similar effects pertain when retrieval inhibition occurs *intentionally*.

To examine this question, we (Knott et al., in press, Experiment 1) set out to replicate our earlier findings for directed forgetting (Howe, 2005), but this time for both children (seven-year-olds) and adults in the same experiment. Here, participants were presented DRM lists and given themes that identified the central meaning or gist of each list, prior to studying the lists. This priming at encoding was used to enhance children's and adults' identification of the lists' gist in order to increase false-memory rates. Interestingly, relative to a standard DRM condition without thematic cuing, regardless of age, participants who received thematic cues generated more false memories, and as expected these effects were larger for children than adults. More importantly, for participants who received the directed-forgetting instructions, true recall rates were lower than those in the control and directed-remembering conditions, regardless of age. For false recall, rates were lower in the directed-forgetting condition for children, but there were no differences for adults relative to the control and directed-remembering groups.

Together, these findings show that children, like adults, exhibit decreases in false memory rates as a result of incidental inhibition of retrieval during testing, both when part-set cues are presented and when retrieval practice is given prior to recall. Moreover, it is clear that although children produce fewer false memories than adults, both children and adults generate their false memories during the encoding process and do so relatively automatically. Age differences seem to exist only when intentional inhibition instructions are given during testing. Here, for children, false items behave as if they were part of the episodic list and can be successfully inhibited when the task requires the children to do so. Such conscious control of false recollection is not always seen in adults, although it is clear that false items can become a part of their conscious awareness, too (McDermott, 1997). Thus, for adults, spontaneous false memories are generated and retrieved automatically, but for children, although false memories may be generated automatically and are subject to incidental retrieval inhibition, automaticity at retrieval, at least in terms of intentional or controlled retrieval processing, undergoes a more protracted period of development.

Many of these results can be accounted for by both AAT and FTT. Both theories converge on the importance of children's knowledge base to changes in the development of the susceptibility to spontaneous false memories. However, it is only AAT that makes predictions about developmental differences in the controlled and automatic inhibition of false information that occurs at retrieval but not encoding. Indeed, any model that accounts for changes in false-memory production with age must contain appropriate assumptions about the development of both domain-specific (e.g., knowledge base) as well as domain-general (e.g., automaticity and speed of processing) features of memory and its development. Clearly, the development of spontaneous false memories depends on the content and organization of children's knowledge base, as well as changes in the speed and automaticity with which children can access and activate concepts and their associative structures in memory.

THE ROLE OF EMOTION IN CHILDREN'S SPONTANEOUS FALSE MEMORIES

There are some very obvious yet important forensic questions that may be answered using the outcomes reviewed in the previous section. However, the relevance of these studies has been questioned—particularly the ecological validity of research that uses simple word lists to study false memories (e.g., Freyd & Gleaves, 1996; Pezdek & Lam, 2007; but see Wade et al., 2007). The first of these ecological validity problems concerning children's spontaneous false memories has to do with how they map onto false memories in the "real world." Although it can be agreed that the DRM procedure is an effective tool when studying the basic memory processes involved in spontaneous memory illusions, forensically relevant false memories frequently involve emotions and are not usually based on affectless associations studied using the DRM method. In order to more closely approximate emotional content in false-memory illusions, researchers have devised lists that are more emotional in nature.

As we saw in the previous chapters, the role of emotion in memory is not straightforward. For example, it may be that, because emotional materials are distinctive, they are more likely to be processed at an item-specific rather than a relational level in memory. That is, the arousal associated with valence may lead to enhanced binding of information in memory, something that increases item-specific memory (e.g., see Mather, 2007). This should improve memory for the item itself and not the context in which it appeared. Moreover, because the processing is at an item-specific level, relational processing is minimized, something that is known to increase true recollection and reduce false memories (e.g., Ghetti et al., 2002; Howe, 2008b).

In the first study of its kind with children, Howe (2007) presented eight- and 12-year-olds with both neutral (e.g., lists with the critical lures *chair, fruit,* and *sweet*) and negative (e.g., lists with the critical lures *anger, cry,* and *lie*) DRM lists. As usual, older children exhibited higher rates of true and false recall than younger children. More importantly, regardless of age, children's true and false recall were higher for neutral information than for negative information. These data also showed that age differences in false recall were larger for neutral than for negative emotional items.

Although these results appear to support the item-specific processing hypothesis, it turns out that they do not. That is, consistent with this hypothesis, false recall levels for critical lures were lower for emotional than for neutral lists. However, inconsistent with this hypothesis, so, too, were true recall rates. Critically, when false alarm rates were calculated for children's recognition scores, the opposite pattern emerged. That is, false alarm rates for critical lures were higher for emotional than non-emotional lists. Thus, although children were better at recalling neutral than emotional information (both true and false), false recognition rates were higher for negative than for neutral information.

These findings have been replicated and extended in our recent series of five experiments (Howe et al., 2010b). In addition to examining true and false memories of emotional information in children and adults, we looked at the persistence of true and false information over time. This additional line of inquiry was prompted by two different kinds of research. First is the finding that false memories persist over retention intervals of varying length. For example, false recall has been found to exceed true recall over intervals of two or more days (McDermott, 1996), and similar results have been obtained for recognition (e.g., Seamon et al., 2002). That true recollection declines over time while false recollection persists is a robust phenomenon that has been obtained in studies with adults (McDermott, 1996; Seamon et al., 2002; Thapar & McDermott, 2001; Toglia et al., 1999) and with children (Brainerd et al., 1995).

A second key finding is that memory for emotional information has been found to be superior to memory for neutral information when tested days, rather than minutes, after study (e.g., LaBar & Cabeza, 2006). This finding is consistent with a number of neurobiological studies that show increases in the recollection of emotional material over time (e.g., Sharot et al., 2007), and it may be linked to differences in consolidation trajectories for emotional and neutral information (see Chapters 7 and 8). It may be that both true and false recollection of emotional information benefits from differences in consolidation over neutral material.

To test this, my colleagues and I (Howe et al., 2010b, Experiments 3–5) had children and adults study neutral and negative emotional DRM lists. Following a test of recall, we gave participants either a recognition test immediately or following a one-week retention interval. The results showed that adults and older children remembered more true and false information than younger children, and that for recall (like Howe, 2007), neutral material was better remembered than emotional information. Also (consistent with Howe, 2007), children and adults falsely recognized more emotional than neutral critical lures. Concerning immediate versus delayed recognition, the results were very clear: regardless of age, true recognition rates declined over the one-week interval regardless of whether the information was neutral or emotional, false recognition rates for neutral information remained unchanged, and false recognition rates for emotional information actually *increased* over time. Consistent with speculation about differences in the consolidation patterns of neutral and emotional material, false memories for negative information increased over time, whereas there was no change for neutral information. That true recognition rates declined over time regardless of valence is consistent with other research in which pure-list (all emotional words) rather than mixed-list (some neutral and some emotional) designs have been used to study memory and emotion (e.g., Comblain et al., 2004). Similar results have been obtained for *implanted* false memories, as will be seen later in this chapter. That negative false memories "grow" over time—both *spontaneous* and *implanted* memory illusions—is somewhat disconcerting, at least from a forensic perspective.

Although this research has shown that emotion is important in memory, particularly to the creation and retention of spontaneous false memories, it is not clear whether this is due to valence, arousal, or both. Remember from earlier chapters, arousal was thought to be a key ingredient in memory for emotional information, particularly as it affected consolidation. In the experiments just reviewed, both valence and arousal were confounded, so it is difficult to tell which one is most important to spontaneous false memories in children, or whether they both are. To help resolve this matter, Brainerd and colleagues (2010) separated arousal and valence and created DRM lists that were high in arousal and positive (e.g., with critical lures such as *love, pretty,* and *baby*); high in arousal and negative (e.g., with critical lures such as *dead, anger, hurt*); low in arousal and positive (e.g., with critical lures such as *nice, soft,* and *sleep*); or low in arousal and negative (e.g., with critical lures such as *trash, fat,* and *shy*). Children (seven- and 11-year-olds) and adults were presented with lists of each type followed by a recognition test. The usual age effects were obtained for both true and false recognition. Importantly, there was a large effect for valence and a more modest effect for arousal. That is, negative lists resulted in higher false-memory rates than positive lists, regardless of arousal, and this valence difference increased with age. That valence trumps arousal in false-memory production is consistent with other findings for adults (e.g., Brainerd et al., 2008b). Thus, at the level of memory performance, negative valence is more important than level of arousal, at least when it comes to children's and adults' spontaneous false-memory illusions.

THE EFFECTS OF STRESS AND MALTREATMENT ON CHILDREN'S SPONTANEOUS FALSE MEMORIES

The second ecological validity problem concerning children's spontaneous false memories has to do with the participants being tested. Oftentimes, complainants in legal cases come from lower socioeconomic backgrounds or perhaps from circumstances that may involve neglect or abuse. It is not clear whether we should generalize our false memory research with children who are from more typical, middle-class backgrounds, to populations that may have actually experienced maltreatment.

As discussed in the last chapter, true recollection in maltreated populations does not differ substantially from true recollection in non-maltreated populations. The question here is whether this holds true for spontaneous false memories. The first study to address this question using a standard DRM paradigm was by my colleagues and I (Howe et al., 2004). We examined both maltreated and non-maltreated children's (five- to 12-year-olds') true and false recall and recognition for neutral lists. The usual age effects were obtained but there were no differences in the rate of false recall and recognition as a function of maltreatment status.

Cicchetti et al. (2010) obtained similar results using a standardized test of verbal recollection, the CVLT-C. Although there were no differences between maltreated and non-maltreated children in true and false recollection rates, differences did emerge as a consequence of variations in neuroendocrine regulation. Specifically, the subgroup of maltreated children who exhibited low levels of morning cortisol was also more susceptible to spontaneous false memories on a recognition test. The importance of neuroendocrine regulation to false recognition rates was clear even when age of onset of maltreatment, the number of developmental periods during which maltreatment was experienced, the recency of maltreatment, and the distinct number and subtypes of maltreatment that had been experienced were controlled. These are the first results to show that the form of cortisol dysregulation known as *hypocortisolism* (see Chapter 8) can exert negative effects on memory accuracy.

As discussed in Chapter 8, perhaps memory differences, in this case differences in false memory rates, between maltreated and non-maltreated children are less apparent with neutral materials but would become more apparent when emotional materials are studied. We (Howe et al., in press) examined this using a directed-forgetting instruction and neutral as well as emotionally negative DRM lists. Maltreated and non-maltreated children (six- to 12-year-olds) learned either a single DRM list or two DRM lists and were instructed to forget the first list or remember both lists in the same paradigm we used before (Howe, 2005). The results showed that like the middle-class children we studied in 2005, both maltreated and non-maltreated children could suppress the output of both true and false memories and did so regardless of valence. Although neutral information was easier to suppress at output than emotional information, all of the children were successful at inhibiting the output of both types of information. Thus, even when emotional information is used, patterns of spontaneous false recollection are similar, regardless of maltreatment status (also see Valentino et al., 2008). As discussed next, similar conclusions can be drawn about *implanted* false memories.

Development of Children's Implanted False Memories

Implanted or suggested false-memory research also addresses an ecological validity concern, inasmuch as these studies have examined memory illusions that involve a portion of an event that has been experienced or the implantation of an entire event that was never experienced. To be clear, although implanted memories may arise because of some external suggestion or misinformation, the basic principles remain the same as those for spontaneous false memories.

That is, the development of false memories, implanted or spontaneous, depends on one's knowledge base, its organization, and the ease and speed with which information can be accessed and activated. These similarities will become obvious in what follows.

As a general rule, younger children are more susceptible to suggestion than older children and adults, although regardless of age almost everyone is susceptible to suggestion and misinformation to varying degrees. To study suggestibility effects, participants are presented with an event (e.g., a video of an event such as a theft, or a live enactment of an event such as a magic show), followed by a retention interval that may involve the presentation of misinformation (often in the form of misleading questions), followed by a memory test (either recall or recognition). When compared to a control condition in which the retention interval does not involve the presentation of misinformation, participants in the suggestibility condition tend to adopt the misinformation and later report it as having been part of the witnessed event (for a review of the early literature on children's suggestibility, see Ceci & Bruck, 1993, 1995). Indeed, misinformation can become incorporated into children's and adults' reports of relatively commonplace events they have witnessed (e.g., watching a film about two people interacting), more traumatic events they have witnessed (e.g., watching a film about a traffic accident), as well as for events that they have participated in (e.g., a medical examination). Alterations in memory are more easily made for peripheral aspects of events but can also change what people remember about core details (e.g., Bruck et al., 1995).

Not only can reports about events that have actually been experienced be influenced by suggestion, but we can also implant entire events that have never been experienced. Indeed, children and adults are able to give highly detailed accounts of events that have never taken place. For example, both children (Pezdek & Hodge, 1999) and adults (see Loftus, 1993) can come to believe that they were lost in a shopping mall when they were young when in fact they had never had such an experience. These descriptions begin somewhat sparsely but with time they develop into very rich and detailed narratives.

Like the suggestibility paradigm, the procedure used to implant memories is very straightforward. Here, children (or adults) are presented with a false event narrative (e.g., being lost in a shopping mall) or a doctored photograph depicting an event (e.g., a picture of the child in a hot air balloon) that is said to have happened to them when in fact it did not (e.g., Pezdek & Hodge, 1999; Wade et al., 2002). Following presentation of this fictitious information, participants are encouraged to "remember" as much as they can about the event. These fictitious events are "remembered" along with events that actually happened, as revealed to the experimenters by the children's parents. In this way, researchers can compare narratives for both actual and false memories.

One variable that has been examined and is claimed to make implantation easier is plausibility (see Pezdek & Hodge, 1999). That is, events that are more plausible (i.e., one could have been lost in a shopping mall) are said to be easier to implant than events that are less plausible (e.g., it is not very likely that one was born on the moon). For example, Pezdek and Hodge (1999) found it easier to implant memories in children for having been lost in a shopping mall than for having experienced a rectal enema.

As it turns out, it is not clear whether the critical feature of this manipulation is plausibility or familiarity. That is, children may be more familiar with, or have more knowledge about, shopping malls than enemas. Research with adults in which these two variables have been disentangled has shown that plausibility and knowledge can both contribute separately to the creation of false memories (Scoboria et al., 2004). Furthermore, research with adults has shown that the absence of knowledge about an event can be used as a basis for rejecting the claim that the event has happened, and hence, cannot serve as the basis of a false recollection (e.g., Ghetti, 2008; Mazzoni & Kirsch, 2002). Because these metamemory judgments are not made as easily by children (e.g., Ghetti & Alexander, 2004), it may be the case that they will form false memories for an event which they have little or no knowledge about.

Recent evidence has shown that for children, event plausibility is not always critical in the creation of false memories. For example, Otgaar and colleagues (2009) found that children (seven- to 12-year-olds) easily created false memories for an implausible event; namely, being abducted by a UFO. Children were asked to recall information about events that actually happened to them (as confirmed by their parents) as well as to "remember" an event that did not happen to them (again, as confirmed by their parents), given a false narrative about an incident that occurred when they were four years old. The false incident was either plausible (i.e., choked on a candy) or implausible (i.e., abducted by a UFO). Half of the children were also given prevalence information about both a true and a false event in the form of a newspaper article that suggested that the event in question (e.g., UFOs being spotted in their town) happened quite frequently during the year in which that child was four years old. The results showed that across two interviews (separated by a week), event plausibility did not affect the development of false memories. That is, children were as likely to create a false memory for "choking on a candy" as they were for "being abducted by a UFO." Although prevalence information affected younger but not older children's willingness to create false memories initially, these effects were not observed during the second interview. Overall, younger children were more susceptible to implantation than older children.

Interestingly, the Otgaar et al. (2009) study accords well with previous research showing that it is not until around eight or nine years of age that children begin to use plausibility in a manner similar to adults when evaluating the veracity of event memories (Ghetti & Alexander, 2004). However, plausibility was still confounded with familiarity. That is, it is likely that children knew more about candies than they did about UFOs, so it is not clear whether the observed effects were due to plausibility, to knowledge, or to both plausibility and knowledge.

To address this question, Otgaar and colleagues (2010) held event plausibility constant while varying event knowledge. Specifically, in a pilot study, a separate group of children rated "receiving a rectal enema" and "fingers caught in a mouse-trap," the two false memory events, as equally plausible, but provided more idea units for getting their "fingers caught in a mousetrap" (high-knowledge event) than for "receiving a rectal enema" (low-knowledge event) when they were asked to provide a narrative about these events. In the experiment, half of the children (seven- and 11-year-olds) were given the standard implantation procedure, and the remaining children were given a more detailed instructional narrative about the false events. Approximately one quarter of the children reported a false memory at both interviews, and there were no age differences in the rates at which children developed false memories. More importantly, children were more likely to create false memories for high-knowledge events (mousetrap) than low-knowledge events (enema). Manipulating additional sug-gestive details in the instructional narratives did not affect (increase or decrease) the probability of developing an implanted false memory.

What these studies make clear is that, like spontaneous false memories, implanted false memories depend on the development of children's knowledge base. Although plausibility may play a role in the development of implanted false memories for older children and adults, it is not as important a variable in the creation of false memories for younger children. However, regardless of age, event knowledge is critical to the establishment of false memories and, as dis-cussed next, part of this event knowledge concerns the emotion that is associ-ated with the to-be-implanted memory.

THE ROLE OF EMOTION IN CHILDREN'S IMPLANTED FALSE MEMORIES

Many of the events used to create implanted memories in children and adults are relatively innocuous (for a review, see Garry & Gerrie, 2005). For example, Strange, Sutherland, and Garry's (2006) target event was having a cup of tea with the British royal family. Others have used what might be considered an arousing event, but one that is positive (e.g., a ride in a hot air balloon; see Wade et al., 2002). Of course, most forensic cases in which questions about false memories arise usually involve negative events (e.g., physical and sexual abuse) and so the extent to which findings from studies such as these are generalizable to the courtroom has been questioned. There is a handful of studies that have examined how easy it is to implant or modify more negative and potentially traumatic memories, although most have been conducted with adults. For example, Hyman, Husband, and Billings (1995) found that adults were equally likely to develop false memories of a negative event as of a positive event. Other, more recent research using misinformation and implantation procedures have shown that negative information can *increase* susceptibility to false-memory illusions (e.g., Nourkova et al., 2004; Porter et al., 2003). These findings are consistent with the DRM outcomes from our (Howe et al., 2010b) series of five experiments reviewed earlier, at least for the results of the recognition test.

One explanation for these counterintuitive findings is that, although the intense emotion associated with negative information can lead to the creation of a memory that is better recalled over time, this emotion does not protect memory from distortion and can actually increase one's susceptibility to false-memory illusions (e.g., Porter et al., 2008). This paradoxical negative emotion (PNE) hypothesis is consistent with an evolutionary perspective inasmuch as it would be adaptive (i.e., enhance survival by avoiding future dangers) to incorporate relevant information about negative events from other reliable sources (also see the section "Potential Benefits and Adaptive Significance of False Memories" later in this chapter).

Although the PNE explanation may account for memories of negative experiences in adults, can it also predict children's recollection of, and susceptibility to, false-memory illusions of negative events? To date, only one study has been published in which children have served as the participants (Otgaar et al., 2008). Using a standard implantation paradigm, children (seven-year-olds) were provided with narratives about true events as well as two false events that had been independently rated as equally plausible but differing in valence: a neutral scenario (i.e., moving to another classroom) and a negative event (i.e., being accused by the teacher of copying off your neighbor). Some of the children were also given photographs of their class from the previous year in order to assist in the induction procedure. The results showed that although the presence or absence of a class photograph did not affect children's susceptibility to false-memory illusions, negative events were easier to implant than neutral ones. Thus, as in adults, negative events are more likely to give rise to false-memory illusions in children than neutral events, at least when using an implanted-memory paradigm.

THE EFFECTS OF STRESS AND MALTREATMENT ON CHILDREN'S IMPLANTED FALSE MEMORIES

That negative events are more sensitive to memory implantation techniques than neutral memories answers one ecological validity concern; but the question remains, are children who have been exposed to more negative events (i.e., maltreatment) and the chronic stress that this entails, any more or less susceptible to false-memory illusions when presented with misinformation? We saw earlier that they were no more or less susceptible to spontaneous false memories, but are they more or less likely than non-maltreated children to succumb to suggestion?

Although there is no published research that has examined maltreated children's susceptibility to implanted memories, there is work on maltreated children's susceptibility to suggestion and misleading information. For example, Eisen et al. (2002) examined maltreated and non-maltreated children's suggestibility concerning an anogenital examination at a hospital and found no differences in their rates of accepting misinformation (see Chapter 8). Eisen et al. (2007) used a similar misinformation procedure and also found no differences in children's (three- to 16-year-olds') suggestibility as a function of maltreatment status. They did, however, obtain some results similar to Cicchetti et al.'s (2010) findings using spontaneous false memories. Specifically, Eisen et al. (2007) found that cortisol level and trauma symptoms were associated with increased memory errors, but only in children who scored higher on dissociative tendencies and not those who scored low on measures of dissociation. Interestingly, unlike some reports concerning memory accuracy in adults (e.g., Alexander et al., 2005), Eisen et al. (2007) found no association between memory accuracy or memory errors as a function of whether children were also suffering from PTSD.

Given these and other results reviewed in this chapter, as well as those reviewed in the immediately preceding chapters, it is apparent that differences in memory performance (both accuracy and errors) are difficult to attribute to maltreatment status. Although neurobiological evidence suggests that the chronic stress associated with child abuse can influence brain structures and systems related to true and false declarative memory, studies of memory performance itself have routinely failed to turn up maltreatment-related changes. Indeed, regardless of whether one is measuring false-memory illusions that occur spontaneously or those that are due to implanting information in memory, maltreated children are no more or less susceptible to these illusions than non-maltreated children.

Potential Benefits and Adaptive Significance of False Memories

It was suggested earlier that perhaps false memories are not as bad as they have been made out to be in the extant literature. Although they clearly lead to inaccuracies about autobiographical experiences, there may also be a positive side to such memory illusions. Indeed, to the extent that true and false memories can be generated through the same spreading activation mechanisms in associative memory, true and false memories may have similar positive benefits on other, related tasks.

For example, Porter et al.'s (2008) PNE hypothesis comes out of a very adaptive consideration; namely, that negative memories can be updated more readily than neutral memories. That is, because survival may depend on avoiding negative or dangerous situations in the future, additional information might be more readily incorporated in such memories than in memories for more mundane and less dangerous events. This additional information, although false with respect to the experiences we have had, nonetheless serves to help us avoid life-threatening circumstances.

Howe and Derbish (2010) have made a similar suggestion. They argue that information that is either survival-related or information that is processed for its survival relevance not only yields better true recollection but is also more susceptible to false-memory illusions. It has been argued that processing information for its survival value rather than for some other purpose (e.g., assessing its pleasantness) makes that information easier to remember later. For example, Nairne, Thompson, and Pandeirada (2007) found that when adults were presented with a set of everyday concepts (e.g., *apple, hammer, dog*), participants who evaluated their importance to a survival scenario (e.g., how important or useful each word is if you had been stranded on a desert island and needed to survive until rescued) remembered more of the words than participants who rated these same words for their pleasantness. Others have extended this to other encoding domains, including rating information for how important it is personally, and have also found that independent of the type (or depth) of semantic processing, items rated for survival are better remembered than items rated for anything else (Kang et al., 2008; Nairne et al., 2008; Weinstein et al., 2008) (also see Chapter 10).

Although much of the research on this recently dubbed *adaptive memory* effect has focused on accuracy, Nairne and colleagues (2007) did find higher rates of semantic intrusions in the survival-processing condition than the other rating conditions. This suggests that survival-related information, while better remembered, is not necessarily more accurate as it may be more prone to semantic intrusions, much like those seen in spontaneous false memories using the DRM paradigm. Indeed, when Howe and Derbish (2010) asked participants to rate DRM lists that were important to survival (e.g., lists with critical lures such as *death, fight, pain*), equally arousing and negative lists (e.g., lists with critical lures such as *sad, lie, bad*), or lists that were relatively neutral (e.g., lists with critical lures such as *money, mountain, school*) either for their relevance to survival, moving to a new house, or pleasantness, they found that survival-related processing produced the best recollection. Moreover, they found that survival-relevant words were better remembered than other words, independent of the type of processing. Thus, processing items for their survival value as well as survival relevant items themselves are better remembered. However, this advantage came at a cost—that is, items processed for survival as well as survival items themselves were more susceptible to the false-memory illusion.

Although these findings make it clear that the "adaptive memory" phenomenon occurs with adults, is there any evidence that children also exhibit this adaptive memory effect? To date, only one study has been conducted with children (Otgaar & Smeets, 2010, Experiment 2). Participants (eight- and 11-year-olds) were asked to rate neutral DRM lists for their survival relevance, relevance to moving house, or pleasantness using a seven-point "smiley scale" (where the smallest "smiley" indicated irrelevance/unpleasantness and the largest "smiley" indicated maximum relevance/pleasantness). Following a distractor task, children were then asked to recall as many of the words as possible. The results showed that like adults', children's true and false recall rates were higher for survival-rating conditions than for the other conditions.

Although the theoretical mechanisms underlying these results are similar to those for other spontaneous false memories observed with both children and adults (also see Howe & Derbish, 2010), the question arises as to why adaptive memory would favor both better recollection of what was present as well as greater spreading activation to neighboring, semantically related information in one's knowledge base that was not presented. What Howe and Derbish (2010) suggested is that activating other survival-relevant knowledge in memory may contribute to one's survival. That is, the rapid spread of activation in memory may serve to prime one's attention to critical aspects of the environment, aspects that may be critical to the detection of things that could be important in escaping danger. Therefore, it is not that false memories themselves are adaptive, but rather, that the rapid and automatic activation of related information that can prime attention for survival-relevant stimuli in the environment may be. Indeed, if one is faced with a predator, it may be adaptive (i.e., enhance survival) if memory can prime one's attention to look for routes of escape, places to hide, weapons for defense, and so forth. That the byproduct of this rapid spreading activation may be a false recollection is a small price to pay for one's continued survival.

Alternatively, false recollection itself may be adaptive. For example, it may be adaptive to falsely recollect the presence of a predator despite only having seen signs (e.g., the predator's tracks, feces) that the predator must have visited that location (e.g., a watering hole) earlier. The individual most likely to survive a subsequent trip to that location may be the one that behaves more cautiously, having misremembered the predator, than the one who remembers accurately that only the signs of a predator had been present earlier. Thus, the tendency to misremember may serve to warn the individual not only about additional hazards that exist currently in the environment, but also about those that can threaten their survival in the future.

Interestingly, there is evidence that the ability to solve problems in a survival-related context is a crucial evolutionary trait (e.g., see Leach & Ansell, 2008). Perhaps an increase in survival-related false memories may not be maladaptive if it helps subsequent problem-solving. Recently, my colleagues and I (Howe, et al., 2010a) have demonstrated that false memories, like true memories, can prime insight-based problem-solving in adults. We gave participants a series of compound remote associates tasks where they had to come up with a single word (e.g., *tree*) that served to integrate the meaning of three other words that had been presented (e.g., *apple, family, house*). For half of the problems, participants had first studied DRM lists where the critical lure was also the solution to the subsequent problems that were presented. For the remaining half of the problems, no prior DRM list was presented. The results showed that for the lists where the critical lure had been falsely remembered, problem solutions were not only more likely but they also occurred more rapidly than for unprimed problems or problems where DRM lists had been presented but the critical lure was not falsely remembered. Recently, similar results have been obtained with children (11-year-olds) (Howe et al., 2011). Thus, like true memories (McDermott, 1997), false memories can serve to prime solutions to insight-based problems in both children and adults.

Although research on the usefulness of false memories is in its infancy, the results obtained to date indicate that both children and adults exhibit the so-called adaptive memory effect. That is, survival-related materials as well as survival-related processing of information results in better true recollection but also in a greater susceptibility to false-memory illusions. The usefulness of survival-related false memories is still speculative, but the theoretical underpinnings are well established. Current and future research in this area is extending our understanding of both the usefulness of false memories in other, problem-solving behaviors, as well as to how useful these memories are in facilitating children's and adults' survival-related problem solutions.

Summary and Conclusions

FINDINGS RECAPITULATED

Children, like adults, are susceptible to both spontaneous and implanted false-memory illusions. Concerning spontaneous false memories, younger children are less susceptible to these illusions than older children and adults. Indeed, this is probably true for any knowledge-base relevant memory phenomenon involving either true or false recollection. Although true and false memories can sometimes be manipulated in opposite directions, oftentimes as true memories increase, so, too, do false memories (also see Wimmer & Howe, 2010). As we saw, this was particularly true when examining the adaptive-memory effect.

Implanted and suggested memories are sometimes more frequent in younger children than in older children and adults, particularly as younger children may be more compliant with interviewers than older children and adults. However, for implanted false memories where knowledge base plays a key role, older children may be more likely to construct entire events that have never happened. Unfortunately, this research is also in its infancy, and our understanding of how children's knowledge base varies systematically with age and its relationship to the content of implanted memories is only just beginning.

The evidence in this chapter has also indicated that emotion, particularly negative emotion, plays an important role in false-memory formation, one that may seem counterintuitive. Specifically, false memories of negative events are easier to implant in both children and adults. Although true memory for negative information may, under certain circumstances, be better than for neutral or even positive information, it is clear that both spontaneous false memories (at least in terms of recognition measures, see Howe, 2007; Howe et al., 2010b) and implanted false memories (Otgaar et al., 2008) are more likely as well. There may be a particular advantage to this association between true and false memories for negative and survival-related information, one that relates directly to the adaptive function of memory (see Howe & Derbish, 2010; Porter et al., 2008).

Finally, the chronic stress associated with maltreatment has not been shown to adversely affect children's susceptibility to false-memory illusions. Maltreatment status is unrelated to changes in rates of spontaneous false recollection and suggestibility, even when emotional materials and events have been examined. Although there is the suggestion that childhood dissociation may be related to lower accuracy and that hypocortisolism is related to higher rates of spontaneous false memories, maltreatment status by itself does not predict higher (or lower) rates of susceptibility to false-memory illusions in childhood.

THEORETICAL EPILOGUE

There is some controversy as to whether a spreading activation account of false memories can adequately capture the findings from the different memory-illusion paradigms without adding additional constraints (e.g., source monitoring) (see comments in Brainerd et al., 2008a). It has been argued that, because there are distinct developmental trajectories for spontaneous (increases with age), suggested (decreases with age), and implanted (increases with age) false memories, one needs at a minimum a dual-process theory in which there are processes that increase the probability of false memories as well as decrease that probability. Brainerd et al.'s (2008a) FTT opponent-process account is one such candidate, as it posits two traces: verbatim and gist. To the extent that gist processes are activated at the expense of verbatim processes, false memories should increase (e.g., gist processes increase over a retention interval as verbatim traces fade). Similarly, to the extent that verbatim processes are activated and trump gist processes, accurate recollection should rule and false recollection should decrease (e.g., as when items are highly distinctive and receive item-specific processing).

However, it is not clear that there really are two distinct trajectories in children's false-memory development. The evidence reviewed in this chapter shows that children's susceptibility to false memories tends to increase with age regardless of which paradigm one selects. That is, even when child-friendly lists were used, older children and adults were still more likely to form spontaneous false memories than younger children. Concerning implantation paradigms, it is well known that although younger children may be more susceptible to suggestion and misinformation than older children and adults, much of this susceptibility has to do with younger children's reduced confidence in their own memories and greater acceptance of information from a more knowledgeable adult (see Bruck & Ceci, 1999). The actual *construction of the false memory* itself is contingent on integrating this new information into a child's knowledge base and developing the false memory from there. Again, the importance of children's knowledge base in the construction of implanted false memories was amply demonstrated in studies that examined the role of preexisting script knowledge (e.g., Otgaar et al., 2010).

Although the nitty-gritty details of FTT versus AAT will not be debated here, as there are clearly more agreements than disagreements (also see Brainerd et al., 2009), it is important to point out that a single-process, spreading activation model can account for all of the findings as well as both developmental trajectories (when they appear) with or without additional assumptions. As already outlined, AAT has always maintained that it is not simply the existence of a knowledge base that is key to memory development, true and false, but also the manner in which that knowledge base is organized and the automaticity with which the concepts and their networks (inter-item links) are accessed and activated. Although both AAT and FTT agree that a mental lexicon (knowledge base) is essential, AAT maintains that a single, integrated trace is constructed, one that contains all of the information (surface and meaning) extracted during the encoding process. AAT also acknowledges that encoding processes can be biased (e.g., by instructions to process information for its meaning, pleasantness, number of vowels, and so forth), and retrieval cues too can bias what is accessed and subsequently output from the integrated memory trace. Indeed, we have shown this in our experiments on adaptive memory (see the previous section in this chapter, and Howe & Derbish, 2010) as well as in our research on the biasing influence of stories on children's true and false memory (Howe & Wilkinson, 2011). We have also demonstrated that to the extent children's knowledge base is involved in the construction of a false memory, as it is in spontaneous and implantation paradigms, their knowledge base certainly accounts for a major proportion of the variance (as we saw in the child-friendly list studies). However, we have also seen that age differences still persist when the knowledge base is taken into account, and that when we examine age differences in automaticity, this remaining variance can be accounted for.

That a single-process model can account for the development of children's spontaneous and implanted false memories can also be seen in the data where true and false memory rates are positively correlated. Although there are conditions in which true and false memories can be forced in different directions (e.g., as when distinctive or item-specific processing is used during encoding; see Ghetti et al., 2002; Howe, 2008b), when relational processing occurs, both true and false memories tend to increase, as we saw in the adaptive-memory paradigm (Howe & Derbish, 2010; Otgaar & Smeets, 2010). Of course, this does not mean that opponent-process models cannot also account for these patterns. However, given that single-process models also predict these outcomes, it may be more parsimonious to assume that only a single process is required.

A single-process spreading activation model also provides a comprehensive account of, and in fact predicted, priming effects for false memories. As seen in the previous section of this chapter, false memories, like true ones, can be used in other higher-order cognitive tasks such as insight-based problem-solving. Creative problem-solving may be particularly well primed by false memories simply because the associations from which they are derived are varied and wide-ranging, including things such as antonymy (e.g., *hot-cold*); entity (i.e., one concept names an entity, *shirt*, and another is a property of that entity, *collar*); introspection (i.e., one concept refers to a mental state, *fear*, and another is a property related to that state, *edginess*); situational (i.e., concepts referring to the same situation such as things to do with medical treatment, *doctor, stethoscope*); synonymy (e.g., *couch-sofa*); and taxonomy (e.g., *four-footed animals, vegetables*) (see Wu & Barsalou, 2009). These associative networks can also be used to account for the development of false memories when children are presented integrated sets of sentences or stories that require deduction, inference, or both. For example, when children are presented the sentences *The cage is on the table; The bird is in the cage; The cat is under the table;* they will later falsely recognize sentences such as, *The cage is above the cat*, during tests of recognition (see Reyna & Kiernan, 1994, 1995). Although such findings are frequently interpreted in terms of gist extraction in the psycholinguistic literature, they are also compatible with spreading activation models in which associative networks are constructed that represent the various relationships described in the sentences (for more details concerning these networks, see Anderson, 1983, 2007).

Similar associative webs can be used to model true and false recall when information is presented in more integrated formats, including stories (see Dewhurst et al., 2007a; Howe & Wilkinson, 2011). Like Reder and her colleagues (Arndt & Reder, 2003; Reder et al., 2009), spreading activation models that include theme nodes in their associative webs have been used effectively to account for the processing of information that is highly interrelated. When several related concepts are encountered, theme nodes can exceed threshold and become active, something that in turn activates other related concepts. The fewer the number of possible themes available, or the more readily the presented information targets the appropriate themes (as when information is presented using stories), the more readily a theme will be activated and hence activate other related concepts as well as reactivate concepts that have just been presented. Homing in on a specific theme can often be difficult for children and is something that story presentation formats can help children, particularly young children (i.e., five-year-olds; see Dewhurst et al., 2007a), focus in on the meaning or overarching theme more rapidly.

The specific details of the excitatory and inhibitory actions of these theme nodes and their links will not be detailed here. However, it should be pointed out that these theme-based associative webs have been used successfully to explain true and false memory differences between survival-related material, which contain few alternative themes, and neutral lists, which usually contain multiple themes. That is, lists with fewer rather than more themes (e.g., see Howe & Derbish, 2010) are more likely to have higher rates of true and false recollection. This is because the presentation of each word activates the single theme rather than multiple themes, resulting in the greater likelihood that such activation will spread to other related concepts in that associative web and reactivate already presented concepts. Similar research examining how stories provide a biasing context in the generation of children's false memories has also produced results consistent with a single-process model when associative webs include theme nodes (see Howe & Wilkinson, 2011).

Although it might be argued that theme nodes are just a reconstituted version of gist-extraction mechanisms common in opponent-processing models, this is not the case. Theme nodes are not constructed in situ or on the fly, given the presentation of a series of related concepts. Indeed, like other nodes in associative webs, theme nodes already exist and are part of one's knowledge base.

There is nothing that needs to be extracted as this information is already embedded in the associative web and may have, at some point earlier in time, served to restructure or reorganize information in the person's knowledge base once that theme had been acquired (e.g., much like different four-footed animals [dogs, cats, etc.] or different vegetables [carrots, celery, etc.] may be grouped together in memory once children learn the appropriate categorical relations).

Finally, there is no reason why AAT, like the Activation-Monitoring Theory (Roediger et al., 2001a), should not take advantage of research on the development of children's memory editing skills. For example, it is well known that children's source monitoring improves with age along with other metamemorial skills that permit children (and adults) to reject false memories at output. Although young children do not have sophisticated source-monitoring skills, when they do develop (at around the age of eight years) they can be used to edit false memories from output queues (see Ghetti, 2008; Mitchell & Johnson, 2009).

Regardless of one's theoretical preference, both the dual-process and single-process models can provide comprehensive accounts of the development of spontaneous and implanted false memories. Both have resulted in extremely productive lines of research, have made unique and testable predictions, and have extended their domain of coverage to higher cognitive processes including reasoning and problem-solving (among others). Whether we need two opposing processes (or possibly more—see Brainerd et al., 2009) or just a single process may be simply a matter of explanatory preference rather than empirical necessity. Regardless, what we can agree on is that the developmental course of false memories depends very much on the content and structure of children's knowledge base, including how it comes to be reorganized with subsequent experience and learning. Moreover, the ease (speed and relative automaticity) with which information can be accessed and activated in memory, particularly the meaning of that information, is critical to the development of both spontaneous and implanted false memories. Finally, as children's memory-editing skills (e.g., source monitoring, metamemory) come online, false memories can be omitted from children's reports despite the fact they were generated automatically during encoding and that they are present in the retrieval queue. Whatever manner in which one prefers to configure these ingredients, these are the very essentials that make up what we know about the development of false-memory illusions in childhood.

PART IV

THE ADAPTIVE NATURE OF MEMORY AND ITS DEVELOPMENT

10

Evolutionary and Adaptive Significance of the Genesis and Early Development of Memory

In a general sense, all evolution is memory.

Biological evolution involves changes in genes that are retained in the genetic structure and replicated if the changes are adaptive. This can be called biological or genetic memory and it has been invoked to explain some universal psychological experiences such as the common fears of falling, dark places, and snakes, among others, and the so-called atavistic dreams related to them.

Cultural evolution involves memory in another sense, namely retention of the habits, customs, myths, and artifacts that are valued by social groups and essentially define them. They could be called social memories that are entrenched in the oral traditions and visual (eventually written) records of a people.
(Paivio, 2007, p. 240)

It is of course a truism to say that memory is adaptive, its evolutionary significance being perhaps, all too self-evident. However, this does not imply that such an observation is trivial as memory has played, and continues to play, a critical role in the evolution of humans and other animals. Although it is not clear when individual memory became an essential evolutionary adaptation, there is some evidence that it may have emerged about 500 million years ago (Gabora & Aerts, 2009; Ginsberg & Jablonka, 2010b; Paivio, 2007). This was an important advance, for as organisms and their memories evolved, the variety and number of fitness-relevant behaviors were greatly enhanced. For many organisms, this included remembering locations where food and water could be obtained; determined the way they looked for mating partners; as well as how they were able to recognize, try to avoid, and the manner in which they reacted to predators (also see Ginsburg & Jablonka, 2010b). Indeed, memory is critical to a number of survival-relevant behaviors, with associations between significant objects (e.g., a predator) and signs of its presence (e.g., rustling grass, paw prints, feces) often being key to avoiding fatal contact.

It has long been surmised that the evolution of memory, at least memory that supported associative learning and the retention of past experiences, opened up the possibility of an entirely new mechanism for adaptive changes in behavior. That is, whereas prior to memory, organisms could only make adaptive behavioral changes phylogenetically (across evolutionary time via the reproduction of surviving individuals), memory afforded the opportunity for organisms to make these adaptive behavioral changes ontogenetically (during their own lifespan) (e.g., see Dennett, 1995). Of course, the picture is more complicated than this, inasmuch as adaptation involves reciprocal relationships between ontogenetic changes and phylogenetic ones.

> For example, if an animal learned that food is usually available in a particular area and consequently it tended to stay there, its offspring would have the same learning environment and learning opportunities. Natural selection would then favor any physiological or morphological features that improved adaptation to this learning environment. The explosion of new behaviors and new ecological opportunities that followed the evolution of associative learning would have been accompanied by an explosion of new, matching, morphological adaptations.
> (Ginsburg & Jablonka, 2010b, p. 15)

Although memory of this sort comes at considerable metabolic expense (e.g., larger brains with increased numbers of neurons), the benefits afforded by this greater expense appear to have outweighed the costs. That is, as the lifespan of organisms increased so that they lived longer and longer, memory for important (e.g., fitness-relevant) events became worthwhile. Indeed, the memory of previous episodes enabled individuals to adapt to new conditions (e.g., behavioral plasticity), with those organisms that had better memory and were, hence, better learners, being more likely to survive and reproduce.

As the neurological structures and processes underlying memory evolved, organisms became more efficient in the storage, retention, and retrieval of larger and larger amounts of information about individual encounters (autobiographical memory). In addition to encoding episodic information about such encounters, commonalities across individual experiences could be extracted and accumulated (semantic memory), contributing to the growing knowledge base about how the world operated and the formation of an integrated worldview. It is this worldview that gives the individual an integrated framework for understanding the world they live in and that guides their behavior (current and future) in that world (also see Gabora & Aerts, 2009). At the very least, this knowledge base forms the representational foundation for cognition; one that includes the prediction of future, survival-relevant events such as where and when to forage for food. Thus, memory has many far-reaching evolutionary consequences and "is the engine of cognitive evolution, the driving force that has led to more intelligent systems" (Paivio, 2007, p. 241).

In this final chapter, I outline a new and different perspective on the genesis and early development of memory, and argue specifically that both the semantic and episodic components of autobiographical memory are essential adaptive mechanisms that help insure our survival. As argued earlier, in memory, we not only store individual episodic experiences, but we also extract from those experiences personal meaning. The recollection of previous episodes and their meanings not only provides a guide and interpretive framework for current behavior, but also guides intentions and future behavior. Autobiographical memory, then, both provides for the recollection of previous, personal experiences and also helps us understand the environment we live in, so we can anticipate and plan for future actions and behaviors. Both predictable and familiar experiences are reconstructed for later inspection (perhaps as scripts or schemas), but equally important, so are the distinctive, unique, and unpredictable experiences that violate our expectations about the world. As seen earlier in this volume, it is these latter types of experiences that remain highly memorable across the lifespan, particularly when they are concerned with unanticipated changes having to do with the self. Of course, both predictable and highly regular aspects of experience and our environment are remembered, along with the experiences that violate our expectations based on these regularities. This, too, is fitness-relevant because organisms need to know what to anticipate in the future, as well as the conditions under which those expectations have been violated, especially as they need to forage and hunt for food, find water, and provide shelter.

I begin by providing a brief overview of what is known about the evolution of memory and its links to associative learning and the establishment of episodic (and semantic) memory. I then illustrate how these advances are associated with the co-emergence of feelings and the evolution of self-consciousness. Altogether, this gives rise to autobiographical memory, both in the classic sense of memories of personal, specific episodes as well as more general, decontextualized knowledge of the world, and I show why it is so important to establish autobiographical memory so very early in life. Next, I return to the literature on adaptive memory: although much of this research has been conducted with adults, there is a burgeoning literature concerning children's adaptive memory. Finally in this chapter, I consider whether autobiographical memory needs to be truth-preserving or whether memories can be adaptive irrespective of their veracity.

A Brief Excursion into the Evolution of Memory

The evolution of memory is thought to have been dependent on the emergence of the neuron and neural communication systems. These changes may have emerged rather rapidly some time over 500 million years ago during what has been called the "Cambrian explosion." Although there are various theories concerning the emergence of memory, most agree that long-term memory evolved in two major phases (Eccles, 1989; Ginsburg & Jablonka 2007a, 2007b, 2010a). In the first phase, memory is thought to be confined to those mechanisms that control short- and long-term habituation and sensitization. As seen earlier in this book, *habituation* can be defined as a decrease in responsiveness (e.g., infant looking) to a repeated stimulus (e.g., visual pattern). This allows the organism to save energy by ignoring environmental stimuli that are already learned or known (i.e., in memory) and focus its attention on and explore novel, less known aspects of the environment. *Sensitization* is essentially the opposite of habituation. Here, the organism's responsiveness to a stimulus increases or the response threshold is lowered following repeated presentations of the same stimuli (see Ginsburg & Jablonka, 2007a).

> The plasticity given by habituation and simple sensitization (through reflex potentiation) is of the fixed-pattern type. What changes, and what is learned and remembered, is the extent of the response (smaller in habituation, larger in sensitization). The organism does not organize new relations, only modulates preexisting, previously selected ones.
> (Ginsburg & Jablonka, 2007a, p. 224)

The second phase is thought to involve the evolution of long-term, stable memory traces that preserve newly learned associations (i.e., associative memory). This advance is thought to be brought about by a number of important neurobiological changes—not the least of which was cephalization—changes that led to better integrated and unitary memory traces (see Eccles, 1989; Ginsburg & Jablonka, 2007b, 2010a). The details of the advances necessary to establish this second phase of memory evolution can be found elsewhere (e.g., Eccles, 1989; Ginsburg & Jablonka, 2007b). For current purposes, the important point is that this form of memory involves the binding of elements into a unified and enduring long-term memory trace. As Ginsburg and Jablonka (2010a, p. 114) point out, the evolution of associative memory provided organisms with at least three advantages not available in earlier forms of memory:

> First, the binding of stimuli, which at the previous stage of evolution (before associative learning had evolved) merely accompanied experiencing,

becomes advantageous, because it makes it possible to distinguish between complex (combined) stimuli. Second, learning-dependent experiencing allows recognition and discrimination on the basis of *partial cues*: for the hungry animal contingent associations (e.g., vibrations) may be recognized and elicit an adaptive response, food-seeking. Third, since for the food-deprived but already experienced [animal], food had become embodied, it gives the animal clues as to *what to do*, since some of the activated traces are associated with successful navigation towards the attractor-related stimuli (food, shelter and their contexts). The animal can now make an *educated guess*, based on its past experience.

(Emphases in the original.)

Importantly, this newly evolved associative-memory system allows the animal not only to remember a past, but also to use this past along with present cues to satisfy its needs in the present and to anticipate the future. This anticipated future might have to do with knowledge of what to do when one is hungry or thirsty again, or where to hide, given cues that a predator might be near. Of additional importance is that associative memory may be at least partly responsible for the emergence of consciousness, particularly self-consciousness. Indeed, Edelman (1989, 2003) has argued that consciousness evolved because memory permitted the mapping of past experiences with those of future needs. I next turn to a consideration of the link between the evolution of associative memory and consciousness.

Memory, Feelings, and the Emergence of Self-consciousness

And the reigning theory in the cognitive sciences—what the biologist Francis Crick called "the astonishing hypothesis"—is that our selves are the results of brain processes.

(Bloom, 2004, p. 213)

In evolutionary terms, feelings and memory are linked. Indeed, it has been hypothesized that the evolution of feelings also went through a two-phase process during evolution (Ginsburg & Jablonka, 2007b). Feelings were first associated with sensory states (e.g., sensations associated with particular reflexes), were transient, and were not stored or associated with any memory of the experiences themselves. Later, once associative memory was established (i.e., in which the remnants of experience were retained in memory traces that outlived the experience itself), these sensations became part of the stored trace for the experience. That is, "when the animal learns a new relation, its neural effects are integrated within the original overall sensation, and this sensation— the feeling—can then be triggered by the newly learned cue, and guide the corresponding behavior upon subsequent encounters" (Ginsburg & Jablonka, 2007b, p. 236).

Many of the affective systems that evolved were probably organized around reflexes that allowed the animal to adapt to its changing environment (e.g., Denton, 2006). Obtaining food may have been associated with a feeling of hunger, pursuing a partner associated with sexual urges, fight or flight associated with fear upon sensing a predator, and so forth. As evolution proceeded, more complex affective categories emerged in tandem with more and more special-ized neural systems and structures (see Cabanac, 1992; Panksepp, 2005).

It may have been that these "first-person" experiences gave rise to conscious-ness, particularly consciousness about a "self" with needs and drives. That is, associative memories that contain records of past experiences, including the affective states that gave rise to a particular response and that could serve to modulate future behaviors in similar circumstances, may have provided a sense of "experiencing" to the organisms that possessed these memories. Although I do not intend to enter into the great debate over the nature of consciousness and the search for its evolutionary origins, suffice it to say that there is reasonable agreement among scholars that memory can be a necessary prerequisite for consciousness and that, importantly, that memory system must be one that binds prior experiences and responses with future needs (Edelman, 2009).

One aspect of this debate that is important to acknowledge is whether such memories give rise to similar feelings and states of consciousness in human and nonhuman animals. Indeed, there is considerable controversy as to whether feelings are similarly experienced in human and nonhuman animals; that is, although most animals experience raw sensory or perceptual feelings, not all have the capacity to reflect upon or have thoughts about these experiences (for recent reviews, see de Waal, 2009; Panksepp, 2005).

Similar controversy arises concerning consciousness more generally (for a recent review, see Edelman, 2009), as well as the emergence of self-consciousness (see Eccles, 1989). For example, Edelman (2009) carefully draws a distinction between sensory or primary consciousness, which may be common to a number of nonhuman animals, and higher-order consciousness, which may be unique to *Homo sapiens* and a few other animals. Perhaps somewhat more contentious is the evolution of self-consciousness. Here, the prevailing view has been that,

Self-awareness is, then, one of the fundamental, possibly the most fundamental, characteristic of the human species. This characteristic is an evolutionary novelty; the biological species from which mankind has descended had only the rudiments of self-awareness, or perhaps lacked it altogether.

(Dobzhansky, 1967, p. 68)

What is not clear is how this squares with the evidence reviewed earlier (Chapter 4) in which a variety of animals, human and nonhuman, exhibit behaviors consistent with self-awareness, such as mirror self-recognition. Although some have argued that despite similarity in the self-recognition response itself, these behaviors may be driven by different underlying mechanisms (see Edelman, 2009, for additional problems). Indeed, it may be that the mirror self-recognition test is a valid index of the emergence of "me" in *Homo sapiens*, who then go on to show other self-relevant behaviors (e.g., embarrassment), but that the passing of this test by nonhuman animals who then do not show these additional self-relevant behaviors is mediated by a simpler, more rudimentary form of primary or sensory consciousness (Edelman, 2009).

However, there is evidence that like humans, some nonhuman animals exhibit self-conscious behaviors (see de Waal, 2009). De Waal (2009) has argued that one of the most important of these behaviors is empathy, something he argues is a co-emergent property of mirror self-recognition. Empathy requires that individuals have a strong sense of self, be aware that others are separate from themselves, and that like themselves, others have affective and cognitive states similar to their own—indeed, empathy requires that the organism be somehow cognizant of the fact that another's states can be similar to its own, given the appropriate circumstances. Consistent with his hypothesis is evidence that such prosocial behaviors are not evident in humans until they pass the mirror self-recognition test (e.g., Bischof-Köhler, 1991, 1994). There is also considerable evidence that nonhuman animals that pass the mirror self-recognition test also exhibit prosocial or helping behaviors, not only within their own species, but also with other species. For example, there are well-documented cases in which dolphins have come to the aid of human swimmers, sometimes protecting them from sharks, other times lifting them to the surface of the water (see de Waal, 2009, for a number of examples across different species). Similarly, elephants in the wild also help one another, even when they are unrelated (e.g., Moss, 1988).

Although evidence for empathy in elephants is mostly anecdotal, empathy in primates has been examined more systematically. Interestingly, chimpanzees (who pass the mirror self-recognition test; see Gallup, 1970, 1979) also exhibit empathy by, for example, offering solace to a bereaved other. Monkeys (who do not pass the mirror self-recognition test; e.g., see Anderson & Gallup, 1999; Gallup, 1982) do not offer such solace, leaving the bereaved other to deal with their internal state by themselves (see de Waal, 2009).

Despite these cross species similarities in mirror self-recognition responses and the co-occurrence of empathic behaviors, few have argued that both human and nonhuman animals possess a qualitatively similar sense of self-consciousness (see Baars, 2005; Panksepp, 2005). I do not intend to argue that there is a cross-species isomorphism in self-consciousness either. The point being made here is simply that there are important cross-species similarities in memory, emotion, and perhaps even self-consciousness. That these characteristics emerged together, not only phylogenetically but also ontogenetically, is perhaps no coincidence. What is not in question, and what serves as the important take-home message, is that the evolution of memory, empathy, and self-consciousness has provided greater plasticity and flexibility in adaptation for those human and nonhuman animals that possess them.

The Importance of Early Memory to Adaptation

> The great evolutionary advantage of human beings is their ability to escape from the constraints of evolution. We can learn about our environment, we can imagine different environments, and we can turn those imagined environments into reality.
>
> (Gopnik, 2009, pp. 7–8)

> Human beings have a much more extended period of immaturity and dependence, a much longer childhood, than other species. . . . This protracted period of immaturity is intimately tied up with the human capacity for change. . . . An animal that depends on the accumulated knowledge of past generations has to have some time to acquire that knowledge. An animal that depends on imagination has to have some time to exercise it. Childhood is that time.
>
> (Gopnik, 2009, p. 10)

The adaptive advantage of having a sophisticated memory system, one that is bound together with self-consciousness, comes at a cost. Although it affords us a greater plasticity and flexibility, these advantages are not present at birth but come later in ontogeny. As seen earlier in this book, for humans, episodic memory begins very early in life. At the very latest, such memories can be formed by the end of the first year of life, and according to some (e.g., Rovee-Collier, 1997), they may be formed within the first six months of life (perhaps even by two months of age). What we have also shown is that, although such memories can and do mediate responses to internal and external stimuli, they are not autobiographical and do not cross the infantile amnesia "barrier." Autobiographical memory does not emerge until the advent of the cognitive self, an achievement that occurs around 18 to 24 months of age.

What happens to these early memories? Perhaps such memories accumulate and are recombined in new distributed structures to form new concepts and relationships between concepts that serve as the infant's knowledge base and the subsequent development of their worldview (Gabora & Aerts, 2009). As Newcombe and colleagues (in press) point out, how infants combine recurring and causally linked information from the experienced world into memory traces is essential to adaptation. Perhaps initially the elements of these co-occurrences are bound together and stored in an episodic manner. If these events tend to co-occur more frequently, their episodic significance may become less important and such memories may become recoded as lawful, semantic memories of how the world operates. As we saw earlier in this book (also see Howe, 2000), one of the key adaptive features of memory lies in its ability to store critical information not only about how the world works, but also how to satisfy one's basic needs such as hunger, thirst, safety, and so forth in the world in which we live.

These memories serve a dual function. First, they provide a "record" of the "rules" governing the environment (semantic/autobiographical memory) in which the infant finds itself (general meanings, schemata, etc.) as well as key individual experiences (episodic/autobiographical memory) that are relevant either as an exception to the rule or as somehow being important to the organism (as in the experiences that are relevant to self transitions as discussed earlier in this book). Second, they provide a kind of "anticipatory map" for future behaviors. Based on previous experience, including both implicit and explicit knowledge of what has been experienced in the past (semantic/autobiographical memory) as well as the exceptions to these rules as embodied in key experiences specific to "me" (episodic/autobiographical memory), we can anticipate what to do in the future when similar conditions (e.g., need states) arise.

As Gopnik (2009, p. 198) has noted, from an evolutionary vantage point, the emphasis on storing information about the past "is rather puzzling. . . . Owning our past is so important because it allows us to own our future." Indeed, planning, as just discussed, is critical to survival. In fact, recent research has shown that retrieving autobiographical memories (recollecting the past) relies on the activation of similar neurological regions to those seen when people are asked to imagine future events (Addis et al., 2009).

That one of memory's most powerful functions lies in the planning of future responses is not a new idea. As Klein and colleagues (2002, p. 313) noted,

> The adaptive function of information storage is intrinsically prospective: It is used to support *future* decisions and judgments, which cannot be known in advance with certainty. To the extent that the character of

subsequent decisions and judgments can be predicted, the memory system can be tailored to flag relevant information and precompute variables that are required to make them.

Although many would agree with this conclusion, how can we reconcile this need for reasonably accurate predictions about the future with the indisputable fact that memories, regardless of whether they are formed and remembered in childhood or adulthood, are fundamentally reconstructive and hence, error prone?

Do Memories Have to Be True to Be Adaptive?

The driving force behind natural selection is survival and reproduction, not truth. All other things being equal, it is better for an animal to believe true things than false things; accurate perception is better than hallucination. But sometimes all things are not equal.

(Bloom, 2004, pp. 222–223)

Like Bloom (2004), McKay and Dennett (2009, p. 493) have noted that it has long been assumed that in order to maximize survival, "humans have been biologically engineered to form true beliefs by evolution." They, too, argue that not all beliefs that are formed by humans are true and that not all false beliefs, or misbeliefs, are necessarily detrimental to our survival. As we will see, similar conclusions obtain for true and false memories. Before discussing the idea that false memories can also have fitness-relevant properties, I present some background on the way researchers have recently been studying adaptive memory in humans.

The adaptive-memory studies reviewed earlier in this book have tended to focus on two very different assumptions about the way evolution has affected memory. The first set of assumptions that has been examined concerns the idea that memory has become specialized through evolution to perform certain specific functions. In this tradition, researchers have studied the recognition of trustworthiness based on the assumption that survival might be enhanced if we can avoid those who are deceptive. Indeed, this line of research has focused on whether there is a "cheater detection module" in memory (e.g., Mehl & Buchner, 2008). Similarly, other researchers have focused on whether evolution shaped memory to be different in each of the sexes, especially in light of differences in the division of labor that occurred during the Pleistocene era. For example, Pacheco-Cobos et al. (2010) examined sex differences in spatial memory and found gender differences that were consistent with the presumed spatial memory requirements of earlier divisions of labor where men hunted mobile, unpredictable prey, whereas women gathered plants that were found in fixed and immobile locations.

A second line of research has examined a slightly different question; namely, whether memory is specialized to retain fitness-relevant, survival information (for a review, see Nairne, 2010). As explained earlier, in this paradigm, participants are given a scenario, such as being stranded on a desert island or in the grasslands, a scenario said to be consistent with our ancestral past, and they are then asked to rate the importance of a list of concepts to their subsequent survival in this environment. Compared to an ancestrally irrelevant but similarly meaningful judgment task (e.g., going on holiday or moving to a new house), these same concepts are better recalled or recognized on a surprise memory test following the rating task. Based on findings such as these, it has been argued that memory is specially adapted to remember survival-relevant information, in part because this information may be especially useful in fitness-relevant, future planning. Findings like these have been obtained in a number of labs and when paradigms (intentional versus incidental memory tasks) and scenarios (ancestrally relevant survival [e.g., grasslands] and ancestrally irrelevant survival [e.g., city streets]) have been varied systematically.

There is disagreement about the importance of an evolutionary interpretation for these latter adaptive-memory findings. For example, Derbish and Howe (2010) have argued that the adaptive-memory scenarios (desert island, grasslands) tend to be less familiar to participants than the non-survival (moving, holiday) and survival-relevant but ancestrally irrelevant scenarios (city streets). Indeed, few of us have been stranded on a desert island, but many of us have gone on holiday or moved house. In the latter cases, participants can solve the rating task by simply accessing autobiographical and semantic representations based on prior experiences. However, in the former case, one cannot rely on autobiographical memory but must instead employ memories of books read (e.g., *Robinson Crusoe*) or movies or television programs watched (e.g., *Gilligan's Island*). The use of such diverse representations (and possibly one's imagination) can lead participants to construct more elaborate, and hence more memorable, representations of the information being processed during the rating task. Indeed, when Derbish and Howe (2010) manipulated the extent of participants' elaboration, regardless of the nature of the scenario, those with more elaborate representations remembered more regardless of the survival relevance of the scenario (desert island versus moving) than those with less elaboration. Moreover, when the familiarity and elaboration requirements of survival-relevant scenarios were equated, as measured by participant ratings, but ancestral relevance differed (desert island versus landing on a foreign planet), so-called adaptive memory differences were again eliminated.

More importantly, it turns out that there are not only more true memories generated using this adaptive memory paradigm, but more false memories as well. As we saw earlier, Howe and Derbish (2010) used Deese/Roediger-McDermott– like lists of concepts that were survival-relevant (e.g., concepts associated with "death"), negatively valenced (e.g., concepts associated with "sad"), and relatively neutral items (e.g., concepts associated with "clothing"). We asked participants to rate these words for their relevance to survival (e.g., desert island) and non-survival (e.g., moving, pleasantness) scenarios. We found that true and false memories were more abundant when items were rated for survival (e.g., desert island) than non-survival scenarios (e.g., moving). Also, there was a separate, independent effect for concept type, such that survival-relevant words also exhibited higher rates of true and false recollection. Recall that Otgaar and Smeets (2010) have replicated these findings with different materials (e.g., categorized lists) and that these increases in true and false remembering were observed for both adults and for children (specifically, eight- and 11-year-olds).

These joint increases in true and false memory need not be interpreted within an evolutionary framework either. Whereas the increases in both true and false memory due to rating tasks can be interpreted in terms of elaboration effects, Howe and Derbish (2010) argued that the material effects can be accounted for by the number of competing themes available in the rated materials. Survival lists contain very few alternative themes, whereas many neutral lists have multiple themes. When we intentionally varied the number of themes available in the different lists, we found that both true and false memory rates were determined by the number of themes that were available in lists of related items and not by whether they were or were not survival-related.

Whether adaptive or not, that both true and false memories are related by a monotonically increasing function in this paradigm raises several concerns. First, what this means is that "adaptive memory" results in reduced, not enhanced, accuracy. If false memories increase at a rate commensurate with true memories, then overall accuracy of memory must decrease. Second, like questions concerning false beliefs, we can ask why false memories would be adaptive at all. Even outside of the adaptive-memory paradigm, we have seen that memories are often inaccurate (see Chapter 9). There we saw that, regardless of age, humans can spontaneously form memories that contain information that is mostly accurate, but some aspects of it can be false. At the other end of the spectrum, we can form autobiographical memories for events that never occurred; that is, "events" that are entirely fictitious. What possible adaptive significance is there for the construction of either entirely, or even just partially, false memories?

According to Newman and Lindsay (2009), the answer is, like that proposed for misbeliefs (see McKay & Dennett, 2009), quite straightforward, especially when it comes to autobiographical memory. To explain, recall that false recollections of our prior experiences can result in a biased recollection of our past self. This, in turn, can be important not only to maintaining our own current self-concept (perhaps painting a rosier picture of ourselves in the past than is warranted), but may also be important in maintaining effective social relations. Such "misrememberings" of the past more frequently involve false memories about the self than false memories about events themselves (see Ross & Wilson, 2000, 2003; Wilson & Ross, 2003, for reviews). Of course, as argued earlier, false memories are simply the byproduct of a highly flexible, powerful, and reconstructive memory system (Newman & Lindsay, 2009). However, they can serve a very adaptive purpose to aid in the revision of our past to facilitate self-enhancement. As Ross and his collaborators (Ross & Wilson, 2000; 2003; Wilson & Ross, 2003) have shown, people frequently revise memories of themselves in the past to be consistent with how they currently view themselves. These systematic revisions of the past may serve a very healthy function inasmuch as they frequently permit a more positive evaluation of one's current self. Moreover, because many of the functions of autobiographical memory are arguably social, at least in later childhood and adulthood, distortions of our past may be quite adaptive as they can serve to nurture social relationships (e.g., Bluck et al., 2005). These distortions may serve to maintain and extend empathy and intimacy in relationships with others, a goal more important perhaps than maintaining an accurate memory of one's past (also see Cuc et al., 2007).

Overall, then, although accuracy in beliefs and memories is often preferred, evolution seems to have provided for relatively advanced cognitive systems that, although being both flexible and powerful, are, as a consequence, prone to error. Although there are examples where such errors are clearly not fitness-relevant, as when people come to believe that they are dead despite being alive (the Cotard delusion) or people who believe that others, particularly relatives, have been replaced by imposters (the Capgras delusion) (see Young, 2000; Young et al., 1992), others may have quite positive effects. For example, like false memories of one's past self, "delusional" positive self-appraisals can lead to a sense of confidence in future tasks. Indeed, such delusional beliefs can include ones where the individual believes that the medicine they are taking can (and then does) cure what is ailing them, even though what they are taking is merely a placebo (see Humphrey 2002, 2004). And still other misbeliefs and false memories can vary in their impact, with some individuals who falsely remember being abducted by aliens developing psychopathologies consistent with such beliefs, and others simply being more flexible in their convictions about the existence of life elsewhere in the universe (see Spanos, 1996). Perhaps false beliefs and false memories themselves, although the product of evolved cognitive systems that are both powerful and complex, are just as adaptive and fitness-relevant as the correct beliefs and true memories generated by those same systems.

Is It Evolution or Is This Simply Another "Just-So" Tautology?

> It is a capital mistake to theorize before one has the data. Insensibly one begins to twist facts to suit theories, instead of theories to suit facts.
>
> Sherlock Holmes in Sir Arthur Conan Doyle's "A Scandal in Bohemia" (1891)

Like other sciences, evolutionary psychology has been criticized for creating post-hoc adaptationist explanations for phenomena in the absence of empirical evidence. These "just so" stories have been criticized for some time, perhaps no more infamously than by Gould and Lewontin (1979), who proclaimed that although adaptation can happen and there do exist such adaptations, you cannot be sure that what you are studying is in fact an adaptation. Because to our knowledge, traits have not been systematically varied over evolutionary time, we must rely on what are called *correlated characters* (e.g., length of a giraffe's neck and available [or preferred] food, the whiteness and strength of bones). Until these traits can be systematically varied in an independent fashion over evolutionary time, or so goes the criticism, we cannot conclude that whiteness and strength or length of neck and food availability (or preference) were naturally selected for (also see Fodor & Piattelli-Palmarini, 2010).

That such evolutionary theories have explanatory value despite the frequent absence of key empirical data does not mean that such theorizing is wrong. Although this debate will continue for some time, many theorists agree that adaptations, even cognitive ones, exist in humans, despite the difficulty inherent in tracing their evolutionary heritage. The absence of such causal evidence, especially in the presence of considerable evidence confirming other empirical predictions, neither negates adaptationist theories nor does it provide confirmation of non-evolutionary speculations (e.g., Barrett, 2011; Block & Kitchen, 2010).

That memory evolved, constrained by natural selection, has led to a number of predictions that have been empirically tested and confirmed. As already seen, although both men and women possess excellent spatial abilities, women are better than men at remembering object locations within a stationary or immobile locale, a spatial memory system that is related to women's earlier role as gatherers. Men, on the other hand, are better than women at tracking and remembering information associated with mobile prey, a spatial memory system that is related to men's earlier role as hunters (New et al., 2007; Pacheco-Cobos et al., 2010; Silverman et al., 2007). Similarly, memory for information processed for its survival value and concepts that are themselves survival-relevant exhibit higher levels of true memory, something perhaps related to the need for memory to be sensitized to processing and remembering fitness-relevant information. That such materials and processing also lead to higher rates of false remembering may simply show that fitness-relevant information is more densely packed in memory, something that is known to increase memorability while at the same time decrease accuracy.

Of additional interest, particularly to the current thesis, are studies relevant to ontological indices of memory as an adaptation and not just those concerned with its importance phylogenetically. Here, some cognitive abilities are thought to have developmental advantages during ontogeny because of their importance or significance during human evolutionary history. Indeed, there appear to be a number of skills that infants can easily acquire, ones that cannot be readily attributed to learning alone. Examples include language; knowledge of aspects of the physical world, including an intuitive sense of motion; and differences between animate and inanimate objects (see Bloom, 2004; Gelman, 2003; Pinker, 1994). In terms of memory per se, as we saw earlier, children benefit from fitness-relevant processing of information in a manner similar to that of adults (increased true and false memories; Otgaar & Smeets, 2010). Finally, infants and children exhibit fearful reactions to evolutionarily significant stimuli, including snakes, spiders, as well as threatening and angry faces (DeLoache & LoBue, 2009; LoBue, 2009; LoBue & DeLoache, 2008, 2010). From an evolutionary perspective, individuals who more quickly recognized and responded to threatening stimuli would be more likely to survive than those who failed to recognize and respond to these threatening stimuli or who did so more slowly.

Of course, none of these outcomes in and of themselves constitutes irrefutable evidence favoring an adaptationist approach. However, arguably, together they do provide a reasonable case for the sculpting of both cognitive and memory processes by pressures associated with natural selection. It may be that memory was shaped to detect, process, and retain survival-relevant information. That is, perhaps memory evolved to help us remember and make plans concerning the what, where, when, who, and how of finding food, water, and opportunities for mating while at the same time recognizing and evading predators. Although initially such memories may have been inherently episodic, as experiences were repeated and general rules were extracted, memories were formed that could provide adequate descriptions of generic events (e.g., locations where food could be gathered reliably or places where water could be routinely found; the pattern of behaviors of predators and locations where they were normally found). That is, as we began to recognize and extract common elements and patterns from the events that were experienced and stored as different episodic memories, semantic representations emerged. Here, too, semantic aspects of autobiographical memory did not replace the episodic components because important exceptions to such generalizations must surely have existed in our past as they do today. These exceptions provide critical information, not only about exceptions to the rules that are important to survival, but also to experiences that are critical to the self. As argued earlier in this chapter, this autobiographical information may be critical in establishing and maintaining social relationships, relationships that serve to maintain intimacy and may have been central to mating and reproduction.

Although memory might have originally been shaped to process and retain such fitness-relevant information, it also functions as a system that can be used to remember information regardless of its fitness relevance. That is, what may have started as the evolution of a system that provided a solution to a specific adaptive problem has now been co-opted and used to remember information more generally (also see Nairne, 2010). Although the evolutionary roots have not been completely erased, as seen in this chapter (and throughout this book), its plasticity and flexibility has perhaps rendered it more useful than originally "intended."

Afterword

As noted at the beginning of this chapter, the importance of memory and associated cognitive systems to the survival of humans and many other animals, as well as its evolutionary significance, is not in question in many academic and scientific circles (also see Klein, 2007). Whether evolutionary sculpting of memory has resulted in specific memory modules (see Barrett & Kurzban, 2006, for a review of adaptive modules more generally), core knowledge (Spelke, 2000), or intuitive theories and innate predispositions (Bloom, 2004; Carey, 1985; Gelman, 2003) will be the fodder for continued and future research. The important point is that memory, particularly of the episodic/autobiographical variety, but also the creation of semantic representations that are derived from cumulative episodes, has provided a degree of flexibility and plasticity critical to an evolution that goes beyond phylogenetic change and one that permits ontogenetic adaptive change. That this memory emerges early in human development may be critical to this adaptation. Although humans do have a relatively protracted infancy and childhood, the early emergence of autobiographical memory signals the infant's preparedness to learn and adapt to the environment in which it finds itself. It is this ability to accumulate experiences, and remember the individual episodes as well as the meanings and general rules that can be extracted from these experiences, that permits maximal flexibility in adapting to one's surroundings.

As self-consciousness emerges and self-experienced memories are dynamically integrated as part of this self across time, the child comes to understand the world in which it lives. This dynamic interplay between the self and its experiences leads to the creation of the individual's understanding of its world, or as Gabor and Aerts (2009) call it, the person's worldview. With this understanding in hand, the child not only remembers its past and interprets its present, but equally important, it can plan for, and to some extent predict, its future. Such future planning has considerable currency in terms of fitness relevance. This is because, if accurate (or at least not so inaccurate as to threaten survival), it may insure access to important resources, enable the evasion of danger, and increase the maintenance of intimacy that is essential to reproduction.

As the chapters in this book have documented, we humans have much in common with our nonhuman counterparts, including a relatively sophisticated memory system. *Homo sapiens* may be the only animal to have developed autobiographical memory in the strictest of sense of this term (i.e., one that includes autonoetic awareness) as well as the only one to also experience what many believe to be a critical emergent property of this system, self-consciousness. However, many of the features of this memory system, ones that we share with other animals, may serve exactly the same purpose regardless of species. That is, they evolved to facilitate adaptation within an ontogenetic timeframe, an advance that is surely fitness relevant.

There is considerable research that lies ahead of us before we can develop a more complete theory of the evolution of memory, especially one that better articulates the similarities and dissimilarities between human and nonhuman animal memory systems. What we do know, as documented in this volume, is that many animals possess a memory system that includes both semantic and episodic, or at least episodic-like, information important to the survival of those animals in the environment in which they find themselves. With this information securely represented in memory, an organism can obtain survival-relevant resources (e.g., food, water, shelter) more reliably and evade dangerous and life-threatening situations in the present as well as in the future. Surely this must be one of the most powerful "adaptive tools" to have evolved over the last 500 million years.

References

Abel, T., Alberini, C., Ghirardi, M., Huang, Y.-Y., Nguyen, P., & Kandel, E. R. (1995). Steps toward a molecular definition of memory consolidation. In D. L. Schacter, J. T. Coyle, G. D. Fischbach, M. M. Mesulam, & L. E. Sullivan (Eds.), *Memory Distortion* (pp. 298–325). Cambridge, MA: Harvard University Press.

Ackil, J. K., van Abbema, D. L., & Bauer, P. J. (2003). After the storm: Enduring differences in mother-child recollections of traumatic and nontraumatic events. *Journal of Experimental Child Psychology, 84*, 286–309.

Addis, D. R., Pan, L., Vu, M.-A., Laiser, N., & Schacter, D. L. (2009). Constructive episodic simulation of the future and the past: Distinct subsystems of a core brain network mediate imagining and remembering. *Neuropsychologica, 47*, 2222–2238.

Ainsworth, M. S., & Bowlby, J. (1991). An ethological approach to personality development. *American Psychologist, 46*, 333–341.

Akirav, I., & Richter-Levin, G. (2002). Mechanisms of amygdala modulation of hippocampal plasticity. *Journal of Neuroscience, 22*, 9912–9921.

Alexander, K. W., Quas, J. A., & Goodman, G. S. (2002). Theoretical advances in understanding children's memory for distressing events: The role of attachment. *Developmental Review, 22*, 490–519.

Alexander, K. W., Quas, J. A., Goodman, G. S., Ghetti, S., Edelstein, R. S., Redlich, A. D., et al. (2005). Trauma impact predicts long-term retention for documented child sexual abuse. *Psychological Science, 16*, 33–40.

Allport, G. W. (1937). *Personality: A Psychological Interpretation*. New York: Holt.

Alpert, J. L., Brown, L. S., Ceci, S. J., Courtois, C. A., Loftus, E. F., & Ornstein, P. A. (1996). *Final Report of the APA Working Group on Investigation of Memories of Childhood Abuse*. Washington, DC: American Psychological Association.

Amabile, T. A., & Rovee-Collier, C. (1991). Contextual variation and memory retrieval at six months. *Child Development, 62*, 1155–1166.

Amsterdam, B. (1972). Mirror self-image reactions before the age of two. *Developmental Psychobiology, 5*, 297–305.

Anastasi, J. S., & Rhodes, M. G. (2008). Examining differences in levels of false memories in children and adults using child normed lists. *Developmental Psychology, 44*, 889–894.

Anda, R. E., Felitti, V. J., Bremner, J. D., Walker, J. D., Whitfield, C., Perry, B. D., Dube, S. R., & Giles, W. H. (2006). The enduring effects of abuse and related adverse experiences in childhood: A convergence of evidence from neurobiology and epidemiology. *European Archives of Psychiatry and Clinical Neurosciences, 256*, 174–186.

Anderson, J., & Gallup, G. G., Jr. (1999). Self-recognition in non-human primates: Past and future challenges. In M. Haug & R. E. Whalen (Eds.), *Animal Models of Human Emotion and Cognition* (pp. 175–194). Washington, DC: American Psychological Association.

Anderson, J. R. (1983). A spreading activation theory of memory. *Journal of Verbal Learning and Verbal Behavior, 22,* 261–295.

Anderson, J. R. (2007). *How Can the Human Mind Occur in the Physical Universe?* New York: Oxford University Press.

Aristotle (c. 345 BC/2001). *On the Soul and Memory and Recollection.* Translated by J. Sachs. Santa Fe, NM: Green Lion Press.

Arndt, J., & Reder, L. M. (2003). The effect of distinctive visual information on false recognition. *Journal of Memory and Language, 48,* 1–15.

Arnold, H. M., & Spear, N. E. (1997). Infantile amnesia: Using animal models to understand forgetting. In P. J. B. Slater, J. S. Rosenblatt, C. T. Snowden, & M. Milinski (Eds.), *Advances in the Study of Behavior* (vol. 26, pp. 251–284). New York: Academic Press.

Asendorpf, J., & Baudonniere, P.-M. (1993). Self-awareness and other awareness: Mirror self-recognition and synchronic imitation among unfamiliar peers. *Developmental Psychology, 29,* 88–95.

Asendorpf, J., Warkentin, V., & Baudonniere, P.-M. (1996). Self-awareness and other awareness II: Mirror self-recognition, social contingency awareness, and synchronic imitation. *Developmental Psychology, 32,* 313–321.

Axelson, D., Dorsaiswamy, P., McDonald, W., Boyko, O., Typler, L., Patterson, L., et al. (1993). Hypercortisolemia and hippocampal changes in depression. *Psychiatry Research, 47,* 163–173.

Baars, B. J. (2005). Subjective experience is probably not limited to humans: The evidence from neurobiology and behavior. *Consciousness and Cognition, 14,* 7–21.

Bachevalier, J. (2008). Nonhuman primate models of memory development. In C. A. Nelson & M. Luciana (Eds.), *Handbook of Developmental Cognitive Neuroscience* (pp. 499–507). Cambridge, MA: MIT Press.

Bachevalier, J., & Mishkin, M. (1984). An early and late developing system for learning and retention in infant monkeys. *Behavioral Neuroscience, 98,* 770–778.

Backhaus, J., Hoeckesfeld, R., Born, J., Hohagen, F., & Junghanns, K. (2008). Immediate as well as delayed post-learning sleep but not wakefulness enhances declarative memory consolidation in children. *Neurobiology of Learning and Memory, 89,* 76–80.

Bagot, R. C., van Hasselt, F. N., Champagne, D. L., Meaney, M. J., Krugers, H. J., & Joels, M. (2009). Maternal care determines rapid effects of stress mediators on synaptic plasticity in adult rat hippocampal dentate gyrus. *Neurobiology of Learning and Memory, 92,* 292–300.

Bahrick, L. E., Hernandez-Reif, M., & Pickens, J. (1997). The effect of retrieval cues on visual preferences and memory in infancy: Evidence for a four-phase attention function. *Journal of Experimental Child Psychology, 67,* 1–20.

Bahrick, L. E., Moss, L., & Fadil, C. (1996). The development of visual self-recognition in infancy. *Ecological Psychology, 8,* 189–208.

Bahrick, L. E., Parker, J. F., Fivush, R., & Levitt, M. (1998). The effects of stress on young children's memory for a natural disaster. *Journal of Experimental Psychology: Applied, 4,* 308–331.

Bahrick, L. E., & Pickens, J. (1995). Infant memory for object motion across a period of three months: Implications for a four-phase attention function. *Journal of Experimental Child Psychology, 59,* 343–371.

Ballesteros, M., Hansen, P., & Soila, K. (1993). MR imaging of the developing human brain: Part 2. Postnatal development. *Radiographics, 13,* 611–622.

Bar-Shakhar, G. (1995). The roles of stimulus novelty and significance in determining electrodermal orienting response: Interaction versus additive approaches. *Psychophysiology, 31,* 402–411.

Barr, R., Dowden, A., & Hayne, H. (1996). Developmental changes in deferred imitation by 6- to 24-month-old infants. *Infant Behavior & Development, 19,* 159–170.

Barr, R., & Hayne, H. (2000). Age-related changes in imitation: Implications for memory development. In C. Rovee-Collier, L. Lipsitt, & H. Hayne (Eds.), *Progress in Infancy Research* (vol. 1, pp. 21–67). Hillsdale, NJ: Erlbaum.

Barr, R., Marrott, H., & Rovee-Collier, C. (2003). The role of sensory preconditioning in memory retrieval by preverbal infants. *Infancy, 7,* 263–283.

Barr, R., Vieria, A. & Rovee-Collier, C. (2001). Mediated imitation in 6-month-olds: Remembering by association. *Journal of Experimental Child Psychology, 79,* 229–252.

Barrett, H. C. (2011). The wrong kind of wrong: A review of *What Darwin Got Wrong. Evolution and Human Behavior, 32,* 76–78.

Barrett, H. C., & Kurzban, R. (2006). Modularity in cognition: Framing the debate. *Psychological Review, 113,* 628–647.

Bates, L. A., Sayialel, K. N., Njiraini, N. W., Moss, C. J., Poole, J. H., & Byrne, R. W. (2007). Elephants classify human groups by odor and garment color. *Current Biology, 17,* 1938–1942.

Bauer, P. J. (2004). Getting explicit memory off the ground: Steps toward construction of a neuro-developmental account of changes in the first two years of life. *Developmental Review, 24,* 347–373.

Bauer, P. J. (2005). Developments in declarative memory: Decreasing susceptibility to storage failure over the second year of life. *Psychological Science, 16,* 41–47.

Bauer, P. J. (2007). Recall in infancy: A neurodevelopmental account. *Current Directions in Psychological Science, 16,* 142–146.

Bauer, P. J. (2009). The cognitive neuroscience of the development of memory. In M. L. Courage & N. Cowan (Eds.), *The Development of Memory in Infancy and Childhood* (pp. 115–144). Hove, UK: Psychology Press.

Bauer, P. J., Burch, M. M., van Abbema, D. L., & Ackil, J. K. (2008). Talking about twisters: How mothers and children converse about a devastating tornado. In M. L. Howe, G. S. Goodman, & D. Cicchetti (Eds.), *Stress, Trauma, and Children's Memory Development: Neurobiological, Cognitive, Clinical, and Legal Perspectives* (pp. 204–235). New York: Oxford University Press.

Bauer, P. J., Stennes, L., & Haight, J. C. (2003). Representation of inner self in autobiography: Women's and men's use of internal states language in personal narratives. *Memory, 11,* 27–42.

Bauer, P. J., van Abbema, D. L., Wiebe, S. A., Cary, M. S., Phill, C., & Burch, M. M. (2004). Props, not pictures, are worth a thousand words: Verbal accessibility of early memories under different conditions of contextual support. *Applied Cognitive Psychology, 18,* 373–392.

Bauer, P. J., Wenner, J. A., Dropik, P. L., & Wewerka, S. S. (2000). Parameters of remembering and forgetting in the transition from infancy to early childhood. *Monographs of the Society for Research in Child Development, 65* (Serial No. 263).

Bauer, P. J., & Wewerka, S. S. (1995). One- to two-year-olds' recall of events: The more expressed, the more impressed. *Journal of Experimental Child Psychology, 59,* 475–496.

Bauer, P. J., & Wewerka, S. S. (1997). Saying is revealing: Verbal expression of event memory in the transition from infancy to early childhood. In P. van den Broek, P. J. Bauer, & T. Bourg (Eds.), *Developmental Spans in Event Comprehension and Representation: Bridging Fictional and Actual Events* (pp. 139–168). Mahwah, NJ: Erlbaum.

Bauer, P. J., Wiebe, S., Carver, L., Lukowski, A., Haight, J., Waters, J., & Nelson, C. A. (2006). Electrophysiological indexes of encoding and behavioral indexes of recall: Examining relations and developmental change later in the first year of life. *Developmental Neuropsychology, 29,* 293–320.

Bauer, P. J., Wiebe, S., Carver, L., Waters, J., & Nelson, C. A. (2003). Developments in long-term explicit memory late in the first year of life: Behavioral and electrophysiological indices. *Psychological Science, 14,* 629–635.

Becker, K., Abraham, A., Kindler, J., Helmeke, C., & Braun, K. (2007). Exposure to neonatal separation stress alters exploratory behavior and corticotropin releasing factor expression in neurons in the amygdala and hippocampus. *Developmental Neurobiology of Aging, 67,* 617–629.

Beckett, C., Maughan, B., Rutter, M., Castle, J., Colvert, E., Groothues, C., et al. (2006). Do the effects of early severe deprivation on cognition persist into early adolescence? Findings from the English and Romanian Adoptees study. *Child Development, 77,* 696–711.

Beers, S. R., & DeBellis, M. D. (2002). Neuropsychological function in children with maltreatment-related post-traumatic stress disorder. *American Journal of Psychiatry, 159*, 483–486.

Belsky, J., & Pluess, M. (2009). The nature (and nurture?) of plasticity in early human development. *Perspectives on Psychological Science, 4*, 345–351.

Bender, B. G., Lerner, J. A., & Poland, J. E. (1991). Association between corticosteroids and psychological change in hospitalized asthmatic children. *Annals of Allergy, 66*, 414–419.

Benes, F. M. (2001). The development of the prefrontal cortex: The maturation of neurotransmitter systems and their interaction. In C. A. Nelson & M. Luciana (Eds.), *Handbook of Developmental Cognitive Neuroscience* (pp. 79–92). Cambridge, MA: MIT Press.

Berenthal, B. I., & Longo, M. R. (2007). Is there evidence of a mirror system from birth? *Developmental Science, 10*, 526–529.

Billingsley, R. L., Smith, M. L., & McAndrews, M. P. (2002). Developmental patterns in priming and familiarity in explicit recollection. *Journal of Experimental Child Psychology, 82*, 251–277.

Bischof-Köhler, D. (1991). The development of empathy in infants. In M. Lamb & M. Keller (Eds.), *Infant Development: Perspectives from German-Speaking Countries* (pp. 245–273). Hillsdale, NJ: Erlbaum.

Bischof-Köhler, D. (1994). Self-objectification and other-oriented emotions: Self-recognition, empathy, and prosocial behavior in the second year. *Zeitschrift fur Psychologie, 202*, 349–377.

Bjorklund, D. F. (1987). How changes in knowledge base contribute to the development of children's memory. *Developmental Review, 7*, 93–130.

Bjorklund, D. F. (2005). *Children's Thinking: Developmental and Individual Differences* (4th ed.). Belmont, CA: Wadsworth/Thompson.

Bjorklund, D. F., Dukes, C., & Brown, R. D. (2009). The development of memory strategies. In M. L. Courage & N. Cowan (Eds.), *The Development of Memory in Infancy and Childhood* (pp. 145–175). Hove, UK: Psychology Press.

Bjorklund, D. F., & Harnishfeger, K. K. (1995). The evolution of inhibition mechanism and their role in human cognition and behavior. In F. N. Dempster & C. J. Brainerd (Eds.), *Interference and Inhibition in Cognition* (pp. 141–173). San Diego, CA: Academic Press.

Blaise, H. J., Koranda, J. L., Chow, U., Haines, K. E., & Dorward, E. C. (2008). Neonatal isolation stress alters bidirectional long-term synaptic plasticity in amygdalo-hippocampal synapses in freely behaving adult rats. *Brain Research, 1193*, 25–33.

Blanchette, I. (2006). Snakes, spiders, guns, and syringes: How specific are evolutionary constraints on the detection of threatening stimuli? *Quarterly Journal of Experimental Psychology, 59*, 1484–1504.

Block, N., & Kitchen, P. (2010). Misunderstanding Darwin: Natural selection's secular critics get it wrong. *Boston Review* (March/April).

Bloom, P. (2004). *Descartes' Baby*. London: Arrow Books.

Bluck, S., Alea, N., Habermas, T., & Rubin, D. C. (2005). A tale of three functions: The self-reported uses of autobiographical memory. *Social Cognition, 23*, 91–117.

Bonne, O., Brandes, D., Gilboa, A., Gomori, J. M., Shenton, M. E., Pitman, R. K., et al. (2001). Longitudinal MRI study of hippocampal volume in trauma survivors with PTSD. *American Journal of Psychiatry, 158*, 1248–1251.

Born, J., Rasch, B., & Gais, S. (2006). Sleep to remember. *The Neuroscientist, 12*, 410–424.

Bourgeois, J.-P. (2001). Synaptogenesis in the neocortex of the newborn: The ultimate frontier for individuation. In C. A. Nelson & M. Luciana (Eds.), *Handbook of Developmental Cognitive Neuroscience* (pp. 23–34). Cambridge, MA: MIT Press.

Bourgeois, J.-P., Goldman-Rakic, P. S., & Rakic, P. (2000). Formation, elimination, and stabilization of synapses in the primate cerebral cortex. In M. Gazzaniga (Ed.), *The New Cognitive Neurosciences* (pp. 45–53). Cambridge, MA: MIT Press.

Bowlby, J. (1969). *Attachment and Loss* (vol. 1). New York: Basic Books.

Bowlby, J. (1980). *Attachment and Loss* (vol. 3). New York: Basic Books.

Bowman, C. (1998). *Children's Past: How Past Life Memories Affect Your Child*. New York: Bantam.

Boyce, W. T., Barr, R. G., & Zeltzer, L. K. (1992). Temperament and the psychobiology of child-hood stress. *Pediatrics, 90*, 483–486.

Brabham, T., Phelka, A., Zimmer, C., Nash, A., Lopez, J. F., & Vazquez, D. M. (2000). Effects of prenatal dexamethasone on spatial learning and response to stress is influenced by maternal factors. *American Journal of Physiology: Regulatory, Integrative, and Comparative Physiology, 279*, R1899–R1909.

Brainerd, C. J., Holliday, R. E., & Reyna, V. F. (2004). Behavioral measurement of remembering phenomenologies: So simple a child can do it. *Child Development, 75*, 505–522.

Brainerd, C. J., Holliday, R. E., Reyna, V. F., Yang, C., & Toglia, M. P. (2010). Developmental reversals in false memory: Effects of emotional valence and arousal. *Journal of Experimental Child Psychology, 107*, 137–154.

Brainerd, C. J., & Reyna, V. F. (2005). *The Science of False Memory*. New York: Oxford University Press.

Brainerd, C. J., Reyna, V. F., & Brandse, E. (1995). Are children's false memories more persistent than their true memories? *Psychological Science, 6*, 359–364.

Brainerd, C. J., Reyna, V. F., & Ceci, S. J. (2008a). Developmental reversals in false memory: A review of data and theory. *Psychological Bulletin, 134*, 343–382.

Brainerd, C. J., Reyna, V. F., & Howe, M. L. (2009). Trichotomous processes in early memory development, aging, and cognitive impairment: A unified theory. *Psychological Review, 116*, 783–832.

Brainerd, C. J., Stein, L. M., & Reyna, V. F. (1998). On the development of conscious and uncon-scious memory. *Developmental Psychology, 34*, 342–357.

Brainerd, C. J., Stein, L. M., Silveira, R. A., Rohenkohl, G., & Reyna, V. F. (2008b). How does negative emotion cause false memories? *Psychological Science, 19*, 919–925.

Braten, S. (2007). On circular reenactment of care and abuse, and on other-centered moments in psychotherapy: Closing comments. In S. Braten (Ed.), *On Being Moved: From Mirror Neurons to Empathy* (pp. 303–314). Philadelphia, PA: John Benjamins.

Brehmer, Y., Li, S. C., Muller, V., von Oertzen, T., & Lindenberger, U. (2007). Memory plastic-ity across the lifespan: Uncovering children's latent potential. *Developmental Psychology, 43*, 465–478.

Bremner, J. D. (2008). The neurobiology of trauma and memory in children. In M. L. Howe, G. S. Goodman, & D. Cicchetti (Eds.), *Stress, Trauma, and Children's Memory Development: Neurobiological, Cognitive, Clinical, and Legal Perspectives* (pp. 11–49). New York: Oxford University Press.

Bremner, J. D., Randall, P., Scott, T. M., Bronen, R. A., Seibyl, J. P., Southwick, S. M., Delaney, R. C., McCarthy, G., Charney, D. S., & Innis, R. B. (1995). MRI-based measurement of hippo-campal volume in patients with combat-related post-traumatic stress disorder. *American Journal of Psychiatry, 152*, 973–981.

Bremner, J. D., Randall, P., Vermetten, E., Staib, L., Bronen, R. A., Mazure, C., et al. (1997). Magnetic resonance imaging-based measurement of hippocampal volume in post-traumatic stress disorder related to childhood physical and sexual abuse. *Biological Psychiatry, 41*, 23–32.

Bremner, J. D., Vermetten, E., Afzal, N., & Vythilingam, M. (2004). Deficits in verbal declarative memory function in women with childhood sexual abuse-related post-traumatic stress disorder. *Journal of Nervous & Mental Disease, 192*, 643–649.

Bremner, J. D., Vythilingam, M., Vermetten, E., Southwick, S. M., McGlashan, T., Nazeer, A., et al. (2003a). MRI and PET study of deficits in hippocampal structure and function in women with childhood sexual abuse and post-traumatic stress disorder. *American Journal of Psychiatry, 160*, 924–932.

Bremner, J. D., Vythilingam, M., Vermetten, E., Southwick, S. M., McGlashan, T., Staib, L. H., et al. (2003b). Neural correlates of declarative memory for emotionally valenced words in women with post-traumatic stress disorder related to early childhood sexual abuse. *Biological Psychiatry, 53,* 879–889.

Bretherton, I., & Waters, E. (Eds.) (1985). Growing points of attachment theory and research. *Monographs of the Society for Research in Child Development, 50* (1–2, Serial No. 209).

Brooks-Gunn, J., & Lewis, M. (1984). The development of early self-recognition. *Developmental Review, 4,* 215–239.

Brosch, T., & Sharma, D. (2005). The role of fear-relevant stimuli in visual search: A comparison of phylogenic and ontogenetic stimuli. *Emotion, 5,* 360–364.

Brown, S. M., Henning, S., & Wellman, C. L. (2005). Mild, short-term stress alters dendritic morphology in rat medial prefrontal cortex. *Cerebral Cortex, 15,* 1714–1722.

Bruce, D., Phillips-Grant, K., Wilcox-O'Hearn, L. A., Robinson, J. A., & Francis, L. (2007). Memory fragments as components of autobiographical knowledge. *Applied Cognitive Psychology, 21,* 307–324.

Bruce, D., Wilcox-O'Hearn, L. A., Robinson, J. A., Phillips-Grant, K., Francis, L., & Smith, M. C. (2005). Fragment memories mark the end of childhood amnesia. *Memory & Cognition, 33,* 567–576.

Bruck, M., & Ceci, S. J. (1999). The suggestibility of children's memory. *Annual Review of Psychology, 50,* 419–439.

Bruck, M., Ceci, S. J., Francoeur, E., & Barr, R. (1995). I hardly cried when I got my shot! Influencing children's reports about a visit to the pediatrician. *Child Development, 66,* 193–208.

Bugental, D. B., Blue, J., Cortez, V., Fleck, K., & Rodriguez, A. (1992). The influence of witnessed affect on information processing in children. *Child Development, 63,* 774–786.

Bullock, M., & Lutkenhaus, P. (1990). Who am I? Self-understanding in toddlers. *Merrill-Palmer Quarterly, 36,* 217–238.

Buss, C., Wolf, O. T., Witt, J., & Hellhammer, D. H. (2004). Autobiographic memory impairment following acute cortisol administration. *Psychoneuroendocrinology, 29,* 1093–1096.

Butterworth, G. E. (1990). Self-perception in infancy. In D. Cicchetti & M. Beeghly (Eds.), *The Self in Transition: Infancy to Childhood* (pp. 119–137). Chicago: University of Chicago Press.

Byrne, R. W., Bates, L. A., & Moss, C. J. (2009). Elephant cognition in primate perspective. *Comparative Cognition & Behavior Reviews, 4,* 65–79.

Cabanac, M. (1992). Pleasure: The common currency. *Journal of Theoretical Biology, 155,* 173–200.

Cahill, L. (2000). Modulation of long-term memory storage in humans by emotional arousal: Adrenergic activation and the amygdala. In J. P. Aggleton (Ed.), *The Amygdala: A Functional Analysis* (pp. 425–445). Oxford, UK: Oxford University Press.

Cahill, L., & McGaugh, J. L. (1996). Modulation of memory storage. *Current Opinion in Neurobiology, 6,* 237–242.

Cahill, L., & McGaugh, J. L. (1998). Mechanisms of emotional arousal and lasting declarative memory. *Trends in Neurosciences, 21,* 294–299.

Cahill, L., Prins, B., Weber, M., & McGaugh, J. L. (1994). β-adrenergic activation and memory for emotional events. *Nature, 371,* 702–704.

Cahill, L., & van Steegeren, A. (2003). Sex-related impairment of memory for emotional events with β-adrenergic blockade. *Neurobiology of Learning and Memory, 74,* 81–88.

Cairns, R. B., & Hood, K. E. (1983). Continuity in social development. In P. Baltes & O. G. Brim (Eds.), *Life Span Development* (vol. 5, pp. 301–358). New York: Academic Press.

Caldwell, M. C., & Caldwell, D. K. (1966). Epimeletic (caregiving) behavior in cetacea. In K. S. Norris (Ed.), *Whales, Dolphins, and Porpoises* (pp. 755–789). Los Angeles, CA: University of California Press.

Campanella, J., & Rovee-Collier, C. (2005). Latent learning and deferred imitation at 3 months. *Infancy, 7,* 243–262.

Campbell, B. A., & Jaynes, J. (1966). Reinstatement. *Psychological Review, 73,* 478–480.

Campbell, B. A., & Spear, N. E. (1972). Ontogeny of memory. *Psychological Review, 79,* 215–236.

Carey, S. (1985). *Conceptual Change in Childhood.* Cambridge, MA: MIT Press.

Carneiro, P., Albuquerque, P., Fernandez, A., & Esteves, F. (2007). Analyzing false memories in children with associative lists specific for their age. *Child Development, 78*, 1171–1185.

Carr, L., Iacoboni, M., Dubeau, M. C., Mazziotta, J. C., & Lenzi, G. L. (2003). Neural mechanisms of empathy in humans: A relay from neural systems for imitation to limbic areas. *Proceedings of the National Academy of Sciences, 100*, 5497–5502.

Carrion, V. G., Weems, C. F., & Reiss, A. L. (2007). Stress predicts brain changes in children: A pilot longitudinal study on youth stress, post-traumatic stress disorder, and the hippocampus. *Pediatrics, 119*, 509–516.

Carver, L. J., Bauer, P. J., & Nelson, C. A. (2000). Associations between infant brain activity and recall memory. *Developmental Science, 3*, 234–246.

Casey, B. J., Tottenham, N., Liston, C., & Durston, S. (2005). Imaging the developing brain: What have we learned about cognitive development? *Trends in Cognitive Sciences, 9*, 104–110.

Ceci, S. J., & Bruck, M. (1993). The suggestibility of the child witness: A historical review and synthesis. *Psychological Bulletin, 113*, 403–439.

Ceci, S. J., & Bruck, M. (1995). *Jeopardy in the Courtroom*. Washington, DC: American Psychological Association.

Ceci, S. J., Fitneva, S. A., & Williams, W. M. (2010). Representational constraints on the development of memory and metamemory: A developmental-representational theory. *Psychological Review, 117*, 464–495.

Ceci, S. J., Papierno, P. B., & Kulkofsky, S. (2007). Representational constraints on children's suggestibility. *Psychological Science, 18*, 503–509.

Chae, Y., Ogle, C. M., & Goodman, G. S. (2009). Remembering negative childhood experiences: An attachment theory perspective. In J. A. Quas & R. Fivush (Eds.), *Emotion and Memory in Development: Biological, Cognitive, and Social Considerations* (pp. 3–27). New York: Oxford University Press.

Chamberlain, D. B. (1990). *Babies Remember Birth*. New York: Ballantine Books.

Chamberlain, D. B. (1998). *The Mind of Your Newborn Baby*. Berkeley, CA: North Atlantic Books.

Cheatham, C. L., & Bauer, P. J. (2005). Construction of a more coherent story: Prior verbal recall predicts later verbal accessibility of early memories. *Memory, 13*, 516–532.

Chen, E., Zeltzer, L. K., Craske, M. G. & Katz, E. R. (2000). Children's memories for painful cancer treatment procedures: Implications for distress. *Child Development, 71*, 933–947.

Chevalier-Skolnikoff, S., & Liska, J. (1993). Tool use by wild and captive elephants. *Animal Behavior, 46*, 209–219.

Chiu, C. Y., Schmithorst, V. J., Brown, R. D., Holland, S. K., & Dunn, S. (2006). Making memories: A cross-sectional investigation of episodic memory encoding in childhood using fMRI. *Developmental Neuropsychology, 29*, 321–340.

Christianson, S.-A. (1992). Emotional stress and eyewitness memory: A critical overview. *Psychological Bulletin, 112*, 284–309.

Christman, S. D., Propper, R. E., & Brown, T. J. (2006). Increased interhemispheric interaction is associated with earlier offset childhood amnesia. *Neuropsychology, 20*, 336–345.

Cicchetti, D., & Beeghly, M. (Eds.) (1990). *The Self in Transition: Infancy to Childhood*. Chicago: University of Chicago Press.

Cicchetti, D., & Rogosch, F. A. (2001). The impact of child maltreatment and psychopathology upon neuroendocrine functioning. *Development and Psychopathology, 13*, 783–804.

Cicchetti, D., Rogosch, F. A., Howe, M. L., & Toth, S. L. (2010). The effects of maltreatment and neuroendocrine regulation on memory performance. *Child Development, 81*, 1504–1519.

Clarke, E. A., & Hanisee, J. (1982). Intellectual and adaptive performance of Asian children in adoptive American settings. *Child Development, 53*, 595–599.

Clayton, N. S., Bussey, T. J., Emery, N. J., & Dickinson, A. (2003). Prometheus to Proust: The case for behavioral criteria for "mental time travel." *Trends in Cognitive Sciences, 7*, 436–437.

Clayton, N. S., Dally, J., Gilbert, J., & Dickinson, A. (2005). Food caching by western scrub-jays (*Aphelocoma californica*) is sensitive to the conditions at recovery. *Journal of Experimental Psychology: Animal Behavior Processes, 31*, 115–124.

Clayton, N. S., & Dickinson, A. (1998). Episodic-like memory during cache recovery by scrub-jays. *Nature, 395*, 272–274.

Clayton, N. S., & Dickinson, A. (1999). Scrub-jays (*Aphelocoma coerulescens*) remember the relative time of caching as well as the location and content of their caches. *Journal of Comparative Psychology, 113*, 403–416.

Clayton, N. S., Emery, N. J., & Dickinson, A. (2006). The prospective cognition of food caching and recovery by Western scrub-jays (*Aphelocoma californica*). *Comparative Cognition & Behavior Reviews, 1*, 1–11.

Clayton, N. S., Yu, K. S., & Dickinson, A. (2001). Scrub jays (*Aphelocoma coerulescens*) form integrated memories of the multiple features of caching episodes. *Journal of Experimental Psychology: Animal Behavior Processes, 27*, 17–29.

Clayton, N. S., Yu, K. S., & Dickinson, A. (2003). Interacting cache memories: Evidence for flexible memory use by western scrub-jays (*Aphelocoma californica*). *Journal of Experimental Psychology: Animal Behavior Processes, 29*, 14–22.

Cleveland, E. S., & Reese, E. (2008). Children remember early childhood: Long-term recall across the offset of childhood amnesia. *Applied Cognitive Psychology, 22*, 127–142.

Coe, C. L., Rosenberg, L. T., & Levine, S. (1988). Effect of maternal separation on the complement system and antibody responses in infant primates. *International Journal of Neuroscience, 40*, 289–302.

Cohen, D., & Gunz, A. (2002). As seen by the other. . . : Perspectives on the self in the memories and emotional perceptions of Easterners and Westerners. *Psychological Science, 13*, 55–59.

Cohen, N. J., & Eichenbaum, H. E. (1993). *Memory, Amnesia, and the Hippocampal System.* Cambridge, MA: MIT Press.

Colombo, J., & Mitchell, D. W. (1990). Individual and developmental differences in infant visual attention: Fixation time and information processing. In J. Colombo & J. W. Fagan (Eds.), *Individual Differences in Infancy: Reliability, Stability, and Prediction* (pp. 193–227). Hillsdale, NJ: Erlbaum.

Colombo, J., & Mitchell, D. W. (2009). Infant visual habituation. *Neurobiology of Learning and Memory, 92*, 225–234.

Comblain, C., D'Argembeau, A., Van der Linden, M., & Aldenhoff, L. (2004). The effect of aging on the recollection of emotional and neutral pictures. *Memory, 12*, 673–684.

Conway, M. A. (1996). Autobiographical knowledge and autobiographical memories. In D. C. Rubin (Ed.), *Remembering Our Past: Studies in Autobiographical Memory* (pp. 67–93). New York: Cambridge University Press.

Conway, M. A. (2005). Memory and the self. *Journal of Memory and Language, 53*, 594–628.

Conway, M. A., & Fthenaki, A. (2000). Disruption and loss of autobiographical memory. In L. S. Cermak (Ed.), *Handbook of Neuropsychology (2nd ed.): Memory and Its Disorders* (pp. 281–312). Amsterdam, Netherlands: Elsevier.

Conway, M. A., & Pleydell-Price, C. W. (2000). The construction of autobiographical memories in the self-memory system. *Psychological Review, 107*, 261–288.

Conway, M. A., & Rubin, D. C. (1993). The structure of autobiographical memory. In A. F. Collins, S. E. Gathercole, M. A. Conway, & P. E. Morris (Eds.), *Theories of Memory* (pp. 103–137). Hillsdale, NJ: Erlbaum.

Cordon, I. M., Pipe, M.-E., Sayfan, L., Melinder, A., & Goodman, G. S. (2004). Memory for traumatic experiences in early childhood. *Developmental Review, 24*, 101–132.

Corkin, S. (1968). Acquisition of a motor skill after bilateral medial temporal-lobe excision. *Neuropsychologica, 6*, 255–265.

Courage, M. L., Edison, S. E., & Howe, M. L. (2004). Variability in the early development of visual self-recognition. *Infant Behavior & Development, 27*, 509–532.

Courage, M. L., & Howe, M. L. (1998). The ebb and flow of infant attentional preferences: Evidence for long-term recognition memory in 3-month-olds. *Journal of Experimental Child Psychology, 70,* 26–53.

Courage, M. L., & Howe, M. L. (2001). Long-term retention in 3.5-month-olds: Familiarization time and individual differences in attentional style. *Journal of Experimental Child Psychology, 79,* 271–293.

Courage, M. L., & Howe, M. L. (2002). From infant to child: The dynamics of cognitive change in the second year of life. *Psychological Bulletin, 128,* 250–277.

Courage, M. L., Howe, M. L., & Squires, S. E. (2004). Individual differences in 3.5-month-olds' visual attention: What do they predict at 1 year? *Infant Behavior & Development, 27,* 19–30.

Cowan, N., & Davidson, G. (1984). Salient childhood memories. *Journal of Genetic Psychology, 145,* 101–107.

Craik, F. I. M., & Bialystok, E. (2006). Cognition throughout the lifespan: Mechanisms of change. *Trends in Cognitive Sciences, 10,* 131–138.

Crawley, R. A., & Eacott, M. J. (2006). Memories of early childhood: Qualities of the experience of recollection. *Memory & Cognition, 34,* 287–294.

Cuc, A., Koppel, J., & Hirst, W. (2007). Silence is not golden: A case for socially shared retrieval-induced forgetting. *Psychological Science, 18,* 727–733.

Cunningham, E., & Janson, C. (2007). Integrating information about location and value of resources by white-faced saki monkeys (*Pithecia pithecia*). *Animal Cognition, 10,* 293–304.

Csikszentmihalkyi, M., & Beatie, O. (1979). Life themes: A theoretical and empirical exploration of their origins and effects. *Journal of Humanistic Psychology, 19,* 45–63.

Dally, J. M., Emery, N. J., & Clayton, N. S. (2006). Food-caching western scrub-jays keep track of who was watching when. *Science, 312,* 1662–1665.

Damasio, A. (1999). *The feeling of what happens: Body and emotion in the making of consciousness.* New York: Harcourt Brace & Company.

Damon, W., & Hart, D. (1988). *Self-understanding in childhood and adolescence.* Cambridge, UK: Cambridge University Press.

Davidson, D., Luo, Z., & Burden, M. J. (2001). Children's recall of emotional behaviors, emotional labels, and nonemotional behaviors: Does emotion enhance memory? *Cognition and Emotion, 15,* 1–26.

Davis, E. L., Quas, J. A., & Levine, L. J. (2008). Children's memory for stressful events: Exploring the role of discrete emotions. In M. L. Howe, G. S. Goodman, & D. Cicchetti (Eds.), *Stress, Trauma, and Children's Memory Development: Neurobiological, Cognitive, Clinical, and Legal Perspectives* (pp. 236–264). New York: Oxford University Press.

Davis, M., Campeau, S., Kim, M., & Falls, W. A. (1995). Neural systems of emotion: The amygdala's role in fear and anxiety. In J. L. McGaugh, N. M. Weinberger, & G. Lynch (Eds.), *Brain and Memory: Modulation and Mediation of Neuroplasticity* (pp. 3–40). New York: Oxford University Press.

DeBellis, M. D., Chrousos, G. P., Dorn, L. D., Burke, L., Helmers, K., Kling, M. A., et al. (1994). Hypothalamic-pituitary-adrenal axis dysregulation in sexually abused girls. *Journal of Clinical Endocrinology and Metabolism, 78,* 249–255.

DeBellis, M. D., Hall, J., Boring, A., Frustaci, K., & Moritz, G. (2001). A pilot longitudinal study of hippocampal volumes in pediatric maltreatment-related stress disorder. *Biological Psychiatry, 50,* 305–309.

DeBellis, M. D., & Keshaven, M. S. (2003). Sex differences in brain maturation in maltreatment-related pediatric post-traumatic stress disorder. *Neuroscience and Biobehavioral Reviews, 27,* 103–117.

DeBellis, M. D., Keshaven, M. S., Clark, D. B., Casey, B. J., Giedd, J. N., Boring, A. M., et al. (1999). Developmental traumatology: Part II: Brain development. *Biological Psychiatry, 45,* 1271–1284.

DeBellis, M. D., Keshaven, M. S., Shifflett, H., Iyengar, S., Beers, S. R., Hall, J., et al. (2002). Brain structures in pediatric maltreatment-related post-traumatic stress disorder: A sociodemo-graphically matched study. *Biological Psychiatry, 52,* 1066–1078.

Debiec, J., LeDoux, J. E., & Nader, K. (2002). Cellular and systems reconsolidation in the hippocampus. *Neuron, 36*, 527–538.

DeCasper, A., & Fifer, W. (1980). Of human bonding: Newborns prefer their mothers' voices. *Science, 208*, 1174–1176.

DeCasper, A. J., & Prescott, P. A. (1984). Human newborns' perception of male voices: Preference, discrimination, and reinforcing value. *Developmental Psychobiology, 17*, 481–491.

DeCasper, A. J., & Spence, M. J. (1986). Prenatal maternal speech influences newborns' perception of speech sounds. *Infant Behavior & Development, 9*, 133–150.

DeCasper, A. J., & Spence, M. J. (1991). Auditory mediated behavior during the prenatal period: A cognitive view. In M. Weiss & P. Zelazo (Eds.), *Newborn Attention: Biological Constraints and the Influence of Experience* (pp. 142–176). Norwood, NJ: Ablex.

Decety, J., & Meyer, M. (2008). From emotion resonance to empathic understanding: A social developmental neuroscience account. *Development and Psychopathology, 20*, 1053–1080.

DeDecker, A., Hermans, D., Raes, F., & Eelen, P. (2003). Autobiographical memory specificity and trauma in inpatient adolescents. *Journal of Clinical Child and Adolescent Psychology, 32*, 22–31.

Deese, J. (1959). On the prediction of occurrence of certain verbal intrusions in free recall. *Journal of Experimental Psychology, 58*, 17–22.

Deffenbacher, K. A., Bornstein, B. H., Penrod, S. D., & McGorty, E. K. (2004). A meta-analytic review of the effects of high stress on eyewitness memory. *Law and Human Behavior, 28*, 687–706.

de Haan, M., Mishkin, M., Baldeweg, T., & Vargha-Khadem, F. (2006). Human memory development and its dysfunction after early hippocampal injury. *Trends in Neurosciences, 29*, 374–381.

de Hoz, L., & Wood, E. R. (2006). Dissociating the past from the present in the activity of place cells. *Hippocampus, 16*, 704–715.

de Kloet, E. R., & Oitzl, M. S. (2003). Who cares for a stressed brain? The mother, the kid, or both? *Neurobiology of Aging, 24* Supplement 1, S61–S65; discussion S67–S68.

Delis, D. C., Kramer, J. H., Kaplan, E., & Ober, B. A. (1994). *CVLT-C Manual*. San Antonio, TX: The Psychological Corporation.

DeLoache, J. S., & LoBue, V. (2009). The narrow fellow in the grass: Human infants associate snakes and fear. *Developmental Science, 12*, 201–207.

Dennett, D. C. (1995). *Darwin's Dangerous Idea: Evolution and the Meaning of Life*. London: Penguin Books.

Denton, D. (2006). *The Primordial Emotions: The Dawning of Consciousness*. New York: Oxford University Press.

Derbish, M.H., & Howe, M.L. (2010). *Is Survival Processing Adaptive or Simply More Elaborative?* Manuscript in preparation.

de Waal, F. M. B. (1996). *Good Natured*. Cambridge, MA: Harvard University Press.

de Waal, F. M. B. (2008). Putting the altruism back into altruism: The evolution of empathy. *Annual Review of Psychology, 59*, 4.1–4.22.

de Waal, F. M. B. (2009). *The Age of Empathy: Nature's Lessons for a Kinder Society*. New York: Harmony Books.

de Waal, F. M. B., Dindo, M., Freeman, C. A., & Hall, M. (2005). The monkey in the mirror: Hardly a stranger. *Proceedings of the National Academy of Sciences U.S.A., 102*, 11140–11147.

Dewhurst, S. A., Barry, C., & Holmes, S. (2005). Exploring the false recognition of category exemplars: Effects of divided attention and explicit generation. *European Journal of Cognitive Psychology, 17*, 803–819.

Dewhurst, S. A., Barry, C., Swannell, E. R., Holmes, S. J., & Bathurst, L. (2007b). The effect of divided attention on false memory depends on how memory is tested. *Memory & Cognition, 35*, 660–667.

Dewhurst, S. A., Bould, E., Knott, L. M., & Thorley, C. (2009). The roles of encoding and retrieval processes in associative and categorical memory illusions. *Journal of Memory and Language, 60*, 154–164.

Dewhurst, S. A., Pursglove, R. C., & Lewis, C. (2007a). Story contexts increase susceptibility to the DRM illusion in 5-year-olds. *Developmental Science, 10*, 274–278.

Diamond, D. M., Fleschner, M., Ingersoll, N., & Rose, G. M. (1996). Psychological stress impairs spatial working memory: Relevance to electrophysiological studies of hippocampal function. *Behavioral Neuroscience, 110*, 661–672.

DiBiase, R., & Lewis, M. (1997). The relation between temperament and embarrassment. *Cognition and Emotion, 11*, 259–271.

Diekelmann, S., & Born, J. (2010). The memory function of sleep. *Nature Reviews Neuroscience, 11*, 114–126.

Dirix, C. E. H., Nijhuis, J. G., Jongsma, H. W., & Hornstra, G. (2009). Aspects of fetal learning and memory. *Child Development, 80*, 1251–1258.

Dobzhansky, T. (1967). *The Biology of Ultimate Concern*. New York: The New American Library.

Dodd, M. D., & MacLeod, C. M. (2004). False recognition without intentional learning. *Psychonomic Bulletin & Review, 11*, 137–142.

Drummey, A. B., & Newcombe, N. S. (1995). Remembering versus knowing the past: Children's explicit and implicit memories for pictures. *Journal of Experimental Child Psychology, 59*, 549–565.

Dudycha, G. J., & Dudycha, M. M. (1933). Some factors and characteristics of childhood memories. *Child Development, 4*, 265–278.

Dudycha, G. J., & Dudycha, M. M. (1941). Childhood memories: A review of the literature. *Psychological Bulletin, 36*, 668–682.

Dufour, V., & Sterck, E. H. M. (2008). Chimpanzees fail to plan in an exchange task but succeed in a tool-using procedure. *Behavioural Processes, 79*, 19–27.

Dyregov, A., Gjestad, R., & Raundalen, M. (2002). Children exposed to warfare: A longitudinal study. *Journal of Traumatic Stress, 15*, 59–68.

Eacott, M. J., & Crawley, R. A. (1998). The offset of childhood amnesia: Memory for events that occurred before age 3. *Journal of Experimental Psychology: General, 127*, 22–33.

Eacott, M. J., Easton, A., & Zinkivskay, A. (2006). Recollection in an episodic-like memory task in the rat. *Learning & Memory, 12*, 221–223.

Eccles, J. C. (1989). *Evolution of the Brain: Creation of the Self*. London: Routledge.

Edelman, G. (1989). *The Remembered Present: A Biological Theory of Consciousness*. New York: Basic Books.

Edelman, G. (2003). Naturalizing consciousness: A theoretical framework. *Proceedings of the National Academy of Sciences U.S.A., 100*, 5520–5524.

Edelman, G. (2009). Animal consciousness. In W. P. Banks (Ed.), *Encyclopedia of Consciousness* (pp. 23–36). New York: Elsevier.

Eichenbaum, H. (1997). Declarative memory: Insights from cognitive neurobiology. *Annual Review of Psychology, 48*, 547–572.

Eichenbaum, H. (2007). Comparative cognition, hippocampal function, and recollection. *Comparative Cognition & Behavior Reviews, 2*, 47–66.

Eichenbaum, H., & Cohen, N. J. (2001). *From Conditioning to Conscious Recollection: Memory Systems of the Brain*. New York: Oxford University Press.

Eichenhoff, M., & Rakic, P. (1991). A quantitative analysis of synaptogenesis in the molecular layer of the dentate gyrus in the rhesus monkey. *Developmental Brain Research, 64*, 129–135.

Eisen, M. L., Goodman, G. S., Qin, J., Davis, S., & Crayton, J. (2007). Maltreated children's memory: Accuracy, suggestibility, and psychopathology. *Developmental Psychology, 43*, 1275–1294.

Eisen, M. L., Qin, J., Goodman, G. S., & Davis, S. L. (2002). Memory and suggestibility in maltreated children: Age, stress, arousal, dissociation, and psychopathology. *Journal of Experimental Child Psychology, 83*, 167–212.

Elhers, A., Hackmann, A., Steil, R., Clohessy, S., Wenninger, K., & Winter, H. (2002). The nature of intrusive memories after trauma: The warning signal hypothesis. *Behavior Research and Therapy, 40,* 995–1002.

Emde, R. N. (1981). Changing models of infancy and the nature of early development: Re-modeling the foundation. *Journal of the American Psychoanalytic Association, 29,* 179–219.

Emery, N. J., & Clayton, N. S. (2001). Effects of experience and social context on prospective caching strategies by scrub jays. *Nature, 411,* 443–446.

Emery, N. J., & Clayton, N. S. (2004). The mentality of crows: Convergent evolution of intelligence in corvids and apes. *Science, 306,* 1903–1907.

Enticott, P. G., Johnson, P. J., Herring, S. E., Hoy, K. E., & Fitzgerald, P. B. (2008). Mirror neuron activation is associated with facial emotion processing. *Neuropsychologia, 46,* 2851–2854.

Etkin, A., & Wager, T. D. (2007). Functional neuroimaging of anxiety: A meta-analysis of emotional processing in PTSD, social anxiety disorder, and specific phobia. *American Journal of Psychiatry, 164,* 1476–1488.

Fantz, R. L. (1957). Form preferences in newly hatched chicks. *Journal of Comparative and Physiological Psychology, 50,* 422–430.

Fantz, R. L. (1958a). Pattern vision in young infants. *Psychological Record, 8,* 43–47.

Fantz, R. L. (1958b). Visual discrimination in a neonate chimpanzee. *Perceptual and Motor Skills, 8,* 59–66.

Fantz, R. L. (1964). Visual experience in infants: Decreased attention to familiar patterns relative to novel ones. *Science, 146,* 668–670.

Faure, J., Uys, J. D. K., Marais, L., Stein, D. J., & Daniels, W. M. U. (2007). Early maternal separation alters the response to traumatization resulting in increased levels of hippocampal neurotrophic factors. *Metabolic Brain Disease, 22,* 183–195.

Feeney, M. C., Roberts, W. A., & Sherry, D. F. (2009). Memory for what, where, and when in the black-capped chickadee (*Poecile atricapillus*). *Animal Cognition, 12,* 767–777.

Ferbinteanu, J., Kennedy, P. J., & Shapiro, M. L. (2006). Episodic memory—From brain to mind. *Hippocampus, 16,* 691–703.

Ferkin, M. H., Combs, A., del Barco-Trillo, J., Pierce, A. A., & Franklin, S. (2008). Meadow voles, *Microtus pennsylvanicus,* have the capacity to recall "what," "where," and "when" of a single past event. *Animal Cognition, 11,* 147–159.

Ferrari, P. F., & Gallese, V. (2007). Mirror neurons and intersubjectivity. In S. Braten (Ed.), *On Being Moved: From Mirror Neurons to Empathy* (pp. 77–88). Philadelphia, PA: John Benjamins.

Fischer, S., Wilhelm, I., & Born, J. (2007). Developmental differences in sleep's role for implicit off-line learning: Comparing children with adults. *Journal of Cognitive Neuroscience, 19,* 214–227.

Fivush, R. (1994). Young children's event recall: Are memories constructed through discourse? *Consciousness and Cognition, 3,* 356–373.

Fivush, R. (2002). Scripts, schemas, and memory for trauma. In N. L. Stein, P. J. Bauer, & M. Rabinowitz (Eds.), *Representation, Memory, and Development: Essays in Honor of Jean Mandler* (pp. 53–74). Mahwah, NJ: Erlbaum.

Fivush, R. (2009). Sociocultural perspectives on autobiographical memory. In M. L. Courage & N. Cowan (Eds.), *The Development of Memory in Infancy and Childhood* (pp. 283–301). Hove, UK: Psychology Press.

Fivush, R., Haden, C. A., & Reese, E. (1996). Remembering, recounting, and reminiscing: The development of autobiographical memory in social context. In D. C. Rubin (Ed.), *Remembering Our Past: Studies in Autobiographical Memory* (pp. 341–359). Cambridge, MA: Cambridge University Press.

Fivush, R., & Hamond, N. (1990). Autobiographical memory across the preschool years: Toward reconceptualizing childhood amnesia. In R. Fivush & J. A. Hudson (Eds.), *Knowing and Remembering in Young Children* (pp. 223–248). New York: Cambridge University Press.

Fivush, R., Hazzard, A., Sales, J. M., Sarfati, D., & Brown, T. (2003). Creating coherence out of chaos? Children's narratives of emotionally positive and negative events. *Applied Cognitive Psychology, 17,* 1–19.

Fivush, R. & Reese, E. (1992). The social construction of autobiographical memory. In M. A. Conway, D. C. Rubin, H. Spinnler, & W. A. Wagenaar (Eds.), *Theoretical Perspectives on Autobiographical Memory* (pp. 115–132). Dordrecht, Netherlands: Kluwer.

Fivush, R., & Reese, E. (2002). Reminiscing and relating: The development of parent–child talk about the past. In J. D. Webster & B. K. Haight (Eds.), *Critical Advances in Reminiscence Work* (pp. 109–122). New York: Springer.

Fivush, R., Sales, J. M., Goldberg, A., Bahrick, L., & Parker, J. (2004). Weathering the storm: Children's long-term recall of Hurricane Andrew. *Memory, 12,* 104–118.

Flint, R. W., Jr., & Riccio, D. C. (1999). Post-training glucose administration attenuates forgetting of passive-avoidance conditioning in 18-day-old rats. *Neurobiology of Learning & Memory, 72,* 62–67.

Flykt, A. (2005). Visual search with biological threat stimuli: Accuracy, reaction times, and heart rate changes. *Emotion, 5,* 349–353.

Foa, E. B., & Rothbaum, B. O. (1998). *Treating the Trauma of Rape.* New York: Guilford Press.

Fodor, J., & Piattelli-Palmarini, M. (2010). *What Darwin Got Wrong.* London: Profile Books.

Fogel, A. (2004). Remembering infancy: Accessing our earliest experiences. In G. Bremner & A. Slater (Eds.), *Theories of Infant Development* (pp. 204–230). Cambridge, UK: Blackwell.

Fogel, S. M., Smith, C. T., & Cote, K. A. (2007). Dissociable learning-dependent changes in REM and non-REM sleep in declarative and procedural memory systems. *Behavioral Brain Research, 180,* 48–61.

Fradet, C., McGrath, P. J., Kay, J., Adams, S., & Luke, B. (1990). A prospective survey of reactions to blood tests by children and adolescents. *Pain, 40,* 53–60.

Fraley, R. C., Garner, J. P., Shaver, P. R. (2002). Adult attachment and the defensive regulation of attention and memory: Examining the role of preemptive and postemptive defensive processes. *Journal of Personality and Social Psychology, 79,* 816–826.

Freud, S. (1905/1953). Three essays on the theory of sexuality. In J. Strachey (Ed.), *The Standard Edition of the Complete Psychological Works of Sigmund Freud* (vol. 7, pp. 135–243). London: Hogarth Press.

Freud, S. (1914/1938). The psychopathology of everyday life. In A. A. Brill (Ed.), *The Writings of Sigmund Freud* (pp. 35–178). New York: Modern Library.

Freud, S. (1916–1917/1963). Introductory lectures on psychoanalysis. In J. Strachey (Ed.), *The Standard Edition of the Complete Psychological Works of Sigmund Freud* (vols. 15–16, pp. 243–496). London: Hogarth Press (Original work published 1916–1917).

Freyd, J. J., & Gleaves, D. H. (1996). "Remembering" words not presented in lists: Relevance to the recovered/false memory controversy. *Journal of Experimental Psychology: Learning, Memory, and Cognition, 22,* 811–813.

Fujioka, T., Fujioka, A., Tan, N., Chowdhury, H., Mouri, H., Sakata, Y., & Nakamura, S. (2001). Mild prenatal stress enhances learning performance in the non-adopted rat offspring. *Neuroscience, 103,* 301–307.

Furlow, B. (2001). You must remember this. *New Scientist, 171* (No. 2308, 15 Sept.), 25–27.

Gabora, L., & Aerts, D. (2009). A model of the emergence and evolution of integrated worldviews. *Journal of Mathematical Psychology, 53,* 434–451.

Gaensbauer, T. J. (1995). Trauma in the preverbal period: Symptoms, memories, and developmental impact. *Psychoanalytic Study of the Child, 49,* 412–433.

Gaensbauer, T. J. (2002). Representations of trauma in infancy: Clinical and theoretical implications for the understanding of early memory. *Infant Mental Health Journal, 23,* 259–277.

Gaensbauer, T. J. (2010). *Mirror Neurons and the Reenactment of Trauma in Early Childhood.* Unpublished manuscript, University of Colorado.

Gaensbauer, T. J., & Siegel, C. H. (1995). Therapeutic approaches to post-traumatic stress disorder in infants and toddlers. *Infant Mental Health Journal, 16,* 292–305.

Gallese, V., Gadiga, L., Gogassi, L., & Rizzolatti, G. (1996). Action recognition in the premotor cortex. *Brain, 119,* 593–609.

Gallo, D. A., Roberts, M. J., & Seamon, J. G. (1997). Remembering words not presented in lists: Can we avoid creating false memories? *Psychonomic Bulletin & Review, 4,* 271–276.

Gallo, D. A., Roediger, H. L., III, & McDermott, K. B. (2001). Associative false recognition occurs without strategic criterion shifts. *Psychonomic Bulletin & Review, 8,* 589–586.

Gallup, G. G., Jr. (1970). Chimpanzees: Self-recognition. *Science, 167,* 86–87.

Gallup, G. G., Jr. (1979). Self-recognition in chimpanzees and man: A developmental and comparative perspective. In M. Lewis & L. Rosenblum (Eds.), *The Child and Its Family: The Genesis of Behavior* (vol. 2, pp. 107–126). New York: Plenum.

Gallup, G. G., Jr. (1982). Self-awareness and the emergence of mind in primates. *American Journal of Primatology, 2,* 237–248.

Garcia-Rill, E., Charlesworth, A., Heister, D., Ye, M., & Hayar, A. (2008). The developmental decrease in REM sleep: The role of transmitters and electrical coupling. *Sleep, 31,* 673–690.

Garry, M., & Gerrie, M. (2005). When photographs create false memories. *Current Directions in Psychological Science, 14,* 321–325.

Gati, I., & Ben-Shakhar, G. (1990). Novelty and significance in orientation and habituation: A feature-matching approach. *Journal of Experimental Psychology: General, 119,* 251–263.

Gelman, S. A. (2003). *The essential Child: Origins of Essentialism in Everyday Thought.* New York: Oxford University Press.

Gerstadt, C. L., Hong, H. Y., & Diamond, A. (1994). The relationship between cognition and action: Performance of 3½- to 7-year-olds on a Stroop-like day-night test. *Cognition, 53,* 129–153.

Ghetti, S. (2003). Memory for non-occurrences: The role of metacognition. *Journal of Memory and Language, 48,* 722–739.

Ghetti, S. (2008). Rejection of false events in childhood: A metamemory account. *Current Directions in Psychological Science, 17,* 16–20.

Ghetti, S., & Alexander, K. W. (2004). "If it happened, I would remember it": Strategic use of event memorability in the rejection of false autobiographical events. *Child Development, 75,* 542–561.

Ghetti, S., & Angelini, L. (2008). The development of recollection and familiarity in childhood and adolescence: Evidence from the dual-process signal detection model. *Child Development, 79,* 339–358.

Ghetti, S., Qin, J., & Goodman, G. S. (2002). False memories in children and adults: Age, distinctiveness, and subjective experience. *Developmental Psychology, 38,* 705–718.

Gibbon, J., Church, R. M., & Meck, W. H. (1984). Scalar timing in memory. *Annals of the New York Academy of Sciences, 423,* 52–77.

Gilbertson, M. W., Shenton, M. E., Ciszewski, A., Kasai, K., Lasko, N. B., Orr, S. P. (2002). Smaller hippocampal volume predicts pathologic vulnerability to psychological trauma. *Nature Neuroscience, 5,* 1242–1247.

Gill, F. B. (1988). Trap line foraging by hermit hummingbirds: Competition for an undefended renewable resource. *Ecology, 69,* 1933–1942.

Ginsburg, S., & Jablonka, E. (2007a). The transition to experiencing: I. Limited learning and limited experiencing. *Biological Theory, 2,* 218–230.

Ginsburg, S., & Jablonka, E. (2007b). The transition to experiencing: II. The evolution of associative learning based on feelings. *Biological Theory, 2,* 231–243.

Ginsburg, S., & Jablonka, E. (2010a). Experiencing: A Jamesian approach. *Journal of Consciousness Studies, 17,* 102–124.

Ginsburg, S., & Jablonka, E. (2010b). The evolution of associative learning: A factor in the Cambrian explosion. *Journal of Theoretical Biology, 266,* 11–20.

Gluck, M. A., & Myers, C. E. (2001). *Gateway to Memory: An Introduction to neural Network Modeling of the Hippocampus and Learning.* Cambridge, MA: MIT Press.

Gold, P. E., & McCarty, R. C. (1995). Stress regulation of memory processes: Role of peripheral catecholamines and glucose. In M. J. Friedman, D. S. Charney, & A. Y. Deutch (Eds.), *Neurobiological and Clinical Consequences of Stress* (pp. 151–162). Philadelphia, PA: Lippincott-Raven.

Gold, P. E., Murphy, J. M., & Cooley, S. (1982). Neuroendocrine modulation of memory during development. *Behavioral and Neural Biology, 35,* 277–293.

Goldman-Rakic, P. S. (1987). Circuitry of primate prefrontal cortex and regulation of behavior by representational memory. In F. Plum (Ed.), *Handbook of Physiology, the Nervous System, and Higher Functions of the Brain* (vol. 5, pp. 373–417). Bethesda, MD: American Physiological Society.

Golier, J. A., Yehuda, R., Lupien, S. J., & Harvey, P. D. (2003). Memory for trauma-related information in Holocaust survivors with PTSD. *Psychiatry Research, 121,* 133–143.

Goodenough, B., Champion, G. D., Laubreaux, L., Tabah, L., & Kampel, L. (1998). Needle pain severity in children: Does the relationship between self-report and observed behavior vary as a function of age? *Australian Journal of Psychology, 50,* 1–9.

Goodenough, B., Kampel, L., Champion, G. D., Laubreaux, L., Nicholas, M. K., Ziegler, J. B., & McInerney, M. (1997). An investigation of the placebo effect and age-related factors in the report of needle pain from venipuncture in children. *Pain, 72,* 383–391.

Goodman, G. S., Ghetti, S., Quas, J. A., Edelstein, R. S., Alexander, K. W., Redlich, A. D., et al. (2003). A prospective study of memory for child sexual abuse: New findings relevant to the repressed-memory controversy. *Psychological Science, 14,* 113–118.

Goodman, G. S., & Quas, J. A. (1997). Trauma and memory: Individual differences in children's recounting of a stressful experience. In N. L. Stein, P. A. Ornstein, B. Tversky, & C. J. Brainerd (Eds.), *Memory for Everyday and Emotional Events* (pp. 267–294). Mahwah, NJ: Erlbaum.

Goodman, G. S., Quas, J. A., Batterman-Faunce, J. M., Riddlesberger, M. M., & Kuhn, J. (1994). Predictors of accurate and inaccurate memories for traumatic events experienced in childhood. *Consciousness and Cognition, 3,* 269–294.

Goodman, G. S., Quas, J. A., & Ogle, C. M. (2010). Child maltreatment and memory. *Annual Review of Psychology, 61,* 325–351.

Gopnik, A. (2009). *The Philosophical Baby: What Children's Minds Tell Us About Truth, Love, and the Meaning of Life.* London: The Bodley Head.

Gottlieb, G. (1985). Development of species identification in ducklings: XI. Embryonic critical period for species-typical perception in the hatchling. *Animal Behavior, 33,* 225–233.

Gould, S. J., & Lewontin, R. C. (1979). The spandrels of San Marco and the Panglossian paradigm: A critique of the adaptationist programme. *Proceedings of the Royal Society B: Biological Sciences, 205,* 581–598.

Greenhoot, A. F., Bunnell, S. L., Curtis, J. S., & Beyer, A. M. (2008). Trauma and autobiographical memory functioning: Findings from a longitudinal study of family violence. In M. L. Howe, G. S. Goodman, & D. Cicchetti (Eds.), *Stress, Trauma, and Children's Memory Development: Neurobiological, Cognitive, Clinical, and Legal Perspectives* (pp. 139–170). New York: Oxford University Press.

Greenough, W. T., Black, J. E., & Wallace, C. S. (1987). Experience and brain development. *Child Development, 58,* 539–559.

Griffiths, D. P., Dickinson, A., & Clayton, N. S. (1999). Declarative and episodic memory: What can animals remember about their past? *Trends in Cognitive Sciences, 3,* 74–80.

Gunnar, M. R., & Donzella, B. (2002). Social regulation of the cortisol levels in early human development. *Psychoneuroendocrinology, 27,* 199–220.

Gunnar, M. R., Tout, K., de Haan, M., Pierce, S., & Stansbury, K. (1997). Temperament, social competence, and adrenocortical activity in preschoolers. *Developmental Psychobiology, 31,* 65–85.

Gunnar, M. R., & Vazquez, D. (2001). Low cortisol and flattening of expected daytime rhythm: Potential indices of risk in human development. *Development and Psychopathology, 13,* 515–538.

Gurvits, T. V., Shenton, M. E., Hokama, H., Ohta, H., Lasko, N. B., Gilbertson, M. W., et al. (1996). Magnetic resonance imaging study of hippocampal volume in chronic, combat related post-traumatic stress disorder. *Biological Psychiatry, 40*, 1091–1099.

Gutteling, B. M., de Weerth, C., Willemsen-Swinkels, S. H., Huizink, A. C., Mulder, E. J., Visser, G. H., & Buitelaar, J. K. (2005). The effects of prenatal stress on temperament and problem behavior of 27-month-old toddlers. *European Child & Adolescent Psychiatry, 14*, 41–51.

Gutteling, B. M., de Weerth, C., Zandbelt, N., Mulder, E. J., Visser, G. H., & Buitelaar, J. K. (2006). Does maternal prenatal stress adversely affect the child's learning and memory at age six? *Journal of Abnormal Child Psychology, 34*, 789–798.

Haden, C. A., Haine, R. A., & Fivush, R. (1997). Developing narrative structure in parent-child reminiscing across the preschool years. *Developmental Psychology, 33*, 295–307.

Hampton, R. R., & Schwartz, B. L. (2004). Episodic memory in nonhumans: What, and where, is when? *Current Opinion in Neurobiology, 14*, 192–197.

Han, J. J., Leichtman, M. D., & Wang, Q. (1998). Autobiographical memory in Korean, Chinese, and American children. *Developmental Psychology, 34*, 701–713.

Hanna, E., & Meltzoff, A. N. (1993). Peer imitation by toddlers in laboratory, home, and day-care contexts: Implications for social learning and memory. *Developmental Psychology, 29*, 702–710.

Hardt, J., & Rutter, M. (2004). Validity of adult retrospective reports of adverse childhood experiences: Review of the evidence. *Journal of Child Psychology and Psychiatry, 45*, 260–273.

Harley, K., & Reese, E. (1999). Origins of autobiographical memory. *Developmental Psychology, 35*, 1338–1348.

Harlow, H. F., & Harlow, M. K. (1966). Learning to love. *American Scientist, 54*, 244–272.

Harlow, H. F., Harlow, M. K., & Suomi, S. J. (1971). From thought to therapy: Lessons from a primate laboratory. *American Scientist, 59*, 538–549.

Hart, J., Gunnar, M., & Cicchetti, D. (1996). Altered neuroendocrine activity in maltreated children related to symptoms of depression. *Development and Psychopathology, 8*, 201–214.

Hartshorn, K., Rovee-Collier, C., Gerhardstein, P. C., Bhatt, R. S., Klein, P. J., Aaron, F., et al. (1998). Developmental changes in the specificity of memory over the first year of life. *Developmental Psychobiology, 33*, 61–78.

Hayne, H. (2004). Infant memory development: Implications for childhood amnesia. *Developmental Review, 24*, 33–73.

Hayne, H. (2007). Infant memory development. In L. M. Oakes & P. J. Bauer (Eds.), *Short- and Long-Term Memory in Infancy and Early Childhood: Taking the First Steps Toward Remembering* (pp. 209–239). New York: Oxford University Press.

Hayne, H., Barr, R., & Herbert, J. (2003). The effect of prior practice on memory reactivation and generalization. *Child Development, 74*, 1615–1627.

Hayne, H., & Herbert, J. (2004). Verbal cues facilitate memory retrieval during infancy. *Journal of Experimental Child Psychology, 89*, 127–139.

Heim, C., Ehlert, U., & Hellhammer, D. (2000). The potential role of hypocortisolism in the pathophysiology of stress-related bodily disorders. *Psychoneuroendocrinology, 25*, 1–35.

Heim, C., Newport, J. D., Mletzko, T., Miller, A. H., & Nemeroff, C. B. (2008). The link between childhood trauma and depression: Insights from HPA axis studies in humans. *Psychoneuroendocrinology, 33*, 693–710.

Henderson, D., Hargreaves, I., Gregory, S., & Williams, J. M. G. (2002). Autobiographical memory and emotion in a nonclinical sample of women with and without a reported history of childhood sexual abuse. *British Journal of Clinical Psychology, 41*, 129–141.

Henri, V., & Henri, C. (1895). On earliest recollections of childhood. *Psychological Review, 2*, 215–216.

Henson, R. (2005). A mini-review of fMRI studies of human medial temporal lobe activity associated with recognition memory. *Quarterly Journal of Experimental Psychology, 58B*, 340–360.

Hepper, P. G. (1997). Memory in utero? *Developmental Medicine and Child Neurology, 39,* 343–346.

Hill, W. L., Borovsky, D., & Rovee-Collier, C. (1988). Continuities in infant memory development. *Developmental Psychobiology, 21,* 43–62.

Höffding, H. (1891). *Outlines of Psychology.* New York: Macmillan.

Hoffman, M. L., Beran, M. J., & Washburn, D. A. (2009). Memory for "what," "where," and "when" information in rhesus monkeys (*Macaca mulatte*). *Journal of Experimental Psychology: Animal Behavior Processes, 35,* 143–152.

Howe, M. L. (1997). Children's memory for traumatic experiences. *Learning and Individual Differences, 9,* 153–174.

Howe, M. L. (1998a). Individual differences in factors that modulate storage and retrieval of traumatic memories. *Developmental and Psychopathology, 10,* 681–698.

Howe, M. L. (1998b). Language is never enough: Memories are more than words reveal. *Applied Cognitive Psychology, 12,* 475–481.

Howe, M. L. (2000). *The Fate of Early Memories: Developmental Science and the Retention of Childhood Experiences.* Washington, DC: American Psychological Association.

Howe, M. L. (2002). The role of intentional forgetting in reducing children's retroactive interference. *Developmental Psychology, 38,* 3–14.

Howe, M. L. (2004a). Early memory, early self, and the emergence of autobiographical memory. In D. Beike, J. M. Lampinen, & D. A. Behrend (Eds.), *The Self and Memory* (pp. 45–72). New York: Psychology Press.

Howe, M. L. (2004b). The role of conceptual recoding in reducing children's retroactive interference. *Developmental Psychology, 40,* 131–139.

Howe, M. L. (2005). Children (but not adults) can inhibit false memories. *Psychological Science, 16,* 927–931.

Howe, M. L. (2006a). Developmental invariance in distinctiveness effects in memory. *Developmental Psychology, 42,* 1193–1205.

Howe, M. L. (2006b). Developmentally invariant dissociations in children's true and false memories: Not all relatedness is created equal. *Child Development, 77,* 1112–1123.

Howe, M. L. (2006c). Distinctiveness effects in children's memory. In R. R. Hunt & J. Worthen (Eds.), *Distinctiveness and Memory* (pp. 237–257). New York: Oxford University Press.

Howe, M. L. (2007). Children's emotional false memories. *Psychological Science, 18,* 856–860.

Howe, M. L. (2008a). The nature of infantile amnesia. In R. Menzel (Ed.), *Learning Theory and Behavior* (pp. 287–297). Volume 1 of *Learning and Memory: A Comprehensive Reference,* 4 vols. (J. Byrne, Ed.). Oxford, UK: Elsevier.

Howe, M. L. (2008b). Visual distinctiveness and the development of children's false memories. *Child Development, 79,* 65–79.

Howe, M. L. (2008c). What is false memory development the development of? Comment on Brainerd, Reyna, and Ceci (2008). *Psychological Bulletin, 134,* 768–772.

Howe, M. L., Candel, I., Otgaar, H., Malone, C., & Wimmer, M. C. (2010b). Valence and the development of immediate and long-term false memory illusions. *Memory, 18,* 58–75.

Howe, M. L., Cicchetti, D., & Toth, S. (2006a). Children's basic memory processes, stress, and maltreatment. *Development and Psychopathology, 18,* 759–769.

Howe, M. L., Cichetti, D., Toth, S. L., Cerrito, B. M. (2004). True and false memories in maltreated children. *Child Development, 75,* 1402–1417.

Howe, M. L., & Courage, M. L. (1993). On resolving the enigma of infantile amnesia. *Psychological Bulletin, 113,* 305–326.

Howe, M. L., & Courage, M. L. (1997a). The emergence and early development of autobiographical memory. *Psychological Review, 104,* 499–523.

Howe, M. L., & Courage, M. L. (1997b). Independent paths in the development of infant learning and forgetting. *Journal of Experimental Child Psychology, 67,* 131–163.

Howe, M. L., Courage, M. L., & Bryant-Brown, L. (1993). Reinstating preschoolers' memories. *Developmental Psychology, 29,* 854–869.

Howe, M. L., Courage, M. L., & Edison, S. (2003). When autobiographical memory begins. *Developmental Review, 23,* 471–494.

Howe, M. L., Courage, M. L., & Peterson, C. (1994). How can I remember when "I" wasn't there: Long-term retention of traumatic experiences and emergence of the cognitive self. *Consciousness and Cognition, 3,* 327–355.

Howe, M. L., Courage, M. L., & Peterson, C. (1995). Intrusions in preschoolers' recall of traumatic childhood events. *Psychonomic Bulletin & Review, 2,* 130–134.

Howe, M. L., Courage, M. L., & Rooksby, M. (2009a). The genesis and development of autobiographical memory. In M. L. Courage & N. Cowan (Eds.), *The Development of Memory in Infancy and Childhood* (pp. 177–196). Hove, UK: Psychology Press.

Howe, M. L., Courage, M. L., Vernescu, R., & Hunt, M. (2000). Distinctiveness effects in children's long-term retention. *Developmental Psychology, 36,* 778–792.

Howe, M. L., & Derbish, M. H. (2010). On the susceptibility of adaptive memory to false memory illusions. *Cognition, 115,* 252–267.

Howe, M. L., Garner, S., Charlesworth, M, & Knott, L. (2011). A brighter side to memory illusions: False memories prime children's and adults' insight-based problem solving. *Journal of Experimental Child Psychology, 108,* 383–393.

Howe, M. L., Garner, S., Dewhurst, S. A., & Ball, L. J. (2010a). Can false memories prime problem solutions? *Cognition, 117,* 176–181.

Howe, M. L., Goodman, G. S., & Cicchetti, D. (Eds.) (2008). *Stress, Trauma, and Children's Memory Development: Neurobiological, Cognitive, Clinical, and Legal Perspectives.* New York: Oxford University Press.

Howe, M. L., & Malone, C. (in press). Mood-congruent true and false memory: Effects of depression. *Memory.*

Howe, M. L., Rabinowitz, F. M., & Grant, M. J. (1993). On measuring (in)dependence of cognitive processes. *Psychological Review, 100,* 737–747.

Howe, M. L., Toth, S., & Cicchetti, D. (2006b). Memory and developmental psychopathology. In D. Cicchetti & D. Cohen (Eds.), *Developmental Psychopathology* (2nd ed.). Volume 2: *Developmental Neuroscience* (pp. 237–257). New York: Wiley.

Howe, M. L., Toth, S., & Cicchetti, D. (in press). Can maltreated children inhibit true and false memories for emotional information? *Child Development.*

Howe, M. L., & Wilkinson, S. (2011). Using story contexts to bias children's true and false memories. *Journal of Experimental Child Psychology, 108,* 77–95.

Howe, M. L., Wimmer, M. C., & Blease, K. (2009b). The role of associative strength in children's false memory illusions. *Memory, 17,* 8–16.

Howe, M. L., Wimmer, M. C., Gagnon, N., & Plumpton, S. (2009c). An associative-activation theory of children's and adults' memory illusions. *Journal of Memory and Language, 60,* 229–251.

Hu, P., Stylos-Allan, M., & Walker, M. P. (2006). Sleep facilitates consolidation of emotional declarative memory. *Psychological Science, 17,* 891–898.

Hudson, J. A. (1988). Children's memory for atypical actions in script-based stories: Evidence for a disruption effect. *Journal of Experimental Child Psychology, 46,* 159–173.

Hudson, J. A. (1990). Constructive processing in children's event memory. *Developmental Psychology, 26,* 180–187.

Huizink, A. C., Dick, D. M., Sihvola, E., Pukkiene, L., Rose, J. K. (2007). Chernobyl exposure as stressor during pregnancy and behavior in adolescent offspring. *Acta Psychiatrica Scandinavia, 116,* 438–446.

Huizink, A. C., Robles de Medina, P. G., Mulder, E. J. H., Visser, G. H. A., & Buitelaar, J. K. (2003). Stress during pregnancy is associated with developmental outcome in infancy. *Journal of Child Psychology and Psychiatry, 44,* 810–818.

Humphrey, N. (2002). *The Mind Made Flesh.* New York: Oxford University Press.

Humphrey, N. (2004). The placebo effect. In R. L. Gregory (Ed.), *Oxford Companion to the Mind* (2nd Ed., pp. 735–736). New York: Oxford University Press.

Hunt, R. R. (2006). The concept of distinctiveness in memory research. In R. R. Hunt & J. B. Worthen (Eds.), *Distinctiveness and Memory* (pp. 3–25). New York: Oxford University Press.

Hupbach, A., Gomez, R., & Nadel, L. (2009). Episodic memory reconsolidation: Updating or source confusion? *Memory, 17*, 502–510.

Huttenlocher, P. R. (1979). Synaptic density in human frontal cortex: Developmental changes and effects of aging. *Brain Research, 163*, 195–205.

Huttenlocher, P. R. (1994). Synaptogenesis, synapse elimination, and neural plasticity in human cerebral cortex. In C. A. Nelson (Ed.), *The Minnesota Symposium on Child Psychology: Vol. 27. Threats to Optimal Development: Integrating Biological, Psychological, and Social Risk Factors* (pp. 35–54). Hillsdale, NJ: Erlbaum.

Huttenlocher, P. R., & Dabholkar, A. S. (1997). Regional differences in synaptogenesis in human cerebral cortex. *Journal of Comparative Neurology, 387*, 167–178.

Hyman, I. E., Husband, T. H., & Billings, F. J. (1995). False memories of childhood experiences. *Applied Cognitive Psychology, 9*, 181–197.

Iacoboni, M. (2007). Face to face: The neural basis of social mirroring and empathy. *Psychiatric Annals, 37*, 236–241.

Irie-Sugimoto, N., Kobayashi, T., Sato, T., & Hasegawa, T. (2007). Evidence of means-end behavior in Asian elephants (*Elephas maximus*). *Animal Cognition, 11*, 1435–1441.

Irie-Sugimoto, N., Kobayashi, T., Sato, T., & Hasegawa, T. (2008). Relative quantity judgment by Asian elephants (*Elephas maximus*). *Animal Cognition, 12*, 193–199.

Isbell, L. (2006). Snakes and agents of evolutionary change in primate brains. *Journal of Human Evolution, 51*, 1–35.

Ito, Y., Teicher, M. H., Glod, C. A., & Ackerman, E. (1998). Preliminary evidence for aberrant cortical development in abused children: A quantitative EEG study. *Journal of Neuropsychiatry and Clinical Neuroscience, 10*, 298–307.

Ito, Y., Teicher, M. H., Glod, C. A., Harper, D., Magnus, E., & Gelbard, H. A. (1993). Increased prevalence of electrophysiological abnormalities in children with psychological, physical, and sexual abuse. *Journal of Neuropsychiatry and Clinical Neuroscience, 5*, 401–408.

Izquierdo, I., & Medina, J. H. (1997). The biochemistry of memory formation and its regulation by hormones and neuromodulators. *Psychobiology, 25*, 1–9.

Jackowski, A. P., Douglas-Palumberi, H., Jackowski, M., Win, L., Schultz, R. T., Staib, L. W., et al. (2008). Corpus callosum in maltreated children with post-traumatic stress disorder: A diffusion tensor imaging study. *Psychiatry Research, 162*, 256–261.

Jacobson, L., & Sapolsky, R. (1991). The role of the hippocampus in feedback regulation of the hypothalamic-pituitary-adrenocortical axis. *Endocrine Reviews, 12*, 118–134.

Jacoby, L. L. (1991). A process dissociation framework: Separating automatic from intentional uses of memory. *Journal of Memory and Language, 30*, 513–541.

Jacoby, L. L., Kelley, C., Brown, J., & Jasechko, J. (1989). Becoming famous overnight: Limits on the ability to avoid unconscious influences of the past. *Journal of Personality and Social Psychology, 56*, 326–338.

James, W. (1890/1961). *The Principles of Psychology*. New York: Henry Holt.

Janov, A. (2000). *The Biology of Love*. Amherst, NY: Prometheus Books.

Janus, L. (1993). Affective learning processes before and during birth. In T. Blum (Ed.), *Prenatal Perception, Learning, and Bonding* (pp. 33–60). Berlin: Leonardo.

Jelicic, M., & Bonke, B. (2004). Memory impairments following chronic stress? A critical review. *European Journal of Psychiatry, 15*, 225–232.

Joh, A., Sweeny, B., & Rovee-Collier, C. (2002). Minimum duration of reactivation at 3 months of age. *Developmental Psychobiology, 40*, 23–32.

Johnson, M. H. (1997). *Developmental Cognitive Neuroscience*. Oxford, UK: Blackwell.

Jones, E. J. H., & Herbert, J. S. (2006). Exploring memory in infancy: Deferred imitation and the development of declarative memory. *Infant and Child Development, 15*, 195–205.

Kaang, B.-K., Lee, S.-H., Kim, H. (2009). Synaptic protein degradation as a mechanism in memory reorganization. *The Neuroscientist, 15*, 430–435.

Kagan, J. (1981). *The Second Year: The Emergence of Self Awareness.* Cambridge, MA: Harvard University Press.

Kagan, J. (1984). Continuity and change in the opening years of life. In R. N. Emde & R. J. Harmon (Eds.), *Continuities and Discontinuities in Development* (pp. 15–39). New York: Plenum.

Kagan, J. (1994). *Galen's Prophecy: Temperament in Human Nature.* New York: Basic Books.

Kagan, J. (1996). Three pleasing ideas. *American Psychologist, 51*, 901–908.

Kahana, M. (2006). The cognitive correlates of human brain oscillations. *Journal of Neuroscience, 26*, 1669–1672.

Kail, R. (1988). Developmental functions for speeds of cognitive processes. *Journal of Experimental Child Psychology, 45*, 281–291.

Kail, R. (1997). Processing time, imagery, and spatial memory. *Journal of Experimental Child Psychology, 64*, 67–78.

Kail, R. (2002). Developmental change in proactive interference. *Child Development, 73*, 1703–1714.

Kandel, E. R., & Squire, L. R. (2000). Neuroscience: Breaking down scientific barriers to the study of brain and mind. *Science, 290*, 1113–1120.

Kang, S. H. K., McDermott, K. B., & Cohen, S. M. (2008). The mnemonic advantage of processing fitness-relevant information. *Memory & Cognition, 36*, 1151–1156.

Kanitz, E., Otten, W., Tuchscherer, M., & Manteufel, G. (2003). Effects of prenatal stress on corticosteroid receptors and monoamine concentrations in limbic areas of suckling piglets (*Sus scrofa*) at different ages. *Journal of Veterinary Medicine, 50*, 132–139.

Kaplan, J. T., & Iacoboni, M. (2006). Getting a grip on other minds: Mirror neurons, intention understanding, and cognitive empathy. *Social Neuroscience, 1*, 175–183.

Karr-Morse, R., & Wiley, M. S. (1997). *Ghosts From the Nursery.* New York: Atlantic Monthly Press.

Kavushansky, A., & Richter-Levin, G. (2006). Effects of stress and corticosterone on activity and plasticity in the amygdala. *Journal of Neuroscience Research, 84*, 1580–1587.

Kerr, D., Campbell, L., Applegate, M., Brodish, A., & Landfield, P. (1991). Chronic stress-induced acceleration of electrophysiologic and morphometric biomarkers of hippocampal aging. *Journal of Neuroscience, 11*, 1316–1322.

Kety, S. S. (1970). The biogenic amines in the central nervous system: Their possible role in arousal, emotion, and learning. In F. O. Schmitt (Ed.), *The Neurosciences: Second Study Program* (pp. 324–335). New York: Rockefeller University Press.

Kihlstrom, J. F., & Harackiewicz, J. M. (1982). The earliest recollection: A new survey. *Journal of Personality, 50*, 134–148.

Kim, J. H., McNally, G. P., & Richardson, R. (2006). Recovery of fear memories in rats: Role of gamma-amino butyric acid (GABA) in infantile amnesia. *Behavioral Neuroscience, 120*, 40–48.

Kim, J. J., Lee, H. J., Han, J.-S., & Packard, M. G. (2001). Amygdala is critical for stress-induced modulation of hippocampal long-term potentiation and learning. *Journal of Neuroscience, 21*, 5222–5228.

Kimball, D. R., & Bjork, R. A. (2002). Influences of intentional and unintentional forgetting on false memories. *Journal of Experimental Psychology: General, 131*, 116–130.

Kinzie, J. D., Sack, W. H., Angell, R. H., Manson, S., & Rath, B. (1986). The psychiatric effects of massive trauma on Cambodian children: I. The children. *Journal of the American Academy of Child and Adolescent Psychiatry, 25*, 370–376.

Kisilevsky, B. S., Hains, S. M. J., Lee, K., Xie, X., Huang, H., Ye, H. H., Zhang, K., & Wang, Z. (2003). Effects of experience on fetal voice recognition. *Psychological Science, 14*, 220–224.

Kitayama, N., Vaccarino, V., Kutner, M., Weiss, P., & Bremner, J. D. (2005). Magnetic resonance imaging (MRI) measurement of hippocampal volume in post-traumatic stress disorder: A meta-analysis. *Journal of Affective Disorders, 88*, 79–86.

Kitchigina, V., Vankov, A., Harley, C., & Sara, S. J. (1997). Novelty-elicited, noradrenaline-dependent enhancement of excitability in the dentate gyrus. *European Journal of Neuroscience,* 9, 41–47.

Klein, P. J., & Meltzoff, A. N. (1999). Long-term memory, forgetting, and deferred imitation in 12-month-old infants. *Developmental Science, 2,* 102–113.

Klein, S. B. (2007). Phylogeny and evolution: Implications for understanding the nature of a memory system. In H. L. Roediger III, Y. Dudai, & M. Fitzpatrick (Eds.), *Science of Memory: Concepts* (pp. 377–381). New York: Oxford University Press.

Klein, S. B., Cosmides, L., Tooby, J., & Chance, S. (2002). Decisions and the evolution of memory: Multiple systems, multiple functions. *Psychological Review, 109,* 306–329.

Kleinknecht, E., & Beike, D. R. (2004). How knowing and doing inform an autobiography: Relations among preschoolers' theory of mind, narrative, and event memory skills. *Applied Cognitive Psychology, 18,* 745–764.

Knott, L. M., & Dewhurst, S. A. (2007). The effects of divided attention at study and test on false recognition: A comparison of DRM and categorized lists. *Memory & Cognition, 35,* 1954–1965.

Knott, L., Howe, M. L., Wimmer, M. C., & Dewhurst, S. A. (in press). The Development of Automatic and Controlled Inhibitory Retrieval Processes in True and False Recall. *Journal of Experimental Child Psychology.*

Kohler, W. (1929). *Gestalt Psychology.* New York: Liveright.

Kohler, W. (1941). On the nature of associations. *Proceedings of the American Philosophical Society, 84,* 489–502.

Kopf, S. R., & Baratti, C. M. (1995). Memory-improving actions of glucose: Improvement of a central cholinergic mechanism. *Behavioral and Neural Biology, 62,* 237–243.

Korneyev, A. Y. (1997). The role of hypothalamic-pituitary-adrenocortical axis in memory-related effects of anxiolytics. *Neurobiology of Learning and Memory, 67,* 1–13.

Krueger, C., Holditch-Davis, D., Quint, S., & DeCaper, A. (2004). Recurring auditory experience in the 28- to 34-week-old fetus. *Infant Behavior & Development, 27,* 537–543.

Krützen, M., Mann, J., Heithaus, M. R., Connor, R. C., Bejder, L., & Sherwin, W. B. (2005). Cultural transmission of tool use in bottlenose dolphins. *Proceedings of the National Academy of Sciences U.S.A., 102,* 8939–8943.

Kuhl, P. K. (1988). Auditory perception and the evolution of speech. *Human Evolution, 3,* 19–43.

Kuhl, P. K. (1993). Effects of linguistic experience in the first half year of life: Implications for a theory of infant speech perception. In B. de Boysson-Bardies, S. de Schonen, P. Jusczyk, P. McNeilage, & J. Morton (Eds.), *Developmental Neurocognition: Speech and Face Processing in the First Year of Life* (pp. 259–274). Dordrecht, Netherlands: Kluwer.

Kuhl, P. K., Williams, K. A., Lacerda, F., Stevens, K. N., & Lindblom, B. (1992). Linguistic experience alters phonetic perception in infants by 6 months of age. *Science, 255,* 606–608.

Kunst-Wilson, W., & Zajonc, R. (1980). Affective discrimination of stimuli that cannot be recognized. *Science, 207,* 557–558.

Kuyken, W., & Brewin, C. R. (1995). Autobiographical memory functioning in depression and reports of early abuse. *Journal of Abnormal Psychology, 104,* 585–591.

Kuyken, W., Howell, R., & Dalgleish, T. (2006). Overgeneral autobiographical memory in depressed adolescents with, versus without, a reported history of trauma. *Journal of Abnormal Psychology, 115,* 387–396.

LaBar, K. S., & Cabeza, R. (2006). Cognitive neuroscience of emotional memory. *Nature Reviews: Neuroscience, 7,* 54–64.

Ladd, C. O., Owens, M. J., & Nemeroff, C. B. (1996). Persistent changes in corticotropin-releasing factor neuronal systems induced by maternal deprivation. *Endocrinology, 137,* 1212–1218.

Lange, A., de Beurs, E., Dolan, C., Lachnit, T., Sjollema, S., & Hanewald, G. (1999). Long-term effects of childhood sexual abuse: Objective and subjective characteristics of the abuse and psychopathology in later life. *Journal of Nervous & Mental Disease, 187,* 150–158.

Lanius, R. A., Williamson, P. C., Densmore, M., Boksman, K., Gupta, M. A., Neufeld, R. W., et al. (2001). Neural correlates of traumatic memories in post-traumatic stress disorder: A functional MRI investigation. *American Journal of Psychiatry, 158,* 1920–1922.

Lanius, R. A., Williamson, P. C., Densmore, M., Boksman, K., Neufeld, R. W, Gati, J. S., et al. (2004). The nature of traumatic memories: A 4-T fMRI functional connectivity analysis. *American Journal of Psychiatry, 161,* 36–44.

Lanius, R. A., Williamson, P. C., Hopper, J., Densmore, M., Boksman, K., Gupta, M. A., et al. (2003). Recall of emotional states in post-traumatic stress disorder: An fMRI investigation. *Biological Psychiatry, 53,* 204–210.

Laor, N., Wolmer, L., Mayes, L. C., Gershon, A., Weizman, R., & Cohen, D. J. (1997). Israeli preschool children under Scuds: A 30-month follow-up. *Journal of the American Academy of Child and Adolescent Psychiatry, 36,* 349–356.

Leach, J., & Ansell, L. (2008). Impairment in attentional processing in a field survival environment. *Applied Cognitive Psychology, 22,* 643–652.

Lecanuet, J., & Schaal, B. (1996). Fetal sensory competencies. *European Journal of Obstetrics, Gynecology, and Reproductive Biology, 68,* 1–23.

Lee, J. L. C. (2009). Reconsolidation: Maintaining memory relevance. *Trends in Neurosciences, 32,* 413–420.

Legerstee, M., Anderson, D., & Schaffer, A. (1998). Five- and eight-month-old infants recognize their faces and voices as familiar and social stimuli. *Child Development, 69,* 37–50.

Lemaire, V., Lamarque, S., Le Moal, M., Pier-Vincenzo, P., & Abrous, D. N. (2006). Postnatal stimulation of the pups counteracts stress-induced deficits in hippocampal neurogenesis. *Biological Psychiatry, 59,* 786–792.

Lepage, J. F., & Theoret, H. (2007). The mirror neuron system: Grasping others' actions from birth? *Developmental Science, 10,* 513–529.

Levine, B. (2004). Autobiographical memory and the self in time: Brain lesion effects, functional neuroanatomy, and lifespan development. *Brain and Cognition, 55,* 54–68.

Levy, F., Melo, A. I., Galef, B. G., Jr., Madden, M., & Fleming, A. S. (2003). Complete maternal deprivation affects social, but not spatial, learning in adult rats. *Developmental Psychobiology, 43,* 177–191.

Lewis, M. (1994). Myself and me. In S. Parker, R. Mitchell, & M. Boccia (Eds.), *Self Awareness in Animals and Humans: Developmental Perspectives* (pp. 20–34). Cambridge, MA: Cambridge University Press.

Lewis, M. (1995). Aspects of the self: From systems to ideas. In P. Rochat (Ed.), *The Self in Infancy: Theory and Research* (pp. 95–115). Amsterdam, Netherlands: Elsevier.

Lewis, M., & Brooks-Gunn, J. (1979). *Social Cognition and the Acquisition of the Self.* New York: Plenum.

Lewis, M., Brooks-Gunn, J., & Jaskir, J. (1985). Individual differences in early visual self-recognition. *Developmental Psychology, 21,* 1181–1187.

Lewis, M., & Carmody, D. P. (2008). Self-representation and brain development. *Developmental Psychology, 44,* 1329–1334.

Lewis, M., & Ramsay, D. S. (1997). Stress reactivity and self-recognition. *Child Development, 68,* 621–629.

Lewis, M., Sullivan, M., Stanger, C., & Weiss, M. (1989). Self-development and self-conscious emotions. *Child Development, 60,* 146–156.

Lickliter, R., & Virkar, P. (1989). Intersensory functioning in bobwhite quail chicks: Early sensory dominance. *Developmental Psychobiology, 22,* 651–667.

Lindblom, B. (1992). Phonological units as adaptive emergents of lexical development. In C. A. Ferguson, L. Menn, & C. S. Gammon (Eds.), *Phonological Development: Models, Research, Implications* (pp. 131–163). Timonium, MD: York.

Lindsay, D. S., Johnson, M. K., & Kwon, P. (1991). Developmental changes in memory source monitoring. *Journal of Experimental Child Psychology, 52,* 297–318.

Liu, D., Dorio, J., Day, J. C., Francis, D. D., & Meaney, M. J. (2000). Maternal care, hippocampal synaptogenesis, and cognitive development in rats. *Nature Neuroscience, 3*, 799–806.

Lloyd, M. E., & Newcombe, N. S. (2009). Implicit memory in childhood: Reassessing developmental invariance. In M. L. Courage & N. Cowan (Eds.), *The Development of Memory in Infancy and Childhood* (pp. 93–113). Hove, UK: Psychology Press.

LoBue, V. (2009). More than just another face in the crowd: Detection of threatening facial expressions in children and adults. *Developmental Science, 12*, 305–313.

LoBue, V., & DeLoache, J. S. (2008). Detecting the snake in the grass: Attention to fear-relevant stimuli by adults and young children. *Psychological Science, 19*, 284–289.

LoBue, V., & DeLoache, J. S. (2010). Superior detection of threat-relevant stimuli in infancy. *Developmental Science, 13*, 221–228.

Loftus, E. F. (1993). The reality of repressed memories. *American Psychologist, 48*, 518–537.

Loftus, E. F., & Loftus, G. R. (1980). On the permanence of stored information in the human brain. *American Psychologist, 35*, 409–420.

Lowe, P. (2001). Ethics specialist blasts "rebirthing." Rocky Mountain News, April 14. Retrieved September 20, 2002, from http://www.rockymountainnews.com/drmn/local/articles/0,DRMN_15_282715,00.html.

Lupien, S. J., Lecours, A., Lussier, I., Schwartz, G., Nair, N., & Meany, M. (1994). Basal cortisol levels and cognitive deficits in human aging. *Journal of Neuroscience, 14*, 2893–2903.

Lupien, S. J., & McEwen, B. S. (1997). The acute effects of glucocorticoids on cognition: Integration of animal and human model studies. *Brain Research Reviews, 24*, 1–27.

Lyons, K. E., Ghetti, S., & Cornoldi, C. (2010). Age differences in the contribution of recollection and familiarity to false-memory formation: A new paradigm to examine developmental reversals. *Developmental Science, 13*, 355–362.

Mabbott, D. J., Rovet, J., Noseworthy, M. D., Smith, M. L., & Rockel, C. (2009). The relations between white matter and declarative memory in older children and adolescents. *Brain Research, 1294*, 80–90.

MacDonald, S., Uesiliana, K., & Hayne, H. (2000). Cross-cultural and gender differences in childhood amnesia. *Memory, 8*, 365–376.

Maguire, E. A. (2001). Neuroimaging studies of autobiographical event memory. *Philosophical Transactions of the Royal Society of London, 356*, 1441–1451.

Mandler, J. M. (2004). *The Foundations of Mind: Origins of Conceptual Thought.* New York: Oxford University Press.

Mandler, J. M. (2007). How do we remember? Let me count the ways. In L. M. Oakes & P. J. Bauer (Eds.), *Short- and Long-Term Memory in Infancy and Early Childhood* (pp. 271–290). New York: Oxford University Press.

Manns, J. R., & Eichenbaum, H. (2006). Evolution of declarative memory. *Hippocampus, 16*, 795–808.

Manns, J. R., Stark, C., & Squire, L. (2000). The visual paired-comparison task as a measure of declarative memory. *Proceedings of the National Academy of Sciences, U.S.A., 97*, 12375–12379.

Mans, L., Cicchetti, D., & Sroufe, L. A. (1978). Mirror reaction of Down's syndrome infants and toddlers: Cognitive underpinnings of self-recognition. *Child Development, 49*, 1247–1250.

Markowitsch, H. J. (2000). Neuroanatomy of memory. In E. Tulving & F. I. M. Craik (Eds.), *The Oxford Handbook of Memory* (pp. 465–484). New York: Oxford University Press.

Marshall, P. J., & Kenney, J. W. (2009). Biological perspectives on the effects of early psychosocial experience. *Developmental Review, 29*, 96–119.

Martin-Ordas, G., Haun, D., Colmenares, F., & Call, J. (2010). Keeping track of time: Evidence for episodic-like memory in great apes. *Animal Cognition, 13*, 331–340.

Mather, M. (2007). Emotional arousal and memory binding: An object-based framework. *Perspectives on Psychological Science, 2*, 33–52.

Mazzoni, G., & Kirsch, I. (2002). Autobiographical memories and beliefs: A preliminary metacognitive model. In T. Perfect & B. Schwartz (Eds.), *Applied Metacognition* (pp. 121–145). Cambridge, UK: Cambridge University Press.

McAdams, D. P. (2001). The psychology of life stories. *Review of General Psychology, 5,* 100–122.

McDermott, K. B. (1996). The persistence of false memories in list recall. *Journal of Memory and Language, 35,* 221–230.

McDermott, K. B. (1997). Priming on perceptual implicit memory tests can be achieved through presentation of associates. *Psychonomic Bulletin & Review, 4,* 582–586.

McDermott, K. B., & Roediger, H. L., III (1998). Attempting to avoid illusory memories: Robust false recognition of associates persists under conditions of explicit warnings and immediate testing. *Journal of Memory and Language, 39,* 508–520.

McDonough, L., & Mandler, J. M. (1994). Very-long-term recall in infants: Infantile amnesia reconsidered. *Memory, 2,* 339–352.

McEwen, B. S., & Sapolsky, R. M. (1995). Stress and cognitive function. *Current Opinion in Neurobiology, 5,* 205–216.

McGaugh, J. L. (1995). Emotional activation, neuromodulatory systems, and memory. In D. L. Schacter, J. T. Coyne, G. D. Fischbach, M.-M. Mesulam, & L. E. Sullivan (Eds.), *Memory Distortion* (pp. 255–273). Cambridge, MA: Harvard University Press.

McGaugh, J. L. (2000). Memory: A century of consolidation. *Science, 287,* 248–251.

McGaugh, J. L. (2003). *Memory and Emotion.* London: Weidenfeld & Nicholson.

McGaugh, J. L., Cahill, L., & Roozendaal, B. (1996). Involvement of the amygdala in memory storage: Interaction with other brain systems. *Proceedings of the National Academy of Science, U.S.A., 93,* 13508–13514.

McGaugh, J. L., McIntyre, C. K., & Power, A. E. (2002). Amygdala modulation of memory consolidation: Interaction with other brain systems. *Neurobiology of Learning and Memory, 78,* 539–552.

McGuigan, F., & Salmon, K. (2004). Time to talk: The influence of the timing of child–adult talk on children's event memory. *Child Development, 75,* 669–686.

McKay, R. T., & Dennett, D. C. (2009). The evolution of misbelief. *Behavioral and Brain Sciences, 32,* 493–561.

McKee, R., & Squire, L. (1993). On the development of declarative memory. *Journal of Experimental Psychology: Learning, Memory, and Cognition, 19,* 397–404.

McLaughlin, K. L., Gomez, J. L., Baran, S. E., & Conrad, C. D. (2007). The effects of chronic stress on hippocampal morphology and function: An evaluation of chronic restraint paradigms. *Brain Research, 1161,* 56–64.

McNally, R. J., Clancy, S. A., Schacter, D. L., & Pitman, R. K. (2000). Cognitive processing of trauma cues in adults reporting repressed, recovered, or continuous memories of childhood sexual abuse. *Journal of Abnormal Psychology, 109,* 355–359.

McNally, R. J., Kaspi, S. P. Riemann, B. C., & Zeitlin, S. B. (1990). Selective processing of threat cues in post-traumatic stress disorder. *Journal of Abnormal Psychology, 99,* 398–402.

McNally, R. J., Litz, B. T., Prassas, A., Shin, L. M., & Weathers, F. W. (1994). Emotional priming of autobiographical memory in post-traumatic stress disorder. *Cognition and Emotion, 8,* 351–367.

McNally, R. J., Metzger, L., Lasko, N. B., Clancy, S. A., & Pitman, R. K. (1998). Directed forgetting of trauma cues in adult survivors of childhood sexual abuse with and without post-traumatic stress disorder. *Journal of Abnormal Psychology, 107,* 596–601.

Meaney, M. J. (2001). Maternal care, gene expression, and the transmission of individual differences in stress reactivity across generations. *Annual Review of Neuroscience, 24,* 1161–1192.

Mehl, B., & Buchner, A. (2008). No enhanced memory for faces of cheaters. *Evolution and Human Behavior, 29,* 35–41.

Meltzoff, A. N. (1988a). Infant imitation after a 1-week delay: Long-term memory for novel acts and multiple stimuli. *Developmental Psychology, 24,* 470–476.

Meltzoff, A. N. (1988b). Infant imitation and memory: Nine-month-olds in immediate and deferred tests. *Child Development, 59,* 217–225.

Meltzoff, A. N. (1990). Toward a developmental cognitive science: The implications of cross-modal matching and imitation for the development of representation and memory in infants. In A. Diamond (Ed.), *The Development and Neural Basis of Higher Cognitive Functions* (vol. 608, pp. 1–29). New York: New York Academy of Sciences.

Meltzoff, A. N. (1995). What infant memory tells us about infantile amnesia: Long-term recall and deferred imitation. *Journal of Experimental Child Psychology, 59*, 497–515.

Meltzoff, A. N., & Brooks, R. (2007). Intersubjectivity before language: Three windows on preverbal sharing. In S. Braten (Ed.), *On Being Moved: From Mirror Neurons to Empathy* (pp. 149–174). Philadelphia, PA: John Benjamins.

Meltzoff, A. N., & Moore, M. K. (1977). Imitation of facial and manual gestures by human neonates. *Science, 198*, 75–78.

Meltzoff, A. N., & Prinz, W. (2002). *The Imitative Mind: Development, Evolution, and Brain Bases.* Cambridge, UK: Cambridge University Press.

Menon, V., Boyett-Anderson, J., & Reiss, A. (2005). Maturation of medial temporal lobe response and connectivity during memory encoding. *Cognitive Brain Research, 25*, 379–385.

Mercado, E., Murray, S. O., Uyeyama, R. K., Pack, A. A., & Herman, L. M. (1998). Memory for recent actions in the bottlenosed dolphin (*Tursiops truncates*): Repetition of arbitrary behaviors using an abstract rule. *Animal Learning & Behavior, 26*, 210–218.

Merritt, K. A., Ornstein, P. A., & Spicker, B. (1994). Children's memory for a salient medical procedure: Implications for testimony. *Pediatrics, 94*, 17–23.

Metzger, R. L., Warren, A. R., Shelton, J. T., Price, J., Reed, A. W., & Williams, D. (2008). Do children "DRM" like adults? False memory production in children. *Developmental Psychology, 44*, 169–181.

Miller, G. E., Chen, E., & Zhou, E. S. (2007). If it goes up, must it come down? Chronic stress and the hypothalamic-pituitary-adrenocortical axis in humans. *Psychological Bulletin, 133*, 25–45.

Milner, B., Corkin, S., & Teuber, H.-L. (1968). Further analysis of the hippocampal amnesic syndrome: 14-year follow-up study of H. M. *Neuropsychologica, 6*, 215–234.

Mitchell, K. J., & Johnson, M. K. (2009). Source monitoring 15 years later: What have we learned from fMRI about the neural mechanisms of source memory? *Psychological Bulletin, 135*, 638–677.

Mizoguchi, K., Ishige, A., Aburada, M., & Tabira, T. (2003). Chronic stress attenuates glucocorticoid negative feedback: Involvement of the prefrontal cortex and hippocampus. *Neuroscience, 119*, 887–897.

Mizoguchi, K., Kunishita, T., Chui, D., & Tabira, T. (1992). Stress induces neuronal death in the hippocampus of castrated rats. *Neuroscience Letters, 138*, 157–164.

Moon, C., & Fifer, W. (2000). Evidence of transnatal auditory learning. *Journal of Perinatology, 20*, 37–44.

Moore, S. A., & Zoellner, L. A. (2007). Overgeneral autobiographical memory and traumatic events: An evaluative review. *Psychological Bulletin, 133*, 419–437.

Moradi, A. R., Doost, H. T., Taghavi, M. R., Yule, W., & Dalgleish, T. (1999). Everyday memory deficits in children and adolescents with PTSD: Performance on the Rivermead Behavioral Memory Test. *Journal of Child Psychology & Psychiatry, 40*, 357–361.

Moradi, A. R., Taghavi, M. R., Neshat-Doost, H., Yule, W., & Dalgleish, T. (2000). Memory bias for emotional information in children and adolescents with post-traumatic stress disorder: A preliminary study. *Journal of Anxiety Disorders, 14*, 521–534.

Morris, G., & Baker-Ward, L. (2007). Fragile but real: Children's capacity to use newly acquired words to convey preverbal memories. *Child Development, 78*, 448–458.

Morrison, C. M., & Conway, M. A. (2010). First words and first memories. *Cognition, 116*, 23–32.

Moscovitz, S. (1983). *Love Despite Hate.* New York: Schocken Books.

Moss, C. (1988). *Elephant Memories: Thirteen Years in the Life of an Elephant Family.* New York: Fawcett Columbine.

Mulcahy, N. J., & Call, J. (2006). Apes save tools for future use. *Science, 312*, 1038–1040.

Mullen, M. K. (1994). Earliest recollections of childhood: A demographic analysis. *Cognition, 52*, 55–79.

Mullen, M. K., & Yi, S. (1995). The cultural context of talk about the past: Implications for the development of autobiographical memory. *Cognitive Development, 10,* 407–419.

Murmu, M. S., Salomon, S., Biala, Y., Weinstock, M., Braun, K., & Bock, J. (2006). Changes in spine density and dendritic complexity in the prefrontal cortex in offspring of mothers exposed to stress during pregnancy. *European Journal of Neuroscience, 24,* 1477–1487.

Nachmias, M., Gunnar, M., Manglesdorf, S., Parritz, R. H., & Buss, K. (1996). Behavioral inhibition and stress reactivity: The moderating role of attachment security. *Child Development, 67,* 508–522.

Nairne, J. S. (2010). Adaptive memory: Evolutionary constraints on remembering. *Psychology of Learning and Motivation, 53,* 1–32.

Nairne, J. S., Pandeirada, J. N. S., & Thompson, S. R. (2008). Adaptive memory: The comparative value of survival processing. *Psychological Science, 19,* 176–180.

Nairne, J. S., Thompson, S. R., & Pandeirada, J. N. S. (2007). Adaptive memory: Survival processing enhances retention. *Journal of Experimental Psychology: Learning, Memory, and Cognition, 33,* 263–273.

Najarian, L. M., Goenjian, A. K., Pelcovitz, D., Mandel, E., & Najarian, B. (1996). Relocation after a disaster: Post-traumatic stress disorder in Armenia after the earthquake. *Journal of the American Academy of Child and Adolescent Psychiatry, 35,* 374–383.

Nash, M. (1987). What, if anything, is regressed about hypnotic age regression? A review of the empirical literature. *Psychological Bulletin, 102,* 42–52.

Nasrallah, H., Coffman, J., & Olson, S. (1989). Structural brain-imaging findings in affective disorders: An overview. *Journal of Neuropsychiatry and Clinical Neuroscience, 1,* 21–32.

Navalta, C. P., Tomoda, A., & Teicher, M. H. (2008). Trajectories of neurobehavioral development: The clinical neuroscience of child abuse. In M. L. Howe, G. S. Goodman, & D. Cicchetti (Eds.), *Stress, Trauma, and Children's Memory Development: Neurobiological, Cognitive, Clinical, and Legal Perspectives* (pp. 50–82). New York: Oxford University Press.

Neal, A., & Hesketh, B. (1997). Episodic knowledge and implicit learning. *Psychonomic Bulletin & Review, 4,* 24–37.

Neisser, U. (Ed.) (1993). *The Perceived Self.* New York: Cambridge University Press.

Neisser, U. (1995). Criteria for an ecological self. In P. Rochat (Ed.), *The Self in Infancy: Theory and Research* (pp. 17–33). Amsterdam, Netherlands: Elsevier.

Nelson, C. A. (1995). The ontogeny of human memory: A cognitive neuroscience perspective. *Developmental Psychology, 31,* 723–738.

Nelson, C. A. (1997). The neurological basis of early memory development. In N. Cowan (Ed.), *The Development of Memory in Childhood* (pp. 41–82). New York: Psychology Press.

Nelson, C. A. (2000). Neural plasticity and human development: The role of early experience in sculpting memory systems. *Developmental Science, 3,* 115–136.

Nelson, C. A., de Haan, M., & Thomas, K. (2006). Neural bases of cognitive development. In W. Damon, R. Lerner, D. Kuhn, & R. Siegler (Eds.), *Handbook of Child Psychology,* 6th ed., vol. 2: *Cognitive, Perception, and Language* (pp. 3–57). Hoboken, NJ: John Wiley.

Nelson, C. A., Zeanah, C. H., Fox, N. A., Marshall, P. J., Smyke, A. T., & Guthrie, D. (2007). Cognitive recovery in socially deprived young children: The Bucharest early intervention project. *Science, 318,* 1937–1940.

Nelson, K. (1989). Monologue as representation of real-life experience. In K. Nelson (Ed.), *Narratives From the Crib* (pp. 27–71). Cambridge, MA: Harvard University Press.

Nelson, K. (1996). *Language in Cognitive Development: The Emergence of the Mediated Mind.* New York: Cambridge University Press.

Nelson, K., & Fivush, R. (2004). The emergence of autobiographical memory: A social cultural developmental theory. *Psychological Review, 111,* 486–511.

New, J., Krasnow, M. M., Truxaw, D., & Gaulin, S. J. C. (2007). Spatial adaptations for plant foraging: Women excel and calories count. *Proceedings of the Royal Society B: Biological Sciences, 274,* 2679–2684.

Newcombe, N. S., Drummey, A. B., Fox, N. A., Lie, E., & Ottinger-Alberts, W. (2000). Remembering early childhood: How much, how, and why (or why not). *Current Directions in Psychological Science, 9,* 55–58.

Newcombe, N., & Fox, N. (1994). Infantile amnesia: Through a glass darkly. *Child Development, 65,* 31–40.

Newcombe, N., & Lie, E. (1995). Overt and covert recognition of faces in children and adults. *Psychological Science, 6,* 241–245.

Newcombe, N. S., Lloyd, M., & Balcomb, F. (in press). Contextualizing the development of recollection: Episodic memory and binding in young children. In S. Ghetti & P. J. Bauer (Eds.), *Origins and Development of Recollection: Perspectives from Psychology and Neuroscience.* New York: Oxford University Press.

Newcombe, N. S., Lloyd, M., & Ratliff, K. R. (2007). Development of episodic and autobiographical memory: A cognitive neuroscience perspective. *Advances in Child Development and Behavior, 35,* 37–85.

Newcomer, J. W., Craft, S., Hershey, T., Askins, K., & Bardgett, M. E. (1994). Glucocorticoid-induced impairment in declarative memory performance in adult humans. *Journal of Neuroscience, 14,* 2047–2053.

Newcomer, J. W., Selke, G., Kelly, A. K., Paras, L., & Craft, S. (1995). Age-related differences in glucocorticoid effect on memory in human subjects. *Society for Neuroscience Abstracts, 21,* 161.

Newman, E. J., & D. S. Lindsay (2009). False memories: What the hell are they for? *Applied Cognitive Psychology, 23,* 1105–1121.

Neylan, T. C., Lenoci, M., Rothlind, J., Metzler, T. J., Schuff, N., Du, A., et al. (2004). Attention, learning, and memory in post-traumatic stress disorder. *Journal of Traumatic Stress, 17,* 41–46.

Nielson, K. A., & Jensen, R. A. (1994). Beta-adrenergic receptor antagonist antihypertensive medications impair arousal-induced modulation of working memory in elderly humans. *Behavioral and Neural Biology, 62,* 190–200.

Nielson, M., Suddendorf, T., & Slaughter, V. (2006). Mirror self-recognition beyond the face. *Child Development, 77,* 1176–1185.

Norman, G., & Eacott, M. J. (2005). Dissociable effects of lesions to the perirhinal cortex and the postrhinal cortex on memory for context and objects in rats. *Behavioral Neuroscience, 119,* 557–566.

Nourkove, V., Bernstein, D. M., & Loftus, E. F. (2004). Altering traumatic memory. *Cognition and Emotion, 18,* 575–585.

Nyberg, L. (1998). Mapping episodic memory. *Behavioral Brain Research, 90,* 107–114.

Oades, R. D. (1979). Search and attention: Interactions of the hippocampal-septal axis, adrenal-cortical, and gonadal hormones. *Neuroscience and Biobehavioral Reviews, 3,* 31–48.

Ohayon, M. M., Carskadon, M. A., Guilleminault, C., & Vitiello, M. V. (2004). Meta-analysis of quantitative sleep parameters from childhood to old age in healthy individuals: Developing normative sleep values across the human lifespan. *Sleep, 27,* 1255–1273.

Ohman, A., Flykt, A., & Esteves, F. (2001). Emotion drives attention: Detecting the snake in the grass. *Journal of Experimental Psychology: General, 130,* 466–478.

Ohman, A., & Mineka, S. (2001). Fears, phobias, and preparedness: Toward an evolved module of fear and fear learning. *Psychological Review, 108,* 483–522.

Oitzl, M. S., Workel, J. O., Fluttert, M., Frosch, F., & de Kloet, E. R. (2000). Maternal deprivation affects behavior from youth to senescence: Amplification of individual differences in spatial learning and memory in senescent Brown Norway rats. *European Journal of Neuroscience, 12,* 3771–3780.

Orbach, Y., Lamb, M. E., Sternberg, K. J., Williams, J. M., & Dawud-Noursi, S. (2001). The effect of being a victim or witness of family violence on the retrieval of autobiographical memories. *Child Abuse & Neglect, 25,* 1427–1437.

Ornstein, P. A. (1995). Children's long-term retention of salient personal experiences. *Journal of Traumatic Stress, 8,* 581–605.

Ornstein, P. A., Baker-Ward, L., Gordon, B. N., Pelphrey, K. A., Tyler, C. S., & Gramzow, E. (2006). The influence of prior knowledge and repeated questioning on children's long-term retention of the details of a pediatric examination. *Developmental Psychology, 42*, 332–344.

Ornstein, P. A., Shapiro, L. R., Clubb, P. A., Follmer, A., & Baker-Ward, L. (1997). The influence of prior knowledge on children's memory for salient medical experiences. In N. L. Stein, P. A. Ornstein, B. Tversky, & C. J. Brainerd (Eds.), *Memory for Everyday and Emotional Events* (pp. 83–112). Mahwah, NJ: Erlbaum.

Osvath, M., & Osvath, H. (2008). Chimpanzee (*Pan troglodytes*) and orangutan (*Pongo abelii*) forethought: Self-control and pre-experience in the face of future tool use. *Animal Cognition, 11*, 661–674.

Otgaar, H., Candel, I., & Merckelbach, H. (2008). Children's false memories: Easier to elicit for a negative than for a neutral event. *Acta Psychologica, 128*, 350–354.

Otgaar, H., Candel, I., Merckelbach, H., & Wade, K. A. (2009). Abducted by a UFO: Prevalence information affects young children's false memories for an implausible event. *Applied Cognitive Psychology, 23*, 115–125.

Otgaar, H., Candel, I., Scoboria, A., & Merckelbach, H. (2010). Script knowledge enhances the development of children's false memories. *Acta Psychologica, 133*, 57–63.

Otgaar, H., & Smeets, T. (2010). Adaptive memory: Survival processing increases both true and false memory in adults and children. *Journal of Experimental Psychology: Learning, Memory, and Cognition, 36*, 1010–1016.

Otsubo, H., & Snead, C. (2001). Magnetoencephalography and magnetic source imaging in children. *Journal of Child Neurology, 16*, 227–235.

Overman, W., Bachevalier, J., & Sewell, F. (1993). A comparison of children's performance on two recognition tasks: Delayed nonmatch-to-sample versus visual paired-comparison. *Developmental Psychobiology, 26*, 345–357.

Pacheco-Cobos, L., Rosetti, M., Cuatianquiz, C., & Hudson, R. (2010). Sex differences in mushroom gathering: Men expend more energy to obtain equivalent benefits. *Evolution and Human Behavior, 31*, 289–297.

Pahl, M., Zhu, H., Pix, W., Tautz, J., & Zhang, S. (2007). Circadian timed episodic-like memory—a bee knows what to do when, and also where. *Journal of Experimental Biology, 210*, 3559–3567.

Paivio, A. (2007). *Mind and Its Evolution: A Dual Coding Approach.* Mahwah, NJ: Erlbaum.

Paldino, A., & Purpura, D. (1979). Quantitative analysis of the spatial distribution of axonal and dendritic terminals of hippocampal pyramidal neurons in immature human brain. *Experimental Neurology, 64*, 604–619.

Paley, J., & Alpert, J. (2003). Memory of infant trauma. *Psychoanalytic Psychology, 20*, 329–347.

Panksepp, J. (2005). Affective consciousness: Core emotional feelings in animals and humans. *Consciousness and Cognition, 14*, 30–80.

Parks, E. D., & Balon, R. (1995). Autobiographical memory for childhood events: Patterns of recall in psychiatric patients with a history of alleged trauma. *Psychiatry, 58*, 199–208.

Parr, L. A., & de Waal, F. B. M. (1999). Visual kin recognition in chimpanzees. *Nature, 399*, 647–648.

Pascalis, O., Hunkin, N., Holdstock, J., Isaac, C., & Mayes, A. (2004). Visual paired comparison performance is impaired in a patient with selective hippocampal lesions and relatively intact item recognition. *Neuropsychologia, 42*, 1293–1300.

Paus, T., Collins, D., Evans, A., Leonard, G., Pike, B., & Zijdenbos, A. (2001). Maturation of white matter in the human brain: A review of magnetic resonance studies. *Brain Research Bulletin, 54*, 255–266.

Payne, K. (2003). Sources of social complexity in the three elephant species. In P. Tyack & F. B. M. de Waal (Eds.), *Animal Social Complexity: Intelligence, Culture, and Individualized Societies* (pp. 57–85). Cambridge, MA: Harvard University Press.

Paz-Alonso, P. M., Ghetti, S., Donohue, S. E., Goodman, G. S., & Bunge, S. A. (2008). Neurodevelopmental correlates of true and false recognition. *Cerebral Cortex, 18*, 2208–2216.

Paz-Alonso, P. M., Larson, R. P., Castelli, P., Alley, D., & Goodman, G. S. (2009). Memory development: Emotion, stress, and trauma. In M. L. Courage & N. Cowan (Eds.), *The Development of Memory in Infancy and Childhood* (pp. 197–239). New York: Psychology Press.

Pederson, C. L., Maurer, S. H., Kaminski, P. L., Zander, K. A., Peters, C. M., Stoke-Crowe, L. A., et al. (2004). Hippocampal volume and memory performance in a community-based sample of women with post-traumatic stress disorder secondary to child abuse. *Journal of Traumatic Stress, 17*, 37–40.

Pelletier, J. G., & Pare, D. (2004). Role of amygdala oscillations in the consolidation of emotional memories. *Biological Psychiatry, 55*, 559–562.

Perner, J., Kloo, D., & Gornik, E. (2007). Episodic memory development: Theory of mind is part of re-experiencing experienced events. *Infant and Child Development, 16*, 471–490.

Perner, J., & Ruffman, T. (1995). Episodic memory or autonoetic consciousness: Developmental evidence and a theory of autobiographical memory development. *Journal of Experimental Child Psychology, 59*, 516–548.

Pezdek, K., & Hodge, D. (1999). Planting false childhood memories in children: The role of event plausibility. *Child Development, 70*, 887–895.

Pezdek, K., & Lam, S. (2007). What research paradigms have cognitive psychologists used to study "false memory" and what are the implications of their choices? *Consciousness and Cognition, 16*, 2–17.

Pfefferbaum, A., Mathalon, D. H., Sullivan, E. V., Rawles, J. M., Zipursky, R. B., & Lim, K. O. (1994). A quantitative magnetic resonance imaging study of changes in brain morphology from infancy to late adulthood. *Archives of Neurology, 51*, 874–887.

Phelps, E. A., & LeDoux, J. E. (2005). Contributions of the amygdala to emotion processing: From animal models to human behavior. *Neuron, 48*, 175–187.

Pillemer, D. B., & White, S. H. (1989). Childhood events recalled by children and adults. In H. W. Reese (Ed.), *Advances in Child Development and Behavior* (vol. 21, pp. 297–340). San Diego, CA: Academic Press.

Pinker, S. (1994). *The Language Instinct*. New York: HarperCollins.

Plato (360 BC/2004). *Theaetetus*. Translated by R. Waterfield. New York: Penguin Classics.

Plotnik, J. M., de Waal, F. B. M., & Reiss, D. (2006). Self-recognition in an Asian elephant. *Proceedings of the National Academy of Sciences U.S.A., 103*, 17053–17057.

Pollak, S. D. (2003). Experience-dependent affective learning and risk for psychopathology in children. *Annals of the New York Academy of Sciences, 1008*, 102–111.

Pollak, S. D., & Kistler, D. J. (2002). Early experience is associated with the development of categorical representations for facial expressions of emotion. *Proceedings of the National Academy of Sciences U.S.A., 99*, 9072–9076.

Pollak, S. D., Nelson, C. A., Schlaak, M. F., Roeber, B. J., Wewerka, S. S., Wiik, K. L., et al. (in press). Neurodevelopmental effects of early deprivation in post-institutionalized children. *Child Development*.

Pollak, S. D., Vardi, S., Bechner, A. M. P., & Curtin, J. J. (2005). Physically abused children's regulation of attention in response to hostility. *Child Development, 76*, 968–977.

Pope, K. S., & Brown, L. S. (1996). *Recovered Memories of Abuse: Assessment, Therapy, Forensics*. Washington, DC: American Psychological Association.

Porter, C., Lawson, J., & Bigler, E. D. (2005). Neurobehavioral sequelae of child sexual abuse. *Child Neuropsychology, 11*, 203–220.

Porter, S., & Peace, K. A. (2007). The scars of memory: A prospective, longitudinal investigation of the consistency of traumatic and positive emotional memories in adulthood. *Psychological Science, 18*, 435–441.

Porter, S., Spencer, L., & Birt, A. (2003). Blinded by emotion? Effect of emotionality of a scene on susceptibility to false memories. *Canadian Journal of Behavioural Sciences, 35*, 165–175.

Porter, S., Taylor, K., & ten Brinke, L. (2008). Memory for media: Investigation of false memories for negatively and positively charged public events. *Memory, 16*, 658–666.

Povinelli, D. J., Landau, K. R., & Perilloux, H. K. (1996). Self-recognition in young children using delayed versus live feedback: Evidence of a developmental asynchrony. *Child Development*, 67, 1540–1554.

Povinelli, D. J., Landry, A. M., Theall, L. A., Clarke, B. R., & Castile, C. M. (1999). Development of young children's understanding that the recent past is causally bound to the present. *Developmental Psychology*, 35, 1426–1439.

Povinelli, D. J., & Simon, B. B. (1998). Young children's understanding of briefly versus extremely delayed images of the self: Emergence of the autobiographical stance. *Developmental Psychology*, 34, 188–194.

Povinelli, D. J., Rulf, A. B., Landau, K. R., & Bierschwale, D. T. (1993). Self-recognition in chimpanzees (*Pan troglodytes*): Distribution, ontogeny, and patterns of emergence. *Journal of Comparative Psychology*, 107, 347–372.

Pratkanis, A. R., Greenwald, A. G., Leippe, M. R., & Baumgardner, M. H. (1988). In search of reliable persuasion effects: III—The sleeper effect is dead: Long live the sleeper effect. *Journal of Personality and Social Psychology*, 54, 203–218.

Prehn-Kristensen, A., Göder, R., Chirobeja, S., Breßmann, S., Ferstl, R., & Baving, L. (2009). Sleep in children enhances preferentially emotional declarative but not procedural memories. *Journal of Experimental Child Psychology*, 104, 132–139.

Price, J. (2008). *The Woman Who Can't Forget: A Memoir*. New York: Free Press.

Prudhomme, N. (2005). Early declarative memory and self-concept. *Infant Behavior & Development*, 28, 132–144.

Pugh, C. R., Tremblay, D., Fleshner, M., & Rudy, J. W. (1997). A selective role for corticosterone in contextual-fear conditioning. *Behavioral Neuroscience*, 111, 503–511.

Pynoos, R. S., & Nader, K. (1989). Children's memory and proximity to violence. *Journal of the American Academy of Child and Adolescent Psychiatry*, 28, 236–241.

Quas, J. A., Bauer, A., & Boyce, W. T. (2004). Physiological reactivity, social support, and memory in early childhood. *Child Development*, 75, 797–814.

Raby, C. R., Alexis, D. M., Dickinson, A., & Clayton, N. S. (2007). Planning for the future by western scrub jays. *Nature*, 445, 919–921.

Raby, C. R., & Clayton, N. S. (2009). Prospective cognition in animals. *Behavioural Processes*, 80, 314–324.

Radley, J. J., Sisti, H. M., Rocher, A. B., McCall, T., Hof, P. R., McEwen, B. S., & Morrison, J. H. (2004). Chronic behavioral stress induces apical dendrite reorganization in pyramidal neurons of the medial prefrontal cortex. *Neuroscience*, 125, 1–6.

Rajaram, S. (1996). Perceptual effects on remembering: Recollective processes in picture recognition. *Journal of Experimental Psychology: Learning, Memory, and Cognition*, 22, 365–377.

Rank, O. (1924/1994). *The Trauma of Birth*. New York: Dover Publications (Original work published in 1924).

Rathbun, C., DeVirgilio, L., & Waldfogel, S. (1958). A restituted process in children following radical separation from family and culture. *American Journal of Orthopsychiatry*, 28, 408–415.

Reder, L. M., Park, H., & Kieffaber, P. D. (2009). Memory systems do not divide on consciousness: Reinterpreting memory in terms of activation and binding. *Psychological Bulletin*, 135, 23–49.

Reese, E. (1999). What children say when they talk about the past. *Narrative Inquiry*, 9, 1–27.

Reese, E. (2009). The development of autobiographical memory: Origins and consequences. *Advances in Child Development and Behavior*, 37, 145–200.

Reese, E., & Cleveland, E. (2007). Mother–child reminiscing and children's understanding of mind. *Merrill-Palmer Quarterly*, 52, 17–43.

Reese, E., Haden, C. A., & Fivush, R. (1993). Mother–child conversations about the past: Relationships of style and memory over time. *Cognitive Development*, 8, 403–430.

Reese, E., Hayne, H., & MacDonald, S. (2008). Looking back to the future: Maori and Pakeha mother–child birth stories. *Child Development*, 79, 114–125.

Reese, E., & Newcombe, R. (2007). Training mothers in elaborative reminiscing enhances children's autobiographical memory and narrative. *Child Development, 78,* 1153–1170.

Reiss, D., & Marino, L. (2001). Mirror self-recognition in the bottlenose dolphin: A case of cognitive convergence. *Proceedings of the National Academy of Sciences U.S.A., 98,* 5937–5942.

Reiss, D., McCowan, B., & Marino, L. (1997). Communicative and other cognitive characteristics of bottlenose dolphins. *Trends in Cognitive Sciences, 1,* 140–145.

Reyna, V. F., & Kiernan, B. (1994). The development of gist versus verbatim memory in sentence recognition: Effects of lexical familiarity, semantic content, encoding instructions, and retention interval. *Developmental Psychology, 30,* 178–191.

Reyna, V. F., & Kiernan, B. (1995). Children's memory and interpretation of psychological metaphors. *Metaphor and Symbolic Activity, 10,* 309–331.

Reynolds, G. D., & Lickliter, R. (2002). Effects of prenatal sensory stimulation on heart rate and behavioral measures of arousal in bobwhite quail embryos. *Developmental Psychobiology, 41,* 112–122.

Reynolds, G. D., & Richards, J. E. (2005). Familiarization, attention, and recognition memory in infancy: An event-related potential and cortical source localization study. *Developmental Psychology, 41,* 598–615.

Reysen, M. B., & Nairne, J. S. (2002). Part-set cuing of false memories. *Psychonomic Bulletin & Review, 9,* 389–393.

Richards, J. E., & Casey, B. J. (1991). Heart rate variability during attentional phases in young infants. *Psychophysiology, 28,* 43–53.

Richardson, D. C., & Kirkham, N. Z. (2004). Multimodal events and moving locations: Eye movements of adults and 6-month-olds reveal dynamic spatial indexing. *Journal of Experimental Psychology: General, 133,* 46–62.

Richardson, R., & Fan, M. (2002). Behavioral expression of conditioned fear in rats is appropriate to their age at training, not their age at testing. *Animal Learning & Behavior, 30,* 394–404.

Richardson, R., & Hayne, H. (2007). You can't take it with you: The translation of memory across development. *Current Directions in Psychological Science, 16,* 223–227.

Richardson, R., Paxinos, G., & Lee, J. (2000). The ontogeny of conditioned odor potentiation of startle. *Behavioral Neuroscience, 114,* 1167–1173.

Richardson, R., Riccio, D. C., & Axiotis, R. (1986). Alleviation of infantile amnesia in rats by internal and external contextual cues. *Developmental Psychobiology, 19,* 453–462.

Richardson, R., Riccio, D. C., & Jonke, T. (1983). Alleviation of infantile amnesia in rats by means of pharmacological contextual state. *Developmental Psychobiology, 16,* 511–518.

Richmond, J., Colombo, M., & Hayne, H. (2007). Interpreting visual preferences in the visual paired-comparison task. *Journal of Experimental Psychology: Learning, Memory, and Cognition, 33,* 823–831.

Richmond, J., & Nelson, C. A. (2007). Accounting for change in declarative memory: A cognitive neuroscience perspective. *Developmental Review, 27,* 349–373.

Richmond, J., Sowerby, P., Colombo, M., & Hayne, H. (2004). The effect of familiarization time, retention interval, and context change on adults' performance on the visual paired-comparison task. *Developmental Psychobiology, 42,* 146–155.

Richter-Levin, G., & Akirav, I. (2003). Emotional tagging of memory formation: In the search for neural mechanisms. *Brain Research Reviews, 43,* 247–256.

Rizzolatti, G., Fogassi, L., & Gallese, V. (2004). Cortical mechanisms subserving object grasping, action understanding, and imitation. In M. S. Gazzaniga (Ed.), *The New Cognitive Neurosciences* (3rd ed., pp. 427–440). Cambridge, MA: MIT Press.

Roberts, K. P., & Blades, M. (1998). The effects of interacting in repeated events in children's eyewitness memory and source monitoring. *Applied Cognitive Psychology, 12,* 489–503.

Roberts, W. A. (2002). Are animals stuck in time? *Psychological Bulletin, 128,* 473–489.

Rochat, P. (1995). Early objectification of the self. In P. Rochat (Ed.), *The Self in Infancy: Theory and Research* (pp. 53–71). Amsterdam, Netherlands: Elsevier.

Rochat, P. (2001). Origins of self-concept. In J. G. Bremner & A. Fogel (Eds.), *Blackwell Handbook of Infant Development* (pp. 125–140). Oxford, UK: Basil Blackwell.

Rochat, P., & Striano, T. (2002). Who is in the mirror? Self-other discrimination in specular images by four- and nine-month-olds. *Child Development, 73*, 35–46.

Roebers, C. M., & Schneider, W. (2002). Stability and consistency of children's event recall. *Cognitive Development, 17*, 1085–1103.

Roediger, H. L., III, Balota, D. A., & Watson, J. M. (2001a). Spreading activation and the arousal of false memories. In H. L. Roediger III, J. S. Nairne, I. Neath, & A. M. Surprenant (Eds.), *The Nature of Remembering: Essays in Honor of Robert G. Crowder* (pp. 95–115). Washington, DC: American Psychological Association.

Roediger, H. L., III, & McDermott, K. B. (1995). Creating false memories: Remembering words not presented on lists. *Journal of Experimental Psychology: Learning, Memory, and Cognition, 21*, 803–814.

Roediger, H. L., III, Rajaram, S., & Srinvas, K. (1990). Specifying criteria for postulating memory systems. *Annals of the New York Academy of Sciences, 608*, 572–595.

Roediger, H. L., III, Watson, J. M., McDermott, K. B., & Gallo, D. A. (2001b). Factors that determine false recall: A multiple regression analysis. *Psychonomic Bulletin & Review, 8*, 385–407.

Roediger, H. L., III, Weldon, M. S., & Challis, B. H. (1989). Explaining dissociations between implicit and explicit measures of retention: A processing account. In H. L. Roediger III & F. I. M. Craik (Eds.), *Varieties of Memory: Essays in Honor of Endel Tulving* (pp. 3–41). Hillsdale, NJ: Erlbaum.

Roozendaal, B., Barsegyan, A., & Lee, S. (2008). Adrenal stress hormones, amygdala activation, and memory for emotionally arousing experiences. *Progress in Brain Research, 167*, 79–97.

Rose, S. A. (1981). Developmental changes in infants' retention of visual stimuli. *Child Development, 52*, 227–233.

Rose, S. A., Feldman, J. F., & Jankowski, J. J. (2001). Attention and recognition memory in the first year of life: A longitudinal study of preterm and full-term infants. *Developmental Psychology, 37*, 135–151.

Rose, S. A., Feldman, J. F., & Jankowski, J. J. (2004). Infant visual recognition memory. *Developmental Review, 24*, 74–100.

Roskoden, T., Linke, R., & Schwegler, H. (2005). Transient early postnatal corticosterone treatment of rats leads to accelerated acquisition of a spatial radial maze task and morphological changes in the septohippocampal region. *Behavioral Brain Research, 157*, 45–53.

Ross, M., & Wilson, A. E. (2000). Constructing and appraising past selves. In D. L. Schacter & E. Scarry (Eds.), *Memory, Brain, and Belief* (pp. 231–259). Cambridge, MA: Harvard University Press.

Ross, M., & Wilson, A. E. (2003). Autobiographical memory and conceptions of the self: Getting better all the time. *Current Directions in Psychological Science, 12*, 66–69.

Rovee-Collier, C. (1997). Dissociations in infant memory: Rethinking the development of implicit and explicit memory. *Psychological Review, 104*, 467–498.

Rovee-Collier, C., & Cuevas, K. (2009a). The development of infant memory. In M. L. Courage & N. Cowan (Eds.), *The Development of Memory in Infancy and Childhood* (pp. 11–41). Hove, UK: Psychology Press.

Rovee-Collier, C., & Cuevas, K. (2009b). Multiple memory systems are unnecessary to account for infant memory development: An ecological model. *Developmental Psychology, 45*, 160–174.

Rovee-Collier, C., & DuFault, D. (1991). Multiple contexts and memory retrieval at 3 months. *Developmental Psychobiology, 24*, 39–49.

Rovee-Collier, C., & Giles, A. (2010). Why a neuromaturational model of memory fails: Exuberant learning in early infancy. *Behavioural Processes, 83*, 197–206.

Rovee-Collier, C., Hayne, H., & Colombo, M. (2001). *The Development of Implicit and Explicit Memory*. Amsterdam, Netherlands: John Benjamins Publishing Company.

Rovee-Collier, C., Schechter, A., Shyi, G., & Shields, P. (1992). Perceptual identification of contextual attributes and infant memory retrieval. *Developmental Psychology, 28*, 307–318.

Rubin, D. C. (2000). The distribution of early childhood memories. *Memory, 8,* 265–269.

Rubin, D. C., Rahhal, T. A., & Poon, L. W. (1998). Things learned in early adulthood are remembered best. *Memory & Cognition, 26,* 3–19.

Russo, R., Nichelli, P., Gibertoni, M., & Cornia, C. (1995). Developmental trends in implicit and explicit memory: A picture completion study. *Journal of Experimental Child Psychology, 59,* 566–578.

Rutter, M. (1981). *Maternal Deprivation Reassessed.* New York: Penguin Books.

Rutter, M. (1998). Developmental catch-up, and deficit, following adoption after severe global early privation. *Journal of Child Psychology and Psychiatry, 39,* 465–476.

Rutter, M. (2006). The psychological effects of early institutional rearing. In P. J. Marshall & N. A. Fox (Eds.), *The Development of Social Engagement: Neurobiological Perspectives* (pp. 355–391). New York: Oxford University Press.

Rutter, M., Beckett, C., Castle, J., Colvert, E., Kreppner, J., Mehta, M., et al. (2007a). Effects of profound early institutional deprivation: An overview of findings from a UK longitudinal study of Romanian adoptees. *European Journal of Developmental Psychology, 4,* 332–360.

Rutter, M., Colvert, E., Kreppner, J., Beckett, C., Castle, J., Groothues, C., et al. (2007b). Early adolescent outcomes for institutionally deprived and non-deprived adoptees. I: Disinhibited attachment. *Journal of Child Psychology and Psychiatry, 48,* 17–30.

Rutter, M., O'Connor, T., & The ERA Study Team (2004). Are there biological programming effects for psychological development? Findings from a study of Romanian adoptees. *Developmental Psychology, 40,* 81–94.

Rutter, M., Sonuga-Barke, E. J., Beckett, C., Castle, J., Kreppner, J., Kumsta, R., et al. (2010). Deprivation-specific psychological patterns: Effects of institutional deprivation. *Monographs of the Society for Research in Child Development, 75* (Whole No. 1).

Sales, J. M., Fivush, R., & Peterson, C. (2003). Parental reminiscing about positive and negative events. *Journal of Cognition and Development, 4,* 185–209.

Sapolsky, R. M., Krey, L., & McEwen, B. S. (1985). Prolonged glucocorticoid exposure reduces hippocampal neuron number: Implications for aging. *Journal of Neuroscience, 5,* 1121–1127.

Sapolsky, R. M., Romero, M., & Munck, A. U. (2000). How do glucocorticoids influence stress responses? Integrating permissive, suppressive, stimulatory, and preparative actions. *Journal of Neuroscience, 10,* 2897–2902.

Schachtel, E. G. (1947). On memory and childhood amnesia. *Psychiatry, 10,* 1–26.

Schacter, D. L., Koustaal, W., & Norman, K. A. (1996). Can cognitive neuroscience illuminate the nature of traumatic childhood memories? *Current Opinion in Neurobiology, 6,* 207–214.

Schechter, N. L., Bernstein, B. A., Beck, A., Hart, L., & Scherzer, L. (1991). Individual differences in children's response to pain: Role of temperament and parental characteristics. *Pediatrics, 87,* 171–177.

Schiffer, F., Teicher, M. H., & Papanicolaou, A. C. (1995). Evoked potential evidence for right brain activity during the recall of traumatic memories. *Journal of Neuropsychiatry and Clinical Neuroscience, 7,* 169–175.

Schin, L. M., Rauch, S. L., & Pitman, R. K. (2006). Amygdala, medial temporal cortex, and hippocampal function in PTSD. *Annals of the New York Academy of Sciences, 1071,* 67–79.

Schmahmann, J. D., Pandya, D. N., Wang, R., Dai, G., D'Arceuil, H. E., de Crespigny, A. J., & Wedeen, V. J. (2007). Association fibre pathways of the brain: Parallel observation from diffusion spectrum imaging and autoradiography. *Brain, 130,* 630–653.

Schmidt, S. R. (2006). Emotion, significance, distinctiveness, and memory. In R. R. Hunt & J. B. Worthen (Eds.), *Distinctiveness and Memory* (pp. 47–64). New York: Oxford University Press.

Schmuckler, M. A. (1995). Self-knowledge of body position: Integration of perceptual and action system information. In P. Rochat (Ed.), *The Self in Infancy: Theory and Research* (pp. 221–242). Amsterdam, Netherlands: North Holland-Elsevier.

Schneider, J. F. L., Il'yasov, K. A., Hennig, J., & Martin, E. (2004). Fast quantitative diffusion-tensor imaging of cerebral white matter from the neonatal period to adolescence. *Neuroradiology*, *46*, 258–266.

Schneider, M. L., Roughton, E. C., Koehler, A. J., & Lubach, G. R. (1999). Growth and development following prenatal stress exposure in primates: An examination of ontogenetic vulnerability. *Child Development*, *70*, 263–274.

Schneider-Rosen, K., & Cicchetti, D. (1991). Early self-knowledge and emotional development: Visual self-recognition and affective reactions to mirror self-images in maltreated and non-maltreated toddlers. *Developmental Psychology*, *27*, 471–478.

Schoener, J. A., Baig, R., & Page, K. C. (2006). Prenatal exposure to dexamethasone alters hippocampal drive on the hypothalamic-pituitary-adrenal axis in adult male rats. *American Journal of Physiology: Regulatory, Integrative, and Comparative Physiology*, *290*, R1366–R1373.

Schwartz, B. L., Hoffman, M. L., & Evans, S. (2005). Episodic-like memory in a gorilla: A review and new findings. *Learning and Motivation*, *36*, 226–244.

Schwartz, E. D., & Kowalski, J. M. (1991). Malignant memories: PTSD in children and adults after a school shooting. *Journal of the American Academy of Child and Adolescent Psychiatry*, *30*, 936–944.

Scoboria, A., Mazzoni, G., Kirsch, I., & Relyea, M. (2004). Plausibility and belief in autobiographical memory. *Applied Cognitive Psychology*, *18*, 791–807.

Scoville, W. B., & Milner, B. (1957). Loss of recent memory after bilateral hippocampal lesions. *Journal of Neurology, Neurosurgery, & Psychiatry*, *20*, 11304–11312.

Seamon, J. G., Luo, C. R., Kopecky, J. J., Price, C. A., Rothschild, L., Fung, N. S., & Schwartz, M. A. (2002). Are false memories more difficult to forget than accurate memories? The effect of retention interval on recall and recognition. *Memory & Cognition*, *30*, 1054–1064.

Seligman, M. (1970). On the generality of laws of learning. *Psychological Review*, *77*, 406–418.

Seress, L., & Abraham, H. (2008). Pre- and postnatal morphological development of the human hippocampal formation. In C. A. Nelson & M. Luciana (Eds.), *Handbook of Developmental Cognitive Neuroscience* (2nd ed.) (pp. 187–211). Cambridge, MA: MIT Press.

Sevelinges, Y., Moriceau, S., Holman, P., Miner, C., Muzny, K., Gervais, R., Mouly, A.-M., & Sullivan, R. M. (2007). Enduring effects of infant memories: Infant odor-shock conditioning attenuates amygdala activity and adult fear conditioning. *Biological Psychiatry*, *62*, 1070–1079.

Sharot, T., Verfaellie, M., & Yonelinas, A. P. (2007). How emotion strengthens the recollective experience: A time-dependent hippocampal process. *PLoS ONE*, *2*(10), e1068. Doi: 10.1371.

Shaw, J. A., Applegate, B., & Schorr, C. (1996). Twenty-one month follow-up study of school-age children exposed to Hurricane Andrew. *Journal of the American Academy of Child and Adolescent Psychiatry*, *35*, 359–364.

Sheffield, E. G., & Hudson, J. A. (1994). Reactivation of toddlers' event memory. *Memory*, *2*, 447–465.

Shettleworth, S. J. (2007). Studying mental states is not a research program for comparative cognition. *Behavioral and Brain Sciences*, *30*, 332–333.

Shin, L., Wright, C., Cannistraro, P. A., Wedig, M. M., McMullin, K., Martis, B., Macklin, M. L., Lasko, N. B., Cavanagh, S. R., Krangel, T. S., Orr, S. P. Pitman, R. K., Whalen, P. J., & Rauch, S. L. (2005). A functional magnetic resonance imaging study of amygdala and medial prefrontal cortex responses to overtly presented fearful faces in post-traumatic stress disorder. *Archives of General Psychiatry*, *62*, 273–281.

Shroder, T. (2001). *Old Souls: Compelling Evidence From Children Who Remember Past Lives*. New York: Simon & Schuster.

Siegel, D. (1995). Memory, trauma, and psychotherapy: A cognitive sciences view. *Journal of Psychotherapy Practice and Research*, *4*, 93–122.

Silverman, I., Choi, J., & Peters, M. (2007). The hunter-gatherer theory of sex differences in spatial abilities: Data from 40 countries. *Archives of Sexual Behavior, 36*, 261–268.

Simcock, G., & Hayne, H. (2002). Breaking the barrier: Children do not translate their preverbal memories into language. *Psychological Science, 13*, 225–231.

Simcock, G., & Hayne, H. (2003). Age-related changes in verbal and nonverbal recall during early childhood. *Developmental Psychology, 39*, 805–814.

Simpson, A., & Riggs, K. J. (2005). Inhibitory and working memory demands of the day-night task in children. *British Journal of Developmental Psychology, 23*, 471–486.

Simpson, J. A., & Rholes, W. S. (1998). *Attachment Theory and Close Relationships.* New York: Guilford.

Singer, R. A., & Zentall, T. R. (2007). Pigeons learn to answer the question "Where did you just peck?" and can report peck location when unexpectedly asked. *Learning & Behavior, 35*, 184–189.

Skeels, H. M. (1966). Adult status of children with contrasting early life experiences. *Monographs of the Society for Research in Child Development, 31*, 1–65.

Skov-Rackette, S. I., Miller, N. Y., & Shettleworth, S. J. (2006). What-where-when memory in pigeons. *Journal of Experimental Psychology: Animal Behavior Processes, 32*, 345–358.

Skronowski, J. J. (2004). Giving sight and voice to blind mutes: An overview of theoretical ideas in autobiographical memory. *Social Cognition, 22*, 451–459.

Sloviter, R. S., Sollas, A. L., Dean, E., & Neubort, S. (1993). Adrenalectomy-induced degeneration in the rat hippocampal dentate gyrus: Characterization of an in vivo model of controlled neuronal death. *Journal of Comparative Neurology, 330*, 324–336.

Sluzenski, J., Newcombe, N. S., & Kovacs, S. L. (2006). Binding, relational memory, and recall of naturalistic events: A developmental perspective. *Journal of Experimental Psychology: Learning, Memory, and Cognition, 32*, 89–100.

Smith, C. (2001). Sleep states and memory processes in humans: Procedural versus declarative memory systems. *Sleep Medicine Reviews, 5*, 491–506.

Smith, G. J., & Spear, N. E. (1981). Role of proactive interference in infantile forgetting. *Animal Learning and Behavior, 9*, 371–380.

Smyke, A. T., Koga, S. F., Johnson, D. E., Fox, N. A., Marshall, P. J., Nelson, C. A., et al. (2007). The caregiving context in institutional-reared and family-reared infants and toddlers in Romania. *Journal of Child Psychology and Psychiatry, 48*, 210–218.

Sokolov, E. N. (1963). *Perception and the Conditioned Reflex.* Oxford: Pergamon Press.

Spanos, N. P. (1996). *Multiple Identities and False Memories: A Sociocognitive Perspective.* Washington, DC: American Psychological Association.

Spelke, E. S. (2000). Core knowledge. *American Psychologist, 55*, 1233–1243.

Spence, M. J. (1996). Young infants' long-term auditory memory: Evidence for changes in preferences as a function of delay. *Developmental Psychobiology, 29*, 685–695.

Spence, M. J., & Freeman, M. S. (1996). Newborn infants prefer the maternal low-pass filtered voice but not the maternal whispered voice. *Infant Behavior and Development, 19*, 199–212.

Spinillo, A., Viazzo, F., Colleoni, R., Chiara, A., Cerbo, R. M., & Fazzi, E. (2004). Two-year infant neurodevelopmental outcome after single or multiple antenatal courses of corticosteroids to prevent complications of prematurity. *American Journal of Obstetrics and Gynecology, 191*, 217–224.

Squire, L. R. (1992). Memory and the hippocampus: A synthesis from findings with rats, monkeys, and humans. *Psychological Review, 99*, 195–231.

Squire, L. R., & Kandel, E. R. (1999). *Memory: From Mind to Molecules.* New York: Scientific American Library.

Squire, L. R., & Zola, S. M. (1996). Structure and function of declarative and nondeclarative memory systems. *Proceedings of the National Academy of Sciences, 93*, 13515–13522.

Sroufe, L. A. (1983). Infant–caregiver attachment and patterns of adaptation in preschool: The roots of maladaptation. In M. Perlmutter (Ed.), *Minnesota Symposium on Child Psychology* (vol. 16, pp. 41–83). Hillsdale, NJ: Erlbaum.

Starkman, M. N., Gebarski, S., Berent, S., & Schteingart, D. (1992). Hippocampal formation volume, memory dysfunction, and cortisol levels in patients with Cushing's syndrome. *Biological Psychiatry, 32,* 756–765.

Stefan, K., Classen, J., Celnik, P., & Cohen, L. G. (2008). Concurrent action observation modulates practice-induced memory formation. *European Journal of Neuroscience, 27,* 730–738.

Stein, M. B. (1997). Hippocampal volume in women victimized by childhood sexual abuse. *Psychological Medicine, 27,* 951–959.

Stein, N. L., & Boyce, W. T. (1995, April). The role of physiological reactivity in attending to, remembering, and responding to an emotional event. In G. S. Goodman & L. Baker-Ward (Chairs), *Children's Memory for Emotional and Traumatic Events.* Symposium conducted at the Society for Research in Child Development Biennial Meeting, Indianapolis, IN.

Stein, N. L., & Liwag, M. D. (1997). Children's understanding, evaluation, and memory for emotional events. In P. van den Broek, P. J. Bauer, & T. Bourg (Eds.), *Developmental Spans in Event Comprehension and Representation: Bridging Fictional and Actual Events* (pp. 199–235). Mahwah, NJ: Erlbaum.

Strack, F., & Forster, J. (1995). Reporting recollective experiences: Direct access to memory systems? *Psychological Science, 6,* 343–351.

Strange, D., Sutherland, R., & Garry, M. (2006). Event plausibility does not determine children's false memories. *Memory, 14,* 937–951.

Stroop, J. R. (1935). Studies of interference in serial verbal reactions. *Journal of Experimental Psychology, 18,* 643–662.

Stuber, M. L., Nader, K., Yasuda, P., Pynoos, R. S., & Cohen, S. (1991). Stress responses after pediatric bone marrow transplantation: Preliminary results of a prospective longitudinal study. *Journal of the American Academy of Child and Adolescent Psychiatry, 30,* 952–957.

Studdert-Kennedy, M. (2002). Mirror neurons, vocal imitation, and the evolution of particulate speech. In M. I. Stamenov & V. Gallese (Eds.), *Mirror Neurons and the Evolution of Brain and Language* (pp. 207–228). Philadelphia, PA: John Benjamins.

Suddendorf, T., & Busby, J. (2003a). Mental travel in animals? *Trends in Cognitive Sciences, 7,* 391–396.

Suddendorf, T., & Busby, J. (2003b). Like it or not? The mental time travel debate: Reply to Clayton et al. *Trends in Cognitive Sciences, 7,* 437–438.

Suddendorf, T., Corballis, M. C., & Collier-Baker, E. (2009). How great is great ape foresight? *Animal Cognition, 12,* 751–754.

Suess, P. E., Porges, S. W., & Plude, D, J, (1994). Cardiac vagal tone and sustained attention in school-age children. *Psychophysiology, 31,* 17–22.

Suomi, S. J., & Harlow, H. H. (1972). Social rehabilitation of isolate reared monkeys. *Developmental Psychology, 6,* 487–496.

Szuran, T. F., Pliska, V., Pokorny, J., & Welzl, H. (2000). Prenatal stress in rats: Effects on plasma corticosterone, hippocampal glucocorticoid receptors, and maze performance. *Physiological Behavior, 71,* 353–362.

Taddio, A., Katz, J., Ilersich, A. L., & Koren, G. (1997). Effect of neonatal circumcision on pain response during subsequent routine vaccination. *Lancet, 349,* 599–603.

Taddio, A., Shah, V., Gilbert-MacLeod, C., & Katz, J. (2002). Conditioning and hyperalgesia in newborns exposed to repeated heel lances. *Journal of the American Medical Association, 288,* 857–861.

Tanapat, P., Hastings, N. B., Rydel, T. A., Galea, L. A. M., & Gould, E. (2001). Exposure to fox odor inhibits cell proliferation in the hippocampus of adult rats via an adrenal hormone–dependent mechanism. *Journal of Comparative Neurology, 437,* 496–504.

Tannenbaum, E. (2009). Speculations on the emergence of self-awareness in big-brained organisms: The roles of associative memory and learning, existential and religious questions, and the emergence of tautologies. *Consciousness and Cognition, 18,* 414–427.

Teicher, M. H. (1994). Early abuse, limbic system dysfunction, and borderline personality disorder. In K. Silk (Ed.), *Biological and Neurobehavioral Studies of Borderline Personality Disorder* (pp. 177–207). Washington, DC: American Psychiatric Press.

Teicher, M. H., Dumont, N. L., Ito, Y., Vaituzis, C., Giedd, J. N., & Andersen, S. L. (2004). Childhood neglect is associated with reduced corpus callosum area. *Biological Psychiatry, 56,* 80–85.

Teicher, M. H., Ito, Y., Glod, C. A., Andersen, S. L., Dumont, N., & Ackerman, E. (1997). Preliminary evidence for abnormal cortical development in physically and sexually abused children using EEG coherence and MRI. *Annals of the New York Academy of Science, 821,* 160–175.

Terr, L. C. (1981). Psychic trauma in children: Observations following the Chowchilla school-bus kidnapping. *American Journal of Psychiatry, 138,* 14–19.

Terr, L. C. (1983). Chowchilla revisited: The effects of psychic trauma four years after a school-bus kidnapping. *American Journal of Psychiatry, 140,* 1543–1550.

Terr, L. C. (1988). What happens to early memories of trauma? A study of twenty children under age five at the time of documented events. *Journal of the American Academy of Child and Adolescent Psychiatry, 27,* 96–104.

Terr, L. C. (1994). *Unchained Memories: True Stories of Traumatic Memories, Lost and Found.* New York: Basic Books.

Terr, L. C., Bloch, D. A., Michel, B. A., & Shi, H. (1996). Children's memories in the wake of *Challenger. American Journal of Psychiatry, 153,* 618–625.

Thapar, A., & McDermott, K. B. (2001). False recall and recognition induced by presentation of associated words: Effects of retention interval and level of processing. *Memory & Cognition, 29,* 424–432.

Thatcher, R. W. (1997). Human frontal lobe development: A theory of cyclical reorganization. In N. A. Krasnegor, R. Lyon, & P. Goldman-Rakic (Eds.), *Development of the Prefrontal Cortex: Evolution, Neurobiology, and Behavior* (pp. 85–113). Baltimore, MD: Paul H. Brookes Publishing Co.

Thomas, L. A., & DeBellis, M. D. (2004). Pituitary volumes in pediatric maltreatment-related post-traumatic stress disorder. *Biological Psychiatry, 55,* 752–758.

Thomas, K. M., & Tseng, A. (2008). Functional MRI methods in developmental cognitive neuroscience. In C. A. Nelson & M. Luciana (Eds.), *Handbook of Developmental Cognitive Neuroscience* (2nd ed.) (pp. 311–323). Cambridge, MA: MIT Press.

Thorndike, E. L. (1905). *The Elements of Psychology.* New York: Seiler.

Toglia, M. P., Neuschatz, J. S., & Goodwin, K. A. (1999). Recall accuracy and illusory memories: When more is less. *Memory, 7,* 233–256.

Toki, S., Morinobu, S., Imanaka, A., Yamamoto, S., Yamawaki, S., & Honma, K.-I. (2007). Importance of early lighting conditions in maternal care by dam as well as anxiety and memory later in life of offspring. *European Journal of Neuroscience, 25,* 815–829.

Toth, J. P., & Hunt, R. R. (1999). Not one versus many, but zero versus any: Structure and function in the context of the multiple memory systems debate. In J. K. Foster & M. Jelicic (Eds.), *Memory: Systems, Process, or Function? Debates in Psychology* (pp. 232–272). New York: Oxford University Press.

Tulving, E. (1984). Precis of elements of episodic memory. *Behavioral and Brain Sciences, 7,* 223–238.

Tulving, E. (1985). How many memory systems are there? *American Psychologist, 40,* 385–398.

Tulving, E. (1989). Remembering and knowing the past. *American Scientist, 77,* 361–367.

Tulving, E. (1993). What is episodic memory? *Current Directions in Psychological Science, 2,* 67–70.

Tulving, E. (2002). Episodic memory: From mind to brain. *Annual Review of Psychology, 53,* 1–25.

Tulving, E., & Markowitsch, H. J. (1998). Episodic and declarative memory: Role of the hippocampus. *Hippocampus, 8,* 198–204.

Tupler, L. A., & DeBellis, M. D. (2006). Segmented hippocampal volume in children and adolescents with post-traumatic stress disorder. *Biological Psychiatry, 59,* 523–529.

Tyano, S., Iancu, I., Solomon, Z., Sever, J., Goldstein, I., Touveianna, Y., et al. (1996). Seven-year follow-up of child survivors of a bus–train collision. *Journal of the American Academy of Child and Adolescent Psychiatry, 35,* 365–373.

Uno, H., Ross, T., Else, J., Suleman, M., & Sapolsky, R. M. (1989). Hippocampal damage associated with prolonged and fatal stress in primates. *Journal of Neuroscience, 9,* 1705–1711.

Usher, J. N., & Neisser, U. (1993). Childhood amnesia and the beginnings of memory for four early life events. *Journal of Experimental Psychology: General, 122,* 155–165.

Valentino, K., Cicchetti, D., Rogosch, F., & Toth, S. (2008). True and false recall and dissociation among maltreated children: The role of self-schema. *Development and Psychopathology, 20,* 213–232.

Valentino, K., Toth, S., & Cicchetti, D. (2009). Autobiographical memory functioning among abused, neglected, and nonmaltreated children: The overgeneral memory effect. *Journal of Child Psychology and Psychiatry, 50,* 1029–1038.

Vallee, M., Maccari, S., Dellu, F. G., Simon, H., Le Moal, M., & Mayo, W. (1999). Long-term effects of prenatal stress and postnatal handling on age-related glucocorticoids secretion and cognitive performance: A longitudinal study in the rat. *European Journal of Neuroscience, 11,* 1906–1916.

van Marle, H. J. F., Hermans, E. J., Qin, S., & Fernandez, G. (2009). From specificity to sensitivity: How acute stress affects amygdala processing of biologically salient stimuli. *Biological Psychiatry, 66,* 649–655.

van Schaik, C. P., Deaner, R. O., & Merrill, M. Y. (1999). The conditions for tool use in primates: Implications for the evolution of material culture. *Journal of Human Evolution, 36,* 719–741.

von Baeyer, C. L., Marche, T. A., Rocha, E. M., & Salmon, K. (2004). Children's memory for pain: Overview and implications for practice. *Journal of Pain, 5,* 241–249.

Vyas, A., Mitra, R., Shankaranarayana, B. S., & Chattaraji, S. (2002). Chronic stress induces contrasting patterns of dendritic remodeling in hippocampal and amygdaloid neurons. *Journal of Neuroscience, 22,* 6810–6818.

Wade, K., Garry, M., Read, J. D., & Lindsay, S. (2002). A picture is worth a thousand lies: Using false photographs to create false childhood memories. *Psychonomic Bulletin & Review, 9,* 597–603.

Wade, K., Sharman, S., Garry, M., Memon, A., Mazzoni, G., Merckelbach, H., & Loftus, E. (2007). False claims about false memory research. *Consciousness and Cognition, 16,* 18–28.

Wagenaar, W. A., & Groeneweg, J. (1990). The memory of concentration camp survivors. *Applied Cognitive Psychology, 4,* 77–87.

Wagner, U., Gais, S., & Born, J. (2001). Emotional memory formation is enhanced across sleep intervals with high amounts of rapid eye movement sleep. *Learning & Memory, 8,* 112–119.

Walker, M. P., & Stickgold, R. (2004). Sleep-dependent learning review and memory consolidation. *Neuron, 44,* 121–133.

Wallin, A. R., Quas, J. A., & Yim, I. S. (2009). Physiological stress responses and children's event memory. In J. A. Quas & R. Fivush (Eds.), *Emotion and Memory in Development: Biological, Cognitive, and Social Considerations* (pp. 313–339). New York: Oxford University Press.

Wang, Q. (2001). Cultural effects on adults' earliest childhood recollection and self-description: Implications for the relation between memory and self. *Journal of Personality and Social Psychology, 81,* 220–233.

Wang, Q. (2004). The emergence of cultural self construct: Autobiographical memory and self-description in American and Chinese children. *Developmental Psychology, 40,* 3–15.

Wang, Q., & Conway, M. A. (2006). Autobiographical memory, self, and culture. In L.-G. Nilsson & N. Ohta (Eds.), *Memory and Society: Psychological Perspectives* (pp. 9–27). Hove, UK: Psychology Press.

Wang, Q., Conway, M. A., & Hou, Y. (2004). Infantile amnesia: A cross-cultural investigation. *Cognitive Sciences, 1,* 123–135.

Wang, Q., & Leichtman, M. D. (2000). Same beginnings, different stories: A comparison of American and Chinese children's narratives. *Child Development, 71,* 1329–1346.

Wang, Q., Leichtman, M. D., & White, S. H. (1998). Childhood memory and self description in young Chinese adults: The impact of growing up an only child. *Cognition, 69,* 73–103.

Wantanabe, Y., Gould, E., & McEwen, B. S. (1992). Stress induces atrophy of apical dendrites of hippocampal CA3 pyramidal neurons. *Brain Research, 588*, 341–345.

Warneken, F., Hare, B., Melis, A. P., Hanus, D., & Tomasello, M. (2007). Spontaneous altruism by chimpanzees and young children. *PLoS Biology, 5*, 1414–1420.

Webb, S., Long, J., & Nelson, C. A. (2005). A longitudinal investigation of visual event-related potentials in the first year of life. *Developmental Science, 8*, 605–616.

Weber, M., McNally, G. P., & Richardson, R. (2006). Opioid receptors regulate retrieval of infant fear memories: Effects of naloxone on infantile amnesia. *Behavioral Neuroscience, 120*, 702–709.

Weinstein, Y., Bugg, J. M, & Roediger, H. L., III (2008). Can the survival recall advantage be explained by basic memory processes? *Memory & Cognition, 36*, 913–919.

Weinstock, M. (2001). Alterations induced by gestational stress in brain morphology and behavior of the offspring. *Progress in Neurobiology, 65*, 427–451.

Werner, E. E., & Smith, R. L. (1982). *Vulnerable but Invincible.* New York: McGraw-Hill.

Wessel, I., Meeren, M., Peeters, F., Arntz, A., & Merckelbach, H. (2001). Correlates of autobiographical memory specificity: The role of depression, anxiety, and childhood trauma. *Behavior Research and Therapy, 39*, 409–421.

Westbrook, R. F., Iordanova, M., Harris, J. A., McNally, G., & Richardson, R. (2002). Reinstatement of fear to an extinguished conditioned stimulus: Two roles for context. *Journal of Experimental Psychology: Animal Behavior Processes, 28*, 97–110.

Whishaw, I. Q., & Wallace, D. G. (2003). On the origins of autobiographical memory. *Behavioral Brain Research, 138*, 113–119.

Wiedenmayer, C. P. (2004). Adaptations or pathologies? Long-term changes in brain and behavior after a single exposure to severe threat. *Neuroscience and Biobehavioral Reviews, 28*, 1–12.

Wilhelm, I., Diekelmann, S., & Born, J. (2008). Sleep in children improves memory performance on declarative but not procedural tasks. *Learning & Memory, 15*, 373–377.

Williams, J. M. G., & Broadbent, K. (1986). Autobiographical memory in suicide attempters. *Journal of Abnormal Psychology, 95*, 144–149.

Williams, L. M. (1994). Recall of childhood trauma: A prospective study of women's memories of child sexual abuse. *Journal of Consulting and Clinical Psychology, 62*, 1167–1176.

Wilson, A. E., & Ross, M. (2003). The identity function of autobiographical memory: Time is on our side. *Memory, 11*, 137–149.

Wimmer, M. C., & Howe, M. L. (2009). The development of automatic associative processes and children's false memories. *Journal of Experimental Child Psychology, 104*, 447–465.

Wimmer, M. C., & Howe, M. L. (2010). Are children's memory illusions created differently than adults'? Evidence from levels-of-processing and divided attention paradigms. *Journal of Experimental Child Psychology, 107*, 31–49.

Winick, M., Meyer, K. K., & Harris, R. C. (1975). Malnutrition and environmental enrichment by early adoption. *Science, 190*, 1173–1175.

Wolf, O. T. (2009). Stress and memory in humans: Twelve years of progress? *Brain Research, 1293*, 142–154.

Wolkowitz, O. M., Reus, V. I., Weingartner, H., Thompson, K., Breier, A., Doran, A., et al. (1990). Cognitive effects of corticosteroids. *American Journal of Psychiatry, 147*, 1297–1303.

Wong, C. T. W., Bottiglieri, T., & Snead, O. C., III. (2003). GABA, γ-hydroxybutyric acid, and neurological disease. *Annals of Neurology, 54*, S3–S12.

Woolley, C. S., Gould, E., & McEwen, B. S. (1990). Exposure to excess glucocorticoids alters dendritic morphology of adult hippocampal pyramidal neurons. *Brain Research, 531*, 225–231.

Wu, L.-L., & Barsalou, L. W. (2009). Perceptual simulation in conceptual combination: Evidence from property generation. *Acta Psychologica, 132*, 173–189.

Yap, C. S. L., & Richardson, R. (2007). The ontogeny of fear-potentiated startle: Effects of earlier-acquired fear memories. *Behavioral Neuroscience, 121*, 1053–1062.

Yap, C. S. L., Stapinski, L., & Richardson, R. (2005). Behavioral expression of learned fear: Updating of early memories. *Behavioral Neuroscience, 119*, 1467–1476.

Yasik, A. E., Saigh, P. A., Oberfield, R. A., & Halamandaris, P. V. (2007). Post-traumatic stress disorder: Memory and learning performance in children and adolescents. *Biological Psychiatry, 61*, 382–388.

Yasuno, F., Hirata, M., Takimoto, H., Taniguchi, M., Nakagawa, Y., Ikerjiri, Y., et al. (1999). Retrograde temporal order amnesia resulting from damage to the fornix. *Journal of Neurology, Neurosurgery, and Psychiatry, 67*, 102–105.

Yeh, T. F., Lin, Y. J., Lin, H. C., Huang, C. C., Hsieh, W. S., Lin, C. H., & Tsai, C. H. (2004). Outcomes at school age after postnatal dexamethasone therapy for lung disease of prematurity. *New England Journal of Medicine, 350*, 1304–1313.

Young, A. W. (2000). Wondrous strange: The neuropsychology of abnormal beliefs. *Mind and Language, 15*, 47–73.

Young, A. W., Robertson, I. H., Hellawell, D., de Pauw, K. W., & Pentland, B. (1992). Cotard delusion after brain injury. *Psychological Medicine, 22*, 799–804.

Zahn-Waxler, C., Radke-Yarrow, M., Wagner, E., & Chapman, M. (1992). Development of concern for others. *Developmental Psychology, 28*, 126–136.

Zeanah, C. H., Nelson, C. A., Fox, N. A., Smyke, A. T., Marshall, P. J., Parker, S. W., et al. (2003). Designing research to study the effects of institutionalization on brain and behavioral development: The Bucharest early intervention project. *Development and Psychopathology, 15*, 885–907.

Zeinah, M., Engel, S., Thompson, P., & Bookheimer, S. (2005). Dynamics of the hippocampus during encoding and retrieval of face–name pairs. *Science, 299*, 577–580.

Zentall, T. R. (2005). Animals may not be stuck in time. *Learning and Motivation, 36*, 208–225.

Zentall, T. R. (2006). Mental time travel in animals: A challenging question. *Behavioural Processes, 72*, 173–183.

Zentall, T. R., Clement, T. S., Bhatt, R. S., & Allen, J. (2001). Episodic-like memory in pigeons. *Psychonomic Bulletin & Review, 8*, 685–690.

Zentall, T. R., Singer, R. A., & Stagner, J. P. (2008). Episodic-like memory: Pigeons can report location pecked when unexpectedly asked. *Behavioural Processes, 79*, 93–98.

Zhang, S., Schwartz, S., Pahl, M., Zhu, H., & Tautz, J. (2006). Honeybee memory: A honeybee knows what to do and when. *Journal of Experimental Biology, 209*, 4420–4428.

Zhang, T. Y., Chretien, P., Meaney, M. J., & Gratton, A. (2005). Influence of naturally occurring variations in maternal care on prepulse inhibition of acoustic startle and the medial prefrontal cortical dopamine response to stress in adult rats. *Journal of Neuroscience, 25*, 1493–1502.

Zinkivskay, A., Nazir, F., & Smulders, T. V. (2009). What-where-when memory in magpies (*Pica pica*). *Animal Cognition, 12*, 119–125.

Zola, S., Squire, L. R., Teng, E., Stefanacci, L., Buffalo, E., & Clark, R. (2000). Impaired recognition memory in monkeys after damage limited to the hippocampal region. *Journal of Neuroscience, 20*, 451–463.

Zola-Morgan, S., & Squire, L. R. (1990). The neuropsychology of memory: Parallel findings in humans and nonhuman primates. *Annals of the New York Academy of Sciences, 608*, 434–455.

Author Index

Subject Index